**IN & OUT
OF THIS
WORLD**

**RELIGIOUS CULTURES OF AFRICAN
AND AFRICAN DIASPORA PEOPLE**

Series editors: Jacob K. Olupona,
Harvard University; Dianne M. Stewart,
Emory University; and Terrence L.
Johnson, Georgetown University

THE BOOK SERIES EXAMINES THE RELIGIOUS,
CULTURAL, AND POLITICAL EXPRESSIONS OF
AFRICAN, AFRICAN AMERICAN, AND AFRICAN
CARIBBEAN TRADITIONS. THROUGH TRANS-
NATIONAL, CROSS-CULTURAL, AND MULTI-
DISCIPLINARY APPROACHES TO THE STUDY
OF RELIGION, THE SERIES INVESTIGATES THE
EPISTEMIC BOUNDARIES OF CONTINENTAL
AND DIASPORIC RELIGIOUS PRACTICES AND
THOUGHT AND EXPLORES THE DIVERSE AND
DISTINCT WAYS AFRICAN-DERIVED RELIGIONS
INFORM CULTURE AND POLITICS. THE SERIES
AIMS TO ESTABLISH A FORUM FOR IMAGIN-
ING THE CENTRALITY OF BLACK RELIGIONS
IN THE FORMATION OF THE "NEW WORLD."

STEPHEN C. FINLEY

IN & OUT OF THIS WORLD

MATERIAL AND EXTRATERRESTRIAL BODIES IN THE NATION OF ISLAM

DUKE UNIVERSITY PRESS · DURHAM AND LONDON · 2022

Designed by MaTThew Tauch
Typeset in Arno Pro and Hepta Slab
by Westchester Publishing Services

Library of Congress Cataloging-in-Publication Data
Names: Finley, Stephen C., author.
Title: In and out of this world : material and extraterrestrial bodies in
the nation of Islam / Stephen C Finley.
Other titles: Religious cultures of African and African diaspora people.
Description: Durham : Duke University Press, 2022. | Series:
Religious cultures of African and African diaspora people | Includes
bibliographical references and index.
Identifiers: LCCN 2022020045 (print) | LCCN 2022020046 (ebook)
ISBN 9781478016137 (hardcover)
ISBN 9781478018773 (paperback)
ISBN 9781478023418 (ebook)
Subjects: LCSH: Islam—United States—History. | African American
Muslims—History. | Muslims—United States— History. | African
Americans—Religion—History. | Black
people—America—Religion—History.| BISAC: RELIGION /
Islam / General | SOCIAL SCIENCE / Black Studies (Global)
Classification: LCC BP67.U6 F565 2022 (print) | LCC BP67.U6
(ebook) | DDC 297.0973—dc23/eng/20220713
LC recordavailableathTTps:// lccn.loc.gov/2022020045
LC ebook recordavailableathTTps:// lccn.loc.gov/2022020046

Cover art: Delano Dunn, *Relieved of the Weight,* 2016.
49 × 40 inches. Paper, Mylar, cellophane, vinyl, shoe polish,
and resin on board. Courtesy of the artist.

To Hattie M. Fuette, my mother, and the memory of my grandparents, Flora Mae Ball and Lovie D. Ball, my cousin, Tony Ward; my aunt Frances Anderson; and Ella Victoria Lane, who always told me to call her "mother"

CONTENTS

ACKNOWLEDGMENTS

This book has already had a lively existence as a manuscript—through various revisions and edits—and it's going to have a wonderful life as a book. None of this would be possible, however, without the support of so many supportive people who contributed to my understanding of the Nation of Islam and to my perseverance.

I thank two people who were most supportive: Lori Latrice Martin and Biko Mandela Gray. Lori and Biko have been steadfast friends who continuously encouraged me through the process of reviews, revisions, and finally, publication. I cannot envision the moment this book was published without them. They have been my greatest interlocutors, scholarly partners, and fans. More than this, they have been the kindest and most loyal friends.

I also thank other friends and family. So many of them are important to me, and I hope that some of them will forgive me if I fail to mention them. My family has been with me through everything, rooting me on, being proud of me, and bragging about their relative who is a Louisiana State University professor. Thank you, Glenn Anderson, Rita Anderson, Rebecca Simmons, Tamara Hunt Ragsdale, Lynnshya Ward, Jadian Anderson, Najya Shomari Finley, Rachel Vincent-Finley, and my aunt Elizabeth Lacy, mother of my closest cousin, the late Latonia "Tony" Ward. I also have to mention my parents, Hattie Mae Fuette and William Walker Finley Jr., and my stepfather, Herman Fuette. My sister, Sonja Kaye Finley, has always been there for me.

Several friends deserve mention: Rev. Dr. Charles Franklin Baugham Sr.; Christophe L. Beard, Dejuana Butler, Thosha Hart, Cleveland Jones Jr., Tanya Ratcliff—all of whom have been friends with me for more than thirty years. I thank Sarah Becker, Eldon V. Birthwright, Glynis Boyd Hughes, Brent Chambliss, MarieHilliard, Joyce Marie Jackson, Jason Jeffries, Terri Laws, Hugh R. Page Jr., Michael Pasquier, Martha Pitts, Marques Redd, Sundria R. Ridgley; Charles M. Stang, and Michele Watkins, as well as Elijah "Eli" Muhammad, who was formerly a member of the United Nation of Islam, led by Royall Jenkins.

Next, I thank fraternity brothers of the Omega Psi Phi Fraternity, Incorporated: the late Harold "Tex" Allen; Juan Barthelemy; Brenton Brock; Kenneth Broughton; Michael Joseph Brown; Eric Bryant; Torland "Hefty" Garrison; Dean Quality Que, Clifford Hodrick; Surry Jackson; Nathan Lawson; Edward Muhammad; Damon Powell; George "Tino" Prince; Anthony Pruitt; Jerome C. Ross; Rev. Dr. Bobbie Joe Saucer; Paul Stephens; the Ten Tested Titans of Tenacity of the Theta Chi Chapter of Prairie View, Texas; Jeffery Williams; Yardley Williams; and, most of all, Gregory Alton "GAP" Parham, who has always been supportive. Indeed, GAP gave me my frat "hits" on both my arms.

I thank the editors of the series Religious Cultures of African and African Diaspora People: Jacob K. Olupona, Dianne M. Stewart, and Terrence L. Johnson. They believed in this book, and Terrence and Dianne are the reasons that this book has been published with Duke University Press. I don't know where I would be without them. Associate Editor Miriam Angress of Duke University Press has been incredibly supportive and patient through all of my challenges and delays. Again, I don't know where I would be without her. She was so kind. Moreover, Annie Lubinsky of Duke University Press made the copy-editing process so much nicer and efficient.

Editing this book to make it publication-ready was a lot of work, and I would not have been able to complete this task without the expertise of Laura Helper, whom Miriam recommended. Laura was professional and kind, and she did lots of the heavy lifting when it comes to editing. She was thorough and precise. She gave me explicit directions and asked probing questions that addressed gaps in my argumentation. This attention made the book better.

Several groups were supportive of this project: the Department of African and African American Studies and the Department of Philosophy and Religious Studies, both at Louisiana State University (LSU), and the Society for the Study of Black Religion.

Two grants and fellowships made the book better. First, I won a statewide competition in 2017 and 2018 from the State of Louisiana Board of Regents called the ATLAS Grant: Awards to Louisiana Artists and Scholars that funded a year for me to rework and expand this manuscript. Moreover, the Manship Fellowship at LSU gave me one summer month to read and write, which resulted in the epilogue.

Several people offered technical input. I thank the reviewers, who were very insightful but fair on multiple rounds of reviews. They gave me expert feedback on the book that made it stronger. I have to thank David

Metcalfe, who created the images for this book and Amanda Speake, master indexer.

I cannot forget Tracey E. Hucks, who pointed me in the direction of Duke University Press and who connected me with Dianne Stewart, who was excited about my book. I will always be indebted to her and to Dianne.

In terms of technical expertise, the book reflects the tutelage and mentorship of Elias K. Bongmba, David Cook, James Faubion, Jeffrey J. Kripal, the late Lawrence Mamiya, William Parsons, and Anthony B. Pinn. I have to thank James H. Cone and Manning Marable, who allowed me to interview them. Neither lived to see the publication of this book.

Finally, Lasambra "Kitty" Finley, the best cat ever, died a month after I turned the final draft in to the press. Kitty was one of my best friends for almost seventeen years. I will never forget him.

BLACK BODIES IN- AND OUT-OF-PLACE

REREADING THE NATION OF ISLAM THROUGH A THEORY OF THE BODY

This is the thinking and attitude of them. To this very day they see you getting out of your place. So forces are working to put black people back in their place.—**MINISTER ISMAEL MUHAMMAD,** Nation of Islam National Assistant Minister, "Farrakhan and the Wheel Part 2"

The Nation of Islam (NOI) is one of the most revered and reviled religious groups in America. For almost a century, the NOI has influenced millions of people in the United States and globally. For example, the NOI attracted support from black people across social class divisions, as well as from other people of color across the globe, especially during times of global unrest such as the Great Depression and World War II.[1] Elijah Muhammad, Malcolm X, and Warith Deen Mohammed were among the most recognizable black figures in their respective eras. The same can be said of the current leader of the NOI, Minister Louis Farrakhan. For some, the name "Farrakhan" and the NOI evoke images of anger and inflammatory rhetoric; for others, they evoke images of a sea of largely black and brown men's faces on the Mall in Washington,

DC, in 1995 for the Million Man March and again in 2015 for its twentieth anniversary. But there is far more to Elijah Muhammad, Malcolm X, Warith Deen Mohammed, and Louis Farrakhan than meets the eye—or even what is covered in the popular press and in academic scholarship. And these men certainly disagreed and critiqued one another.

In and Out of This World offers a new reading of the Nation of Islam as a religious organization shaped by a set of complex religious ideas and practices, new racial grammars, cosmologies, and racial uplift ideologies. Understanding the NOI as a religious nationalist group challenges existing scholarship that defines it as primarily—if not exclusively—black nationalist. For Carolyn Moxley Rouse, the author of *Engaged Surrender: African American Women and Islam*, for instance, it is a foregone conclusion that the NOI is a black nationalist movement.[2] I have serious doubts about the claim and the utility of this classification; regarding the NOI as a political black nation-state obscures the depth and complexity of the religious meanings of its activities, despite the fact that nearly every book and article about the NOI treats this political category as a given. Most important, this book argues that what motivated the NOI was (re)forming black embodiment, or efforts to retrieve, reclaim, and reform black bodies from the discursive white normative gaze, bodies first formed in and by the pain and performance for white pleasure during the period of enslavement in America.[3]

The exigencies of race and racism forced the NOI to engage the body. Understood as material and symbol, the body was the central concern for all four of its most influential members. While historical moments—both within and beyond the NOI—may have offered new challenges due to changing temporal, political, and institutional realities, the body remained the central focus in NOI discourses and rituals as it attempted to reconstitute bodies that had been constructed in and by white supremacy, slavery, and violence.

The NOI was only partially successful in its reformative efforts, however: in many ways, it internalized the dynamics and values of white supremacy and, as a consequence, reproduced and redeployed its own system of intra-"race" marginalization and an ambiguous but hierarchical "class" ordering in the NOI and African American community. Such intraracial discrimination was predicated on what I call an *ideal embodied economy* that ranked bodies based on indicators such as "gender," sexuality, and skin complexion. Having co-opted many white middle-class American principles and practices, the NOI converted deeply entrenched matters of "race" into class discourses. Nonetheless, the NOI regards race and gender markers of the body as critically important to its project. Contending explicitly with matters directly affecting the materiality and meaning of black embodiment is what made the NOI relevant—and anathema—to America at the same time.

In these pages, I offer a theoretical interpretation of the Nation of Islam—that is, a fresh look at its religious practices and discourses in light of its historical, social, and cultural setting in America. I take on, straightforwardly, what these aspects of its religion mean, how they function, and why they matter. My comparative method is influenced by the history of religions. I also draw from a perspective that is informed by psychoanalysis in various modalities, including classical analysis and object relations theory. What will be more apparent in my interpretive project, however, is my use of theories of religion; social theory, especially that of Mary Douglas and Pierre Bourdieu and, to a degree, W. E. B. Du Bois and Franz Fanon; and philosophy of race. Finally, I employ a form of literary ethnography, quoting the speeches and writings of important figures in a way that preserves and represents their voices. Far too often, translations and interpretations of primary texts miss or misrepresent the original meaning, which is why I privilege and prefer primary texts. Such a complex array of resources is necessary to make sense of the religion of the NOI because it was a religious group that, like other African American communities, had to confront the religious meaning of black bodies in a context in which they were controlled, policed, and violated precisely because of their racialized attributes. Anything less does not begin to scratch the surface of understanding the NOI or the meaning of black embodiment for the group. Embodiment is critical because bodies are what are at stake, both physically and discursively, which is to say, the body is understood as made up of flesh and bones, but social meanings are attached to various bodies based on such characteristics, including race and religion. The NOI talks about the body in both ways and reproduces the body in its discourses and rituals.

Black Bodies *In-* and *Out-*of-Place

This text advances a novel theory of embodiment drawn from Douglas's notion of dirt that I call "Black Bodies *In-* and *Out-*of-Place." Douglas's notion of "dirt" in *Purity and Danger: An Analysis of Concepts of Pollution and Taboo* attempts to explain every culture's concern with purity and contagion.[4] She insists that it is primarily symbolic rather than a regard for actual dirt, suggesting that "the more deeply we go into this and similar rules, the more obvious it becomes that we are studying symbolic systems."[5] Douglas's claim is simple: what is seen as a pollutant and hence as *dangerous* to established social systems is that which does not fit fully into a type, lies outside of a class, or, in her words, is ambiguous, anomalous, marginal, or transitional.[6] In short, "Dirt is matter out of place."[7] As "out of place," dirt speaks to contagion.[8]

In the United States, black bodies are framed as contaminating, recalcitrant, or disobedient. They are not easily structured and relegated to particular spaces in which they are expected to stay in place. Police and other white people *perceived* Trayvon Martin's, Emmett Till's, Rekia Boyd's, Sandra Bland's, and other black bodies—including my own—as being *out-of-place*, not belonging, and engaging in activities that were viewed as violating established social conventions that regulate space and activity.

My contention here is that one of the primary ways that identities of black bodies were named out-of-place was through a white gaze that supersaturated them with multiple negative meanings that served the maintenance of whiteness.[9] This is not to deny the relationship between phenotypical whiteness and the performance of whiteness: whiteness is embodied, discursive, and performed. It is only to suggest that there is no absolute correspondence between the two. One need not be "white" phenotypically to perform white behaviors, though the correlation between the discursive and the embodied are intimate. One needs only to acquiesce to the cultural norm of white bodies as the standard of beauty and humanity. In other words, when meaning is created, it can be said that whiteness is seen as the highest valued body, the ideal to which all nonwhite bodies should aspire. Philosophies and theologies that participated in normalizing and stabilizing white supremacy contributed to the proliferation of black inferiority that dehumanized and constructed black bodies as other.[10] This book disputes that black bodies are seen as "dangerous" a priori; rather, they are deemed such only as they traverse the dominant social classificatory system or fail to fit neatly into given taxonomic categories that are meant to govern their meaning and activity and to protect a given social system and cosmology.[11]

In the NOI we find discursive, ritual, and doctrinal claims about what it means for a black body to be perceived performing not only out-of-place but in-place as well. Black bodies "in-place" were bodies that were racialized and whose identities and meanings were viewed as fixed. For the NOI, these black bodies could be perceived as *socially* in-place in that *physical* bodies operated in defined but limited spheres of activity, which rendered them acceptable and innocuous to white communities. In addition, black bodies could be perceived as symbolically in-place if they bought into and internalized *discourses* and *ideas* of black inferiority; if they were seen as compliant and displayed overly deferential *attitudes* toward whites. Therefore, black bodies that would have been seen by the NOI as in-place symbolically or socially were those that embraced any intellectual state or condition that made them complacent about their subjugation to whites. Christianity, for Elijah Muhammad, was a major sanitizing ideology that rendered black bodies socially and symbolically in-place, in that it was seen as deeply rooted in white ways of living in the world and seeing the world.

In contrast to the white gaze, collective NOI discourses about black embodiment *deplored* bodies that were in-place because they did not challenge or dislodge the racist system of classification in any meaningful way. What the NOI thought was pitiful and ugly was this in-place black body that was constructed in slavery and oppression and the representation of it as slavish, buffoonish, docile, and submissive. The in-place body was the one that danced a jig, ate slave food (such as greens, black-eyed peas, and pork) under the guise of "soul food," and was depicted as animalistic. Furthermore, in-placeness, for instance, was represented as black women constantly available for sexual encounters with white men and as black men who were seen as hypersexual, unintelligent brutes.[12] Largely defined by the racist social system, these in-place black bodies posed no threat to the system and were viewed as acting in accordance with prevailing negative discourses about black people.

As a consequence, the NOI sought to reconstitute such distorted black bodies socially and symbolically. According to Elijah Muhammad:

> Beauty appearance is destroyed in us—not just our facial appearance, but the most beautiful appearance about us, our characteristics (the way we act and practice our way of life). We achieve one of the greatest beauties when we achieve the spiritual beauty and characteristics through practicing them. We achieve the spiritual beauty through practicing or carrying into practice the spiritual laws. . . . We know that we have been made ugly by our enemies . . . by not practicing culture that would beautify [us].[13]

Muhammad appeals to the categories of *in-placeness* and *out-of-placeness* as social and symbolic when he suggests that beauty is something that is physical (social) and spiritual and cultural (symbolic). The NOI was responding to this in-place body that it perceived as mangled and undesirable but that it wanted to reimagine and re-present as an agential, resistant body that was black and beautiful (read: male, heterosexual, middle class, etc.)—in short, a black body out-of-place.

Douglas's notion of dirt allows us to see that structuring and ordering social relationships, activities, discourses, and attitudes protect the system in ways that render black embodiment innocuous, so that while black bodies are potentially *dangerous* due to their recalcitrance, their in-placeness renders them negated, abject, and antiseptic. The system reacts violently to black bodies that are perceived as symbolically out-of-place; and in the NOI we have a perfect illustration of this, given the violent responses to its mythology of Yakub (a black scientist who some followers of the NOI believed created the white race) and intellectual and rhetorical critiques of American culture and government.

The Body as a Physical Reality and Social Symbol

The NOI is viewed as dangerous for symbolic reasons, not simply social (i.e., biological or physical) ones that involved the activity of its members' physical bodies. In short, treatment of the physical body and the meaning of the body socially and religiously reflect the concerns and anxieties of a given social system.[14] The body is both material and metaphor, or *social* and *symbolic*, where the social refers to the activity of physical bodies and the symbolic indicates the attitudinal, intellectual, linguistic expressions of bodies.

The NOI was responding to imposed racialized conditions of existence that distorted and disfigured black bodies: slavery, lynching, symbolic violence, systematic oppression, and now, the destructiveness, control, and mass containment of the prison-industrial complex that legal scholar Michelle Alexander calls "The New Jim Crow."[15] This is not to suggest, however, that the bodies that the NOI constructed in an attempt to refashion "blackness" were all positive. In fact, it projected some of its responses to the experiences of racism, as this book argues, onto marginalized members of African American communities such as women, African American Christians, and poor people. The processes that the NOI employed to reconstitute black bodies and develop new religious identities often obscured the fact that it (re)produced oppressive discourses and practices.

What remained stable in the NOI were continuous and consistent attempts to disrupt constructions of black bodies as physical entities (social) and as symbols (symbolic) viewed as the consequences of a system of racism that constituted them as obsequious and inferior, which then affected their vitality and longevity. To be sure, the body, as material and metaphor, was the concern for the NOI throughout its history and in the four transformative moments that are the focus of this book.

Moreover, the NOI used creative and esoteric symbols to resignify race and *blackness* as something transcendent. For instance, the NOI used religious concepts and symbols from various other religious traditions, and it connects the meaning of black bodies in this world to cosmic and otherworldly ideas. One finds the curious discourses on unidentified flying objects (UFOs) that the NOI calls the Mother Plane or the Mother Wheel, heroic characters from Islam, and extraterrestrials—transcendental symbols—that give its world coherence and that make sense of white supremacy and the ever-present violence that is directed at black bodies in the United States. Viewing the NOI as *religious nationalists, In and Out of This World* takes these symbols, as well as the practices and discourses of the NOI, seriously and creatively ties their usage to how the NOI reconstituted the meaning of black bodies in response to concrete matters that affect the quality of life and health of black bodies in the world.

From a black person's customary treatment in a shopping mall to the killings of Trayvon Martin, Rekia Boyd, Tamir Rice, Alton Sterling, Breonna Taylor, Ahmaud Arbery, and George Floyd, among others, and from the violent perception and treatment of Barack Obama to two young black people going to a football game, the truth is that black people are constantly navigating spaces and places in ways that speak to a host of different existential, political, social, and—in the case of the NOI—theological/religious dimensions of black life. This book names this navigation; it speaks to what it means to be deemed dangerous or not, and it speaks to the very real consequences of living or being out-of-place. In this regard, black bodies *in-place* and *out-of-place* is no mere binary of in-placeness and out-of-placeness. Rather, these terms name a complex matrix of perceptions of black bodies, which are constructed in a system of white supremacy and its attendant privileges. These perceptions provide a means of protecting and guaranteeing the reproduction of the system and its privileges by policing its boundaries from contamination.

Thus, black bodies can be seen as being socially out-of-place and symbolically out-of-place, socially in-place and symbolically in-place, or any combination of these. When black bodies are interpreted as behaving in ways that do not fit neatly into historical notions of blackness that are seen as real in the gaze of white supremacy—that is, lived performances of blackness that may be ambiguous, anomalous, transitional, or marginal—they are perceived as out-of-place and as dangerous. This ordering and policing of bodies is not simply about maintaining the current social order. It is about (re)producing in the lived world an underlying and overarching assumption about the place of black bodies that is metaphysical; this ordering speaks to a worldview that transcends the logic and fact of experience; it is a cosmology. Black bodies that were reconstituted by the religion of the NOI in response to the taxonomy of white supremacy, I argue, were and still are perceived as out-of-place in this culture and are, as such, *dangerous* to its maintenance. As a result, white responses to them are vociferous and violent. However, the system rewards nonthreatening black bodies *in-place*. These are the bodies that the NOI sought to (re)construct in its own image of what was beautiful and respectable. In so doing, the NOI's discourses on the body speak to the existential tightrope of being black and religious in a world marked by white supremacy.

Structure of the Book

Recalcitrant bodies, or black bodies that the system perceives as disobedient and resistant, are out-of-place socially and symbolically; therefore, the system reacts to enact a type of social homeostasis that renders black bodies in-place socially and symbolically so that they are no longer a threat or a *danger* to the system. These "tamed" bodies are now desirable to the vested interests of white supremacy, since they safeguard it from perceived contamination. But the NOI sees these in-place black bodies as a distortion or "fall" of black humanity and seeks to reconstruct them.

In chapter 1, "Elijah Muhammad, The Myth of Yakub, and the Critique of 'Whitenized' Black Bodies," an exploration of Elijah Muhammad's theological and discursive assault on in-place black bodies reveals that they were conditioned by the excessive violence toward and lynching of African Americans that he witnessed and that were otherwise part of the everyday reality of African Americans in the southern United States, including in Georgia, the location of Muhammad's birth. Furthermore, after he joined the NOI and became its leader, the myth of Yakub—the main theological, cosmological, and theodicean narrative—gave coherence to his world and helped to explain the violence directed at black bodies.

The myth of Yakub, which explained the origins of the world and the races, also informed Elijah Muhammad's perspective on in-place black bodies. Subsequently, this mythology shaped his critique of such "whitenized" black bodies. These black bodies, as described in the Yakub narrative, were aesthetically disfigured, psychologically infirm, and religiously demonic. Such was the disposition of bodies that, for Muhammad, had been fixed in-place by white supremacy or, in the language of the NOI, by the devil and his tricks. Muhammad's attention to mythology and religion indicate his privileging of black bodies that would be seen as out-of-place symbolically. The chapter (re)constructs NOI mythology from multiple and disparate sources to make sense of the role it played in the religion of the NOI; in particular it demonstrates the mythology's connection to Muhammad's critique of black bodies in-place.

Chapter 2, "Elijah Muhammad, Transcendent Blackness, and the Construction of Ideal Black Embodiment," shows that ideal or ultimate black bodies for Elijah Muhammad were religious bodies that privileged what would have been perceived by the dominant culture as symbolic out-of-placeness. Muhammad was not necessarily interested in political engagement with an unjust system; instead, he was remaking black bodies that would be prepared for the world to come, a new world after the age of white domination, a world that would disclose black bodies as preeminent and beautiful. The chapter argues first that Muhammad sought to reimagine what black bodies could be and that he used a variety of philosophical and theological resources and rituals in this endeavor. Second, for him, ideal bodies had specific social and symbolic characteristics, constituting a distinct, ideal black bodily economy that distinguished NOI bodies from other black bodies through ritualized and mythologized differentiation. The construction of "the body" here is complex, given that the ritual and discursive sources that constituted these bodies varied depending on whether Muhammad's concern was for the body as a biological reality or the body as symbolization of the NOI collective and cosmology. Restricting these black bodies to the symbolic gestures of resistance rather than to the overtly social ones meant that these bodies were not to engage in mainstream political activities such as taking part in the civil rights movement. They were fashioned for religious and aesthetic purposes. For Muhammad, it was futile to engage in such political work, since the Mother Plane (UFO), an otherworldly but material (transcendent and immanent) vehicle, would come at the end of the age and create a new world and bring ideal black embodiment to fruition. Muhammad's construction of ideal black bodies constitutes a bodily economy that structures class in the NOI based on physical and symbolic factors, such as gender and intellectual ability.

The chapter introduces the notion of *transcendent blackness* to describe the meaning of blackness in the NOI. It means that these ideal black bodies were not simply signified by African Americans but, according to Muhammad, were "black, brown, red, and yellow," suggesting a more vast conception of *black* as a surplus category of race that included Native Americans, Asians, Latinos, and beyond.[16] In addition, blackness had extraterrestrial meaning, since black bodies were related to beings on other planets and were ultimately defined in relation to the Mother Plane, which was the most technological and scientific creation in the history of the cosmos.

Chapter 3, "Malcolm X and the Politics of Resistance: Visible Bodies, Language, and the Implied Critique of Elijah Muhammad," argues that Malcolm X, for many years the national representative of the Honorable Elijah Muhammad, inverted or reversed the paradigm of Muhammad. That is, he privileged the social over the symbolic, so that he made black bodies in the NOI publicly visible: by way of his proselytic work in which the NOI grew in membership and in temples and through which he became known to the American public, and by way of his own linguistic resistance through his lectures and speeches. Malcolm X longed to be engaged socially (i.e., bodily) in the struggle for justice, not just symbolically as a distant critic; Muhammad prevented him from doing so. Malcolm X functioned as— indeed, became—a black body out-of-place socially (not just symbolically) in the eyes of the white American public, not just symbolically.

While his speeches and interviews may have led to uneasiness in the media and the populace, Malcolm's rhetoric exceeded simple symbolic gesturing. The chapter argues that he became an active participant in the civil and human rights movements through his speeches and televised interviews. He made explicit his critique of Muhammad and his desire for bodily participation in future struggles for justice after he left the NOI. The chapter counters dominant narratives about Malcolm X that suggest his critique of Muhammad's theology and political practices appeared only after he left the NOI. Such a narrative is not only false, it fails to consider how much of what he did after he left the NOI was still consistent with the teachings of Elijah Muhammad.

Chapter 4, "Warith Deen Mohammed and the Nation of Islam: Race and Black Embodiment in 'Islamic' Form," contends that, in his appropriation of Sunni Islam for the NOI, Warith Deen Mohammed (a.k.a. Wallace D. Muhammad) critiqued both Elijah Muhammad and Malcolm X in his construction of black ("Islamic") bodies out-of-place. On the one hand, he disagreed with his father, Elijah Muhammad; for the younger man,

Islam was something much more concrete and fixed (e.g., the Five Pillars) and not esoteric and "spooky," as he claimed his father's religion to be.[17] Furthermore, religion was not something private and exclusive as it was for Muhammad—it was universal. But this Sunni notion of the universality (*ummah*) of religion also posed problems for Mohammed, who recognized the effects of racism on African Americans, and he sought to address their particular (*asabiya*) needs with a relevant form of Islam.[18] Therefore, his attention to and assault on racism was an attempt to recast black bodies *symbolically* and *socially* to dislodge them from the negative associations of inferiority that were attached to them vis-à-vis the racist social system. Mohammed's desire to see African Americans "cultured" through and in Islam was a response that was meant to disrupt the reproduction of black bodies in-place symbolically, and his emphasis on diet, proper attire, and clean living, as well as on voting and participation in social activism and the political process, implies his significant but unequal concern for black (physical) bodies *socially*. Hence, he signifies the importance of black bodies out-of-place socially and symbolically, with the aesthetic difference of moving the NOI to a Sunni form of Islam to, ostensibly, make it cultured and politically active. In doing so, however, Mohammed critiqued Malcolm X, for whom religion and social responsibility were somewhat separate (which required that Malcolm found the Muslim Mosque, Inc. [religious] and the Organization for Afro-American Unity [sociopolitical] separately). Subsequently, Mohammed embraced a distinctive tradition within African American Islam, and within the NOI in particular, that was consistent with that of Elijah Muhammad and Malcolm X and held the ostensible universal (i.e., Islam) and the obvious particularism (i.e., race, culture) in tension. That is, the body and the significance of race remained the central focus of the religious meanings that Mohammed employed, even throughout his transition to a manner of religion that was more closely related to international forms of Sunni Islam. Thus, his consistent attention to race in his early years indicate his privileging, like his father, of the symbolic over the social.

Chapter 5, "Mothership Connections: Louis Farrakhan as the Culmination of Muslim Ideals in the Nation of Islam," pays special attention to Louis Farrakhan, arguing that his Islamic thought and praxis was and is the aggregate of all his predecessors: Elijah Muhammad, Malcolm X, and Warith Deen Mohammed. Farrakhan gives his most poignant expression of the nature and meaning of the black body in his discourses on his mystical experiences with the Mother Plane, or what he calls the Mother Wheel, a UFO.[19] Embodying an aggressive discursive, intellectual, and confrontational engagement with America and the US government, Farrakhan's numinous and sociopolitical response to the meaning of the Wheel reveals the pinnacle of black bodies out-of-place socially and symbolically.

Most important, Farrakhan claims to have been taken into a UFO on September 17, 1985.[20] While few studies on Farrakhan and the NOI give sustained theoretical attention to his "abduction narrative," this esoteric, mystical, and epistemological experience of the Wheel is Farrakhan's organizing metaphor for interpreting black bodies—and it, indeed, provides the necessary narrative that gives ultimate coherence and purpose to his life and ministry. Finally, as the culmination of all of his predecessors, Farrakhan elevates social and symbolic out-of-placeness to equal status as he attempts to construct a form of Islam that is sensitive to the social and historical circumstances of African Americans while, at the same time, connecting them more strongly to Muslims in the international religious milieu. *Race* is a significant metaphysical category for Farrakhan as he connects the ultimate meaning of black bodies to the Mother Wheel that he also views as empowering and protecting him to speak and act on behalf of colonized people of the world—people whom, like Elijah Muhammad, he recognizes as "black."

In the conclusion, "(Re)forming Black Bodies, White Supremacy, and the Nation of Islam's Class(ist) Response," I argue that what the Nation of Islam was attempting to accomplish was to (re)form black embodiment that, according to the NOI, had been disfigured in every conceivable way by a white supremacist culture that affected and structured all major aspects of black social life, including religion. Christianity, for the NOI, participated in this grotesque construction of black bodies socially and symbolically in-place, not simply through its images of a white Jesus or white depictions of the Divine in the broader sense, but also in the meaning that it attached to black bodies and in the ways in which it constricted the activities of African Americans to keep them from attaining their own liberation. "Islam," in its various forms, by contrast, was viewed, in general terms, as the appropriate vehicle that could raise the status of black bodies—culture them, beautify them, ennoble them—and give them the motivational, ideological, and metaphysical grounding to push toward their fullness with regard to their material existences. The result was the construction of a *classed* black body within the NOI that structured class in terms of which bodies could be in leadership roles; the NOI rendered other bodies, especially Christian ones, as an inferior class. Indeed, it was strategies such as these, whose primary intent may have been subversive to the dominant order, that invariably reproduced and re-created the very inequality the NOI sought to ameliorate and destabilize.

Pierre Bourdieu's monumental social theory in *Outline of a Theory of Practice and Distinction: A Social Critique of the Judgement of Taste* gives me a way to talk about this classed body hierarchy and the ways in which it structured class discourses that were directed not at white bodies but at black bodies both within and outside the NOI. The problem, as I see it, is that this classed body and these conversations did violence to other black bodies: they collapsed African American complexity and diversity, ontologized an ideal black body as if it corresponded to something real in the world, and legitimized class distinctions that were based on the approximation of bodies to this ideal. As a result, they rendered particular black embodiments problematic and left unmarked and stable intersecting— white supremacist, classist, sexist, homophobic—systems of oppression. Therefore, such discourses based on this economy functioned to make a qualitative class distinction between NOI bodies and other black bodies and can generally be seen, I maintain, in the thought of Elijah Muhammad, Malcolm X, Warith Deen Mohammed, and Louis Farrakhan.[21]

"Wheels, Wombs, and Women: An Epilogue" points to critical directions of research that *In and Out of This World* reveals, particularly the lack of attention to women in the NOI and their embodiment. I review recent scholarship on women in the NOI.[22] The book locates this discussion in UFOs and in Louis Farrakhan's recent speech commemorating the twentieth anniversary of the Million Man March, in which he frequently made reference to African American women and respectability. That is to say that he pointed to women in the NOI as models for how African American women should present themselves: as domesticated and cleanly dressed. Moreover, he made several references to "wombs," rendering women's bodies not as their own but as metaphysical. They are viewed as the vessels in which and through which black masculinity and order in black communities might be ensured. Such a discourse is connected to his UFO (Wheel) narrative, in which he imagines himself reborn in a symbolic womb (i.e., the UFO) and emerging as a sage. Therefore, he, rather than women, is the real exemplar of women's bodies, an example to black people of the positive results of control and management of the physical bodies of black women in service of their religious and metaphysical purposes. In short, Wheels, Wombs, and Women are interconnected, which means that in the NOI women's bodies are not their own. The emphasis, then, is on the symbolic, since women's bodies are objectified and have a reduced meaning that is framed in androcentric terms.

"The 'Louis Farrakhan' That the Public Does Not Know, or Doesn't Want to Know?: An Afterword" is an immediate and contemporary excursus on Farrakhan and the NOI that positions this book as indispensable for future study since it takes on common misconceptions and myths through an examination and interpretation of what may have been Farrakhan's last major public speech, "The Criterion: An Announcement to the World," on July 4, 2020. At the time of its delivery, he was eighty-seven years old. Couched against the background of the COVID-19 pandemic, Farrakhan addresses his legacy; interprets what he has been doing for three decades as leader of the NOI; and assesses the implications of that for the NOI, the United States, and the world. He addresses such matters as George Floyd and police brutality; the representation of him as antiwhite, anti-Jewish, anti-LGBTQ+, anti-women; the pandemic and why the NOI opposes the COVID-19 vaccines; and, of course, the significance of UFOs for understanding him, the NOI, and as I argue in this book, black embodiment. It is a dynamic, complex, and amazing speech that is stark in its universality. It calls for peace on Earth through justice. What's more, readers will likely not recognize it as the "Farrakhan" they have come to "know" through the media and negative tropes that are a flattened stand-in for him, his religious thought, and his religious group.

More than the usual recounting of historical data about the NOI's beliefs and practices, *In and Out This World* initiates a theory and method-based trajectory in the study of the NOI and embodiment that will commence a reassessment of scholarship in the field. This book is well positioned to alter fundamentally how members, sympathizers, critics, students, and scholars of the NOI understand the meaning of black embodiment in the Nation of Islam and America.

ELIJAH MUHAMMAD, THE MYTH OF YAKUB, AND THE CRITIQUE OF "WHITENIZED" BLACK BODIES

The religious mythology of the Nation of Islam (NOI), as expressed in Elijah Muhammad's teachings on Yakub, advanced a new religious and racial lexicon and grammar that allowed members to reenvision their own humanity in the face of white supremacy and antiblackness in America. Their discourses of black "alien" life on other planets afforded them the language to reformulate the meaning of black embodiment. This new linguistics may be the most creative contribution of the NOI; its founder, Master Fard Muhammad; and Elijah Muhammad to African American religion and to Afrofuturism. The aesthetics of this mythology populate their religious imaginings of what black embodiment can be. The NOI's mythology is connected to its doctrines and practices, especially its opposition to Christianity as a genocidal ideology that colonizes black bodies and to the black embodiment that emerged from slavery and violence; both slavery and Christianity, the NOI charges, fix black bodies in-place.

Little scholarly attention has been given to the subject of the Yakub myth and theodicy, which has led to great misunderstanding about the nature and function of the narrative. For instance, Steven Tsoukalas, author of *The Nation of Islam: Understanding "Black Muslims,"* contends that "orthodox" Islam does not substantiate the narrative, which, according to Tsoukalas, does not concern the Nation of Islam. Tsoukalas is right here, but what he does not address is how the story is theodicean, which I counter in this book and elsewhere with my notion of *theological phenomenology*, a term that describes Elijah Muhammad's practice of *description* and meaningful *interpretation*. That is, the story of Yakub describes intense and overwhelming white racial terror in multiple forms and then offers a definitive response, in the mythology of Yakub, about the meaning of black suffering.[1]

Sherman A. Jackson, author of *Islam and the Problem of Black Suffering*, tries to fill the gap between Islamic theologies and black suffering. In this chapter, this is precisely what I argue the Yakub mythology accomplishes. It describes black suffering and attempts to give it coherence and meaning.[2] This is precisely what I mean when I say the Yakub myth is theological phenomenology.

Elijah Muhammad's views, as noted in the introduction, were shaped by the excessive violence against and lynching of black bodies that he witnessed in the US South and especially in Georgia, where he was born. After he joined the NOI and became its leader in 1933, the myth of Yakub gave coherence to his world and helped to explain the violence that African Americans experienced; it also informed his perspective that black bodies in-place, or knowing their place, were "whitenized," or treasonous. Rejecting white supremacy's attempts to make black bodies docile, Christian, and inferior, the Yakub narrative described these whitenized bodies as aesthetically disfigured, psychologically infirmed, and religiously demonic. Such was the disposition of bodies that had been fixed in-place by white supremacy or—in the language of the NOI—by the devil and his tricks.

Black bodies in-place were an embodiment that the NOI despised as inferior to Muslim bodies. For Muhammad, the epitome of such "inferior" bodies were African American Christians. What made these bodies ideologically "white" was their acceptance of the religion used by whites to make black people slaves to white people and to fix that enslavement as divinely ordered and enduring. Hence, Muhammad privileged the symbolic over the social: negative meanings attached to black bodies (symbolic) were more significant to him than physical bodies directly engaging in and challenging structures of oppression (social). They were only *so-called Negroes*.[3] Muhammad uses this term often in his writings as a rhetorical device to call into question the appropriateness of the name "Negro," which, for him, was slave nomenclature. So-called Negroes were odious to him due to their perceived complicity with the devil and *his* white social and religious systems. Although for Muhammad, many people in black communities had been tricked by the devil, no class of African Americans were more conned than African American male Christian preachers, especially those of the civil rights movement of the 1950s and 1960s.[4] He contends:

> Yet there are some leaders so ignorant and so in love and fear of the white man that they preaches [*sic*] the doctrine of equal brotherhood. They want brotherhood with their enemy before they ask for brotherhood with their own kind. Old preachers, Christian, so called Christian church preachers, black preachers, preaching such doctrine that we are all brothers, classifying himself and his followers with being the brother of the devil and the lovers and admirers, worshipers of real devils, their slave masters, regardless to what evil their slave masters do to them they fear to charge him with it, they fear to go from it, *they fear to ask for a place other than the place that the slave master prepare* [sic] *for them: that's a place of torment, worry, grief, and sorrow*.[5]

These African Americans (Christians and preachers) perversely desired to linger in the abyss of abjection—that is, in the oppressive and constrictive social and symbolic "places" to which they were relegated—rather than transverse the boundaries that rendered them subservient. The quote also indicates Muhammad's awareness that the social order functions to relegate black bodies to in-placeness—to keep them in their place—and for him, being in-place meant that black people would experience torment and grief.

Cosmology and the "Original Man": The Yakub Myth and Anthropological Reversal

Elijah Muhammad became the Messenger of Allah and the "absolute" leader of the NOI after the "disappearance" of Master Fard Muhammad in 1933.[6] Master Fard Muhammad was the founder of what at the time was called Allah's Temple of Islam and later became the NOI. The organization was started on July 4, 1930. Master Fard Muhammad was a man of ambiguous racial heritage. Some scholars argue that he was from New Zealand, while others suggest he was from Pakistan. New evidence suggests that

Master Fard Muhammad was of African ancestry at least in part. He conducted services in Detroit. His mission was to find the lost nation of black people in the wilderness of North America and restore them (i.e., black bodies) to their cosmic and natural state.[7] Elijah Muhammad's wife, Clara, encouraged her husband to hear Master Fard Muhammad speak, and the two engaged on at least one important occasion: Elijah Muhammad reportedly asked Master Fard Muhammad questions about his identity as the long-awaited Messiah, to which Master Fard Muhammad responded that Elijah Muhammad had perceived that correctly and should keep it a secret. Subsequently, Elijah Muhammad became his primary disciple. This relationship continued for about three years before Master Fard Muhammad dropped out of public view under mysterious circumstances. The accounts of what happened to him varied depending on the source. For example, the NOI claimed that Master Fard Muhammad ascended to heaven, while federal law enforcement agencies said that he was not who he claimed to be and ended up in a prison in California. The details of the transition are not clear, but Elijah Muhammad became the group's leader after Master Fard Muhammad's disappearance. Almost immediately, Elijah Muhammad took aim at reforming bodies that he saw as being in-place.

Elijah Muhammad was vociferously opposed to black bodies that he interpreted as being in-place symbolically, finding them grotesque and antithetical to their divine nature. The narrative and metaphysical account of the history and origins of the world expressed in the story of Yakub was the basis for his critique of this whitenized black embodiment—which functioned ideologically to maintain white domination.[8] Perhaps because of the omnipresence of violence in everyday life, which gave rise to a sense of terror, the mythology of Yakub became foundational.

Elijah Muhammad understood violence as part of the existential fact of blackness. It was unavoidable, inevitable, ubiquitous. Such a comprehensive and systematic conception of the world as brutal affects black people in devastating ways in that, as for Muhammad, the possibility of violence becomes a necessary everyday consideration in one's life choices. Likewise, the political philosopher Iris Young argues that violence is systemic because it is directed at members of a particular group for no other reason than that they are members of that group. Women, for instance, have reasons to fear rape. African Americans, she contends, are subject to violence just because they are black: "Regardless of what a Black man has done to escape the oppressions of marginality and powerlessness, he lives knowing he is subject to attack or harassment."[9] This violence is an informal and extrajudicial form of public administration, a way to relegate and police the activities of a group that implies an understanding that bodies are metaphors. In practical terms, this means, "If they do it to you, they'll do it to me," as a friend of mine once said. It is a form of terrorism, as Young argues: "The oppression of violence consists not only in direct victimization, but in the daily knowledge shared by all members of oppressed groups that they are *liable* to violation, solely on account of their group identity. Just living under such a threat of attack on oneself or family or friends deprives the oppressed of freedom and dignity, and needlessly expends their energy."[10]

Muhammad would become familiar with such ever-present terror and the threat of violence.[11] As the grandson of slaves and the great-grandson of a slave master, Muhammad was profoundly influenced and emotionally scarred by the violent terror that he experienced as a child and young adult growing up in Georgia.[12] The journalist Karl Evanzz suggests that for African Americans, the period of Muhammad's childhood was the most violent and aggressive period of lynching, with one-third of all lynchings after 1882 carried out between 1890 and 1900.[13] During the year of Muhammad's birth, 1897, at least 123 African Americans were lynched.[14] Three weeks after Muhammad (then Elijah Poole) was born, Georgia's governor W. Y. Atkinson spoke of such lynching as necessary due to the rise in the African American population in the state: he claimed that such violence protected the virtue of white women.[15] On numerous occasions, Muhammad witnessed evidence or heard stories of local lynchings of African Americans in his hometown of Cordele and in nearby towns.[16] As a child (sometime between 1903 and 1905), for example, he ventured into town and encountered a white man who opened his hand to show him the ear of a black man, apparently one of several lynching trophies that the man possessed.[17] On another occasion, in 1907, a large crowd of whites had lynched a black youth whom they accused of raping a young white girl. Muhammad gazed in astonishment as the adolescent body dangled from a tree branch. "He cried for the dead youth and the rest of the blacks in Cordele, who in his view, allowed the killing to take place," Evanzz writes.[18] The perpetrators faced only minimal threat of consequences, legal or otherwise, because of the important role lynchings played in maintaining the status quo. It is little wonder that they happened so frequently and that African Americans very seldom acted to protect themselves against them.[19] Not only was the lynching itself a shock to young Muhammad's sense of safety and well-being, but the apparent helplessness of black people was traumatic.[20]

Perhaps the greatest trauma for Elijah was the lynching of his close friend and neighbor Albert Hamilton in 1912. White locals had "identified" Hamilton as the "big burly Negro" who had attacked a young white girl.[21] Police arrested and imprisoned him at the Crisp County Jail, where three black men had been lynched a week earlier. A white mob overran the jail, dragging Hamilton out of the building and through the black section of Cordele, called "Negro town." There they shot him more than three hundred times and hanged him. They took photographs of the lynching, from which they made and sold hundreds of postcards in nearby towns.[22] The spectacle was meant to be an example to other black people (again, a form of public administration meant to keep black bodies in-place). Young Elijah "cried all the way home," he said later, and swore retribution: "If I ever got to be a man, I told myself, I would find a way to avenge him and my people."[23] The historian Claude Andrew Clegg III writes: "This traumatic experience stayed with Elijah for the rest of his life and certainly made him more susceptible to black separatist doctrines."[24]

Such horrendous events punctuated Elijah's young adult life, too. More than a decade later, in 1919, he would marry Clara Belle Evans, whom he had met at a Cordele dance; in that year's infamous "Red Summer," more African Americans were lynched in eight months than in any full year of the preceding decade.[25] These included the lynching of several black men and the burning of several black churches and lodges in nearby Millen and Milan, Georgia.[26] Elijah and Clara moved to Macon in mid-September, thinking it would be less violent than Cordele partly due to its large black population.[27] Unfortunately, lynching was also prevalent in Macon. Elijah learned of another lynching in the vicinity of Macon on October 7, 1919, his twenty-second birthday. On a day that should have been a joyous celebration, a white mob kidnapped a black prisoner, Eugene Hamilton, from police custody and shot him.[28] The lynching made a lie the idea of "safety in numbers."[29] In fact, the day before Hamilton was murdered, Evanzz documents, two other black men were burned alive. As if that were not enough, another man had been lynched near Sandersville, Georgia, where Elijah was born, only two days earlier—on Sunday, October 5—for a total of "four racially motivated murders in the state in three days."[30] Nowhere in Georgia was safe for black people.

So in April 1923, Elijah left his family in Georgia for Detroit, seeking greater social and economic possibilities.[31] After several months, he had saved enough money to send for his family. But they soon learned that poverty, racial violence, and even the Ku Klux Klan were as bad in Michigan as they had been in Georgia. In fact, the Klan and other white terrorist organizations were as large, and at least as powerful and influential, there as they were in the South.[32]

These traumas formed a lens through which Elijah Muhammad would view America and white people throughout his life. In a speech that he delivered in the mid-1960s, for instance, he explains, "This is the American so-called Negro: Robbed so complete today that even after reading the history of how their fathers were brought here, put on the block and sailed [sic] off as animals, and have been lynched and burned to the stake for every century since he has been here. And today he is being beaten and killed, shot down on the streets and on the highways throughout the government of America without hinderance [sic] by his slave masters children."[33] Muhammad suggests that the American experience has stripped away humanity and dignity from African Americans. Their history is characterized by slavery and lynching, he declares, and, he intimates, the ethos of American culture promotes violence against black bodies even beyond those practices—or, at least, it does nothing to curtail it. Furthermore, this manner of interpreting the world is what made the myth of Yakub compelling and at the same time so necessary: it offered an explanation for the social order, for racial violence, and ultimately, for the subjugation of black people in America. It was a theodicy, or what I call *theological phenomenology*. I use this term to describe violence against African Americans and then make it coherent in an otherwise absurd world.[34]

To this end, the saga of Yakub is a complex and sometimes conflicting and confusing narrative that attempts to explain the transatlantic middle passage, slavery, lynching, and oppression at the hands of whites: the problem of evil. It affirms that God is good, but in a key reversal of common theological conceptions of race, it asserts that God is on the side of the NOI, God's chosen and "original" people.[35] Effectively reversing centuries of racial discourse and theological anthropology that rendered black people divinely inferior, the story explains that white people behaved in a racially aggressive manner because it was their nature as "made," rather than "created," people.[36]

Muhammad told the story of Yakub in speeches, newspaper articles, sermons, and radio addresses, citing it as a history and science of the entire universe.[37] This narrative and its periodization were divinely inspired, Muhammad said. He located its genesis with the appearance of Master Fard Muhammad—Allah-in-person, the Great Mahdi, and founder of the NOI—in 1930: "Allah came to us from the Holy City Mecca, Arabia in 1930.

He used the name Wallace D. Fard, often signing it W. D. Fard. In the third year (1933), He signed his name W. F. Muhammad which stands for Wallace Fard Muhammad. He came alone. He began teaching us the knowledge of ourselves, of God and the devil, of the measurement of the earth, of other planets, and of the civilizations of some of the planets other than the earth."[38] The theodicean account that Master Fard Muhammad would transmit to Elijah Muhammad for the three years in which he learned from Master Fard—part history, science, cosmology, numerology, and theological anthropology—would transform Muhammad's reality and give it a coherence and consciousness that the unlettered man had never before experienced. The world was no longer absurd, and the racial violence and oppression made perfect sense, now that he understood "Mr. Yakub."

Elijah Muhammad had absolute certainty that this was the truth because it had been given to him by Fard, who had revealed that he was God. He said that he had asked Fard, "Who are you?" and Fard replied, "I am the one the world had been expecting for the past 2,000 years. . . . My name is Mahdi; I am God."[39] In Muhammad's mind, it was simple: Allah, who came to him in the person of Master Fard Muhammad, in a rather mundane and ordinary way, gave to him the secrets of the universe: "He gave the exact birth of the white race, the name of their God who made them (i.e., Yakub) and how; and the end of their time; the judgment, how it will begin and end."[40] Allah told him (literally, in face-to-face conversations) the secret of how African Americans were made slaves and kept slaves through Christianity and how America would meet its doom.[41] Consequently, Muhammad had access to the mysteries of the universe— all of which are woven together in the elaborate narrative of Yakub.

THE SELF-CREATION OF GOD AND THE COSMOS

The Yakub narrative uses highly symbolic language that I organize into five periods:[42] the self-creation of God and the origin of the cosmos more than seventy-six trillion years ago and the creation of the Original People on Earth, Mars, and Venus; a plot to destroy the Original People of the Earth sixty-six trillion years ago; an era fifty thousand years ago when the remnants of the Original People lived in the Nile Valley, or "East Asia"; a six hundred-year process, six thousand years ago, during which a black renegade scientist named Yakub made the white race; and, finally, the coming of the Mother Plane that destroys this present age and ushers in the new millennium (Ch. 2).[43] This thematic organization of the mythology is unique to this book.

According to the narrative, the literal and scientific history of African Americans, the "so-called American Negro," goes back roughly seventy-six trillion years, when the universe was filled with darkness and lacked materiality and temporality because nothing moved.[44] This was prior to the invention of writing, so not much is known about it, except that the only existence other than the void of the darkness was an atom, Muhammad insists. He avoids nagging questions of scientific cosmology such as the origin of the atom, which became significant given that, for him, Allah (God) created everything.

The origin of atoms was the question that the physicist Fred Hoyle was exploring. Hoyle was a proponent of the steady state theory of the universe (a refutation of the Big Bang), which he called the "continuous creation": matter always existed and was continuously being created. This neutralized the need to explain the origin of the atom.[45] For Muhammad, time simply began when the original atom began to move, and the atom subsequently developed flesh, blood, brains, and power—consciousness.[46] This was the "beginning" of God, Allah. From this self-creation, God then turned his attention to creating other "gods." Muhammad suggests that these were the original black people but fails to explain why they were called gods.[47]

Then God created the cosmos—an elaborate cosmogony that included a seven-planet solar system, each of which sustained animate life-forms such as gods (i.e., people). The original gods lived on planet Earth, which at the time consisted of what later became the Earth and the Moon. Ruled from "Asia," Earth was the homeland of the thirteen tribes into which Allah organized the gods "united by skin color (black), religion (Islam), and disposition (righteous)."[48] Of the other planets, Mars was by far the most significant, and the gods who lived there, while less intelligent than the beings of Earth, were believed to live as long as 1,200 years, although most lived for two hundred years. About this planet and its inhabitants, Muhammad had much to say—for example:

> God taught me that He has pictures of the Martian people, and the devil [white people] believes it, because they have come so near to looking at the surface of Mars to look for creatures on it. They believe that they are there. They [the beings on Mars] are very wise, very skillful, so Allah taught me. They hear his [white people's?] planes coming. They could hide away. They live on that planet 1000 [sic] of our Earth years, so he may have seen a plane from the Earth yesterday. If they don't want to be seen by you, they don't have to let you see them. That's the truth. You have people

on Mars! Think how great you are. Ask the white man if he has any out there. We have life on other planets, but he don't.[49]

Extending black life beyond the United States—and, indeed, planet Earth—had aesthetic implications for black bodies. These were bodies that were not wholly defined by earthbound racist discourses and, by implication, were the sites of ultimate reality in the universe. Moreover, Mars was important because its black people were those who lived the longest and grew the largest. They may have represented how robust black bodies could be physically. Such life indicates that black bodies are superior, given that whites are limited to earthly existence and black people are interstellar. But Muhammad also maintained that white people were aware of black life on Mars.

Clegg, the author of several books about Elijah Muhammad, including *An Original Man*, suggests that, in constructing this astrobiological aspect of the mythology, Master Fard Muhammad capitalized on fantasies and fears that circulated in the early twentieth century. He points out that life in the cosmos was a theme promulgated by American cinema, itself a developing art form. While Clegg makes an interesting point concerning the role of cinema in diffusing cultural trends—one will also recognize parallels between H. G. Wells's UFO and the Mothership that Minister Louis Farrakhan describes (see chapter 5)—it should also be noted that movies such as *The Birth of a Nation* (1915), *Hallelujah* (1929), *Imitation of Life* (1934), and hundreds of other "race films" also marketed notions of race en masse during the same time period, which contributed to this mythology's easy conflation of race and cosmology.[50]

The story continues its cosmic theme while returning to the notion of "writing." As such, written script was invented several trillion years later, after the beginnings of the universe, due to the need to chronicle the future. The saga contends that 30 percent of the population was always discontented, and everyone was mortal, even though they were righteous and peaceful.[51] In a sense, the story wants to communicate that a type of human fall was inevitable, given the language it uses to describe the Original People as discontented and mortal. These gods of Earth were not eternal—they lived only two hundred to three hundred years, and then they died. As a result, twenty-three god-scientists wrote the future history, and the twenty-fourth analyzed what was written, perhaps made necessary by their own mortality.[52] Elijah Muhammad does not explain why the chroniclers were called "god-scientists," but he does specify that time progressed in

25,000-year cycles, in each of which a god was chosen to reveal the will of Allah.[53] The 25,000-year dispensations that were written by twenty-four scientists correspond to the circumference of the Earth—roughly 24,000 miles—and the twenty-four hours in a day.[54] By using the term *god-scientist*, he may have been attempting to communicate that these original black people were educated and systematic in their approach to the construction of knowledge. Subsequently, the texts that they developed became the Qur'an and the Bible in their modern and organized forms.

RENEGADE BLACK SCIENTISTS AND
THE DESTRUCTION OF THE ORIGINAL PEOPLE

The story is challenging to reconstruct because it has no singular coherent source or record; instead, it has multiple fragmented ones. What seems to happen at this point, however, is that another god-scientist enters the narrative. This scientist is a predecessor of Yakub and, like Yakub, is a renegade black scientist who appeared on the scene sixty-six trillion years ago. Apparently angered over the linguistic and philosophical heterogeneity of the Original People and desiring to rule, he devised a plan in which he drilled a deep hole in the Earth, filled it with an explosive that was 30 percent more powerful than dynamite, and detonated it, which separated the planet into the Earth and the Moon.[55] More specifically, the Moon was split off, or "deported": "The Blasting away of MOON [*sic*] by an enemy . . . robbed the MOON of its life (water) and poured it onto this part of planet Earth. . . . [T]his man or God who in his frenzy to try to force all the people to believe as he believed and to speak the same language with no difference in dialect, caused the deportation of the MOON from the Earth."[56] Prior to the explosion, the Earth and the Moon formed one planet; the "deportation" of the Moon explains their separation. One of the original thirteen tribes was killed in this explosion because the tribe ended up on the Moon, which did not have enough water to sustain life. Nonetheless, the twelve remaining tribes survived on Earth.

EAST ASIA AND THE ORIGINAL PEOPLE
OF THE EARTH

The most resilient of the twelve tribes, the Tribe of Shabazz, went on a quest to find and settle the richest land on Earth. This search led the tribe to the Nile Valley, which the story calls "East Asia," from where they also founded a sister civilization in Mecca.[57] The narrative foregrounds Egypt and Mecca—one cultural and the other religious—as central locations for the black race. Describing the story in *Message to the Blackman in America*, Muhammad passes over trillions of years of "history" and takes up the issue of East Asia, which apparently is where the Tribe of Shabazz lived for millennia. The NOI came to identify itself as the Lost-Found Tribe of Shabazz.

At this juncture, while this mythology still functioned as both a theodicy and a counter-hegemonic discourse *contra* racist Western ideologies, the story reveals the depth to which Master Fard Muhammad and Elijah Muhammad had internalized notions that suggested "black" features were inferior and a distortion of the white norm. In an effort to explain black bodily phenotypes, the legend apologizes for stereotypical African characteristics in a way that offers a classical illustration of Du Boisian "double consciousness," or the practice of seeing oneself through the "revelation of the other world."[58]

The saga intimates that fifty thousand years ago, a dissatisfied scientist from the Tribe of Shabazz encouraged members of the clan to move their families to the "jungle" of East Asia (Africa) to make the Original People "tough and hard . . . to prove to us that we could live there and conquer the wild beasts."[59] This jungle experience adversely affected black features, which is the "origin of our kinky hair" and other distinctions generally described in negative terms.[60] Muhammad offers an example of this contention: "The Origin of our kinky hair, says Allah, came from one of our dissatisfied scientists, 50,000 years ago, who wanted to make all of us tough and hard in order to endure the life of the jungles of East Asia (Africa) and to overcome the beasts there. But he failed to get the others to agree with him. He took his family and moved into the jungle to prove to us that he could live there and conquer the wild beasts."[61]

Muhammad implies here that black hair, which he describes negatively as "kinky," is the result of a "jungle" experience and as such represents a devolution in black physiology. Malcolm X, one of Muhammad's most important disciples, goes on to say that "nappy hair" is a result of "living in a rough climate," and that the remnants of their primordial hair can be seen in the eyebrows of black people, which are straight-haired.[62] No one explains how what is characterized as the degeneration of physical features of one family was transmitted to the greater black populace, especially since the majority of the Tribe of Shabazz refused to follow this dissatisfied scientist.

The tale unwittingly affirms negative meanings ascribed to black bodies by suggesting that their (African) traits signify corruption, distortion, and wildness and thus also acquiesces to the popular conception that Africa was characterized by "jungles" populated by savage people. Clegg notes the dynamic: "Yet, in a regrettable way, the attempt of Fard Muhammad to rationalize the origins of Negroid features denigrated natural characteristics of blacks from tropical Africa. To depict this part of the continent as uncivilized enough to strip away both the Caucasian features and Islamic culture of the Original People reinforced myths and racist stereotypes about Africa that were already popular in the Western world."[63] These are the very notions that the saga intended to counteract by positively associating Islam as the natural religion of the black race and to reclaim Egypt, which has been ascribed to many cultures and peoples other than indigenous Africans, as the classical African civilization.[64] To this end, the story's repudiation of Africa and Africans—even calling Africa "East Asia"—was an effort to distance African Americans from *some of* the negative Western stereotypes associated with Africa and blackness. This is to say that the NOI had assimilated Western ideas about blackness from which it then needed to distance itself to valorize black bodies.

The NOI seemed unaware of the contradiction. Fard and Elijah Muhammad would continue to propagate the saga in an effort to valorize black bodies and to reimagine them.

YAKUB, THE MAKING OF THE WHITE RACE, AND GENOCIDE

As the story goes, Yakub, the latest and the most significant of the god-scientists, was born near Mecca about six thousand years ago in the current 25,000-year cycle.[65] This event was prophesied by the twenty-four scientists 8,400 years before his birth.[66] Muhammad claims: "Six thousand years ago, or to be more exact 6,600 years ago, as Allah taught me, our nation gave birth to another God whose name was Yakub. He started studying the life germ of man to try making a new creation (new man) whom our twenty-four scientists had foretold 8,400 years before the birth of Mr. Yakub, and the Scientists were aware of his birth and work before he was born, as they are today of the intentions or ideas of the present world."[67] Known as the "Big Head" for his superior intellectual abilities and his arrogance or wisdom, Yakub was one of the 30 percent of those who were discontented.[68] Gifted with superior genius, he studied genetics (i.e., "the germ of man"), again as the collective of god-scientists had prophesied.

To be sure, from the time of his youth, Yakub was intent on making trouble for the Original People, and his studies and unusual creativity would ultimately serve his goal of human destruction. He devised his plan from an unusual source, using his keen insight to discern a metaphorical relationship between magnetic and human attraction that would be the basis of a diabolical scheme. Muhammad explains: "Allah said: 'When Yakub was six years old, one day, he was sitting down playing with two pieces of steel. He noticed the magnetic power in the steel attracting the other. He looked up at his uncle and said: "Uncle, when I get to be an old man, I am going to make a people who shall rule you." The uncle said: "What will you make; something to make mischief and cause bloodshed in the land?" Yakub said: "Nevertheless, Uncle, I know that which you do not know."'[69] This episode with the magnets was a revelatory object lesson for Yakub: the magnets symbolized the power of attraction. From them, Yakub saw how an "unlike" people could attract, manipulate, and rule the Original People with lies and tricks.[70]

By eighteen, Yakub had finished his formal education at the colleges and universities of his land, and he was esteemed as a brilliant scientist. Subsequently, he engaged in the study of eugenics to make such an "unlike" people who could dominate the Original People (see figure 1.1). By studying the Original Man's "germ," or chromosomes, under a microscope, Yakub discovered that there were two "people" in him—one black and one brown, which correspond to dominant and recessive genes and traits. Through a type of genetic engineering called grafting, he determined that he could "make" a (white) race of people who could rule and ultimately destroy the black nation:[71] "He said if he could successfully separate the one from the other he could graft the brown germ into its last stage, which would be white. With his wisdom, he could make the white, which he discovered was the weaker of the black germ (which would be unalike) rule the black nation for a time (until a greater one than Yakub was born)."[72]

The source of Elijah Muhammad's knowledge of rudimentary genetics is uncertain. Since he claimed to have learned such mysteries from Master Fard in the early 1930s, perhaps one of them had encountered the work of the geneticist Gregor Mendel or related work in the agricultural sciences, since "grafting" is both an agrarian concept and a term of nineteenth-century race studies. Notwithstanding the ambiguity of the sources and terms, Muhammad suggests that Yakub discovered that he could engineer genetic traits, and he set out to make converts so that he might create a community from among the Original People that would carry out his vision. He did so by seducing them with a corrupted form of Islam that

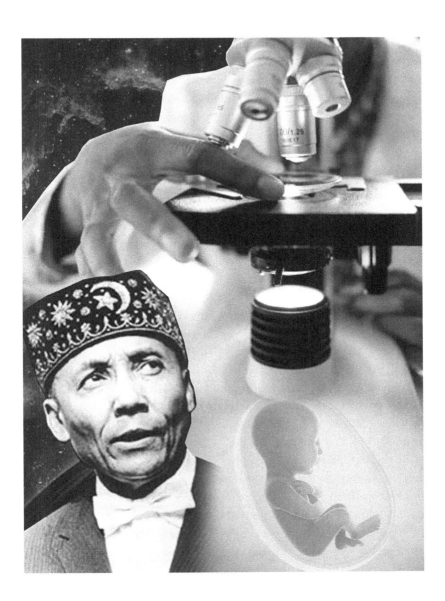

1.1

Elijah Muhammad proclaimed that Master Fard Muhammad taught him about Yakub, a renegade black scientist who made white people in a genetic engineering process after discovering "germs" (i.e., genes) by examining the germs of the original family of "black" people under a microscope. Collage created for the author by David Metcalfe.

promised riches and luxury to those who would follow his leadership.[73] This corrupted Islam may have been a reference to the Islam of the Arabs, but it is unclear whether this was intended as a critique of them.

Fearing the power that Yakub might develop with his seductive doctrine and noticing his constantly growing audience, the King of Mecca (the city in which Yakub was born and raised) jailed Yakub and his followers. But converts believed that they could graft an unlike kind to rule the Original People, and they continued to proliferate by way of wealth-based proselytizing that promised riches to converts.[74] This notion of wealth and prosperity may have functioned as critical commentary on the rise of the Christian and Religious Science gospel of wealth that was being taught by preachers such as Frederick J. Eikerenkoetter (a.k.a. Reverend Ike), whose ministry was contemporaneous with the rise of the NOI. As the story continues, the king—concerned that such a crowd could easily be led to sedition—exiled Yakub and his 59,999 followers (60,000 with Yakub) to Pelan, an island in the Aegean Sea that is known as Patmos in the Bible.[75] "Patmos" was an obvious reference to the Christian Bible: it was the island on which the writer, called "John," allegedly composed the apocalyptic Book of Revelation.

The King of Mecca supported the exiles with finances and technology for twenty years, helping them to establish their own civilization in exchange for their cooperation with the exile. This aspect of the story corresponds to—and may serve as the justification for—Muhammad's demand that the US government support an independent African American religious nation financially for twenty to twenty-five years.[76] Moreover, the king was so afraid of Yakub that he was willing to make any deal with him and his followers.[77] Yakub promised his people that if they chose him as their king, he would share with them the esoteric knowledge that would give them the power to rule the people who had banished them. These events occurred about 6,000 years ago.

More specifically, Yakub set about organizing a genocidal civilization that privileged those who could participate in the destruction of the black race, the "Original Man." Through the process of grafting, he would separate the black germ from the brown germ; from the brown germ would come the red, and from the red, the yellow—a six hundred-year procedure until, finally, the white race was *made*. Though Yakub died at the age of 150, he had by then passed on his secret knowledge to his followers. To guarantee the method, Yakub's people would forbid black people to marry one another and would kill all the black babies that were born (and save the brown ones). The nurses would tell the new parents that the black babies had died and gone on to a better place—that is, heaven. Thus, the story implicated doctors, nurses, ministers, cremators, and even notions such as heaven in the conspiracy.[78]

This story indicates an anxiety that black bodies are in constant jeopardy. Though black bodies for the Nation of Islam included bodies that were phenotypically "brown," "yellow," and "red," the "black," or the darkest of black bodies, were the most at risk of genocide. Furthermore, the story could function ideologically to support interdictions against miscegenation and exogamy, which in the earlier scenario could be read as protecting black bodies against the possibility of genetic extinction. This episode of the story may suggest Muhammad's concern that African Americans were under attack systematically, given that religious, medical, funerary, and other institutions were conspiring to severely curtail their ability to reproduce, if not to outright eliminate them. Finally, such institutionalization of violence against black bodies would mean that no one individual or organization had to maintain the system of destruction, for it was so strategically embedded in the structures of the society that it would continue to function after the death of its chief architect, Yakub. Important at this point is the notion that ideology and theology, including concepts such as heaven, obfuscate insidious practices that support the system of racial annihilation. Christianity, then, and those who embrace it can serve only evil and violent purposes against African Americans. For this reason, Muhammad saw black people who are Christians as the ultimate betrayers of other black people and as utterly whitenized ideologically. From his perspective, black Christians were the quintessential black bodies in-place, both socially and symbolically.

Muhammad explained the final stage of grafting: "The Yakub made devils were really pale white, with really blue eyes; which we think are the ugliest colors for a human eye. They were called Caucasian—which means, according to some Arab scholars, 'One whose evil effect is not confined to one's self alone, but affects others.'"[79] It is in this culminating scene, in which white people are made, where we can most clearly see the anthropological reversal that underlies the Yakub myth. That is to say, Muhammad, and presumably Fard, signify on hundreds of years of racial and theological discourses that argued for the inferiority of black bodies and black intellect and, to paraphrase the scholar of religion Anthony

Pinn, flipped it on its head, reversing Cornel West's notion of the normative gaze.[80] Instead of the standard and the most beautiful, or the ideal for humanity (i.e., blond hair and blue eyes), whiteness is in fact a derogation of original black humanity.

The "devils" (i.e., because they were "made") would terrorize and attempt to dominate the Original People for six thousand years, first by returning to Mecca (Paradise) in 4 BCE with a vengeful intent and being repelled by the King of Mecca to West Asia (Europe).[81] The devils caused the black nations to fight one another, an enduring legacy to this day for the so-called Negroes who cannot unite.[82] In West Asia (i.e., Europe), the white race would undergo a progressive degeneration toward incivility and animality until finally they were living in caves with dogs, running around nude, eating raw meat, climbing trees, walking on their hands and feet, and engaging in all sorts of immorality and savagery, and subsequently no longer resembling the people Yakub made.[83] They even tried to graft themselves back into the black race, and a few of them were lucky enough to begin the process, getting only as far as the gorilla, however.[84] Muhammad discussed the possibility of salvation for the white race and suggested that it was possible through grafting them back into the black race—that is, by reversing the process of genetic engineering.[85] I want to read this desire to (re)incorporate the other as relating psychoanalytically to the desire to return to a state in which there was no subject-object differentiation between white and black people, if humanity's origins, indeed, have one source, which is generally accepted as Africa (and as expressed in the mythology). Furthermore, the mythology may express a desire to "save" what whites represent symbolically (i.e., evil) because this can be read as a segment of what is black, having originated from black and existing in the black self so that it is present in white selves. In the language of psychoanalytic object relations, Yakub can be interpreted as expressing unconscious desire to reincorporate that which has been lost—in this case, a primordial state in which black people were more "human" and whites were more "animal."

The *made* (white) race became so pathetic that Allah sent a series of prophets to raise its level of civilization so that the prophecy that they would rule the black nation for six thousand years could be fulfilled. The first of these prophets was Musa (Moses), a "mulatto" sage, who around 2000 BCE brought whites out of the caves and taught them how to cook meat and avoid pork. Later, Allah sent Jesus, but they (whites, Jews) killed him with a knife or sword against a wooden wall.[86] Muhammad clarifies:

Jesus, who had been simply a mortal man of flesh and blood, was deified by conspirators, who sought to obscure the reality of Allah. December 25, the birthday of the wicked Nimrod, was designated Christmas, or the date of birth for Jesus, who was actually born in September. Additionally, a book, the Bible, that mixed spiritual truth and secular falsehood was promulgated as the authoritative text regarding the history of God and the creation, the life of Jesus and other prophets, and the nature of heaven and hell. The unholy conspiracy, later known as Christianity, was spearheaded by the pope of Rome, who is symbolized in the Book of Revelation as the dragon or devil. The Christian church [is] a masterpiece of tricknology.[87]

Finally, in 622 CE (1 AH), Allah sent Muhammad Ibn Abdullah—the Prophet Muhammad—to counter the pernicious teachings of Christianity, the conspiratorial ideas that were meant to deceive the Original People, and the European whites rejected him. Muhammad was so dejected that he died of grief ten years later (632 CE/10 AH). In short, Allah was attempting to redeem whites through these various prophets. Here the narrative makes Allah and black people tacitly responsible for the destruction and oppression of the black race. Thus, the mythology fails to resolve yet another significant conflict, given that the nature of the *made* European race is to be destructive, having been made that way by a fallen black scientist, and God was responsible for their survival. After conquering the Muslim armies, these Europeans then moved westward to a new land in America. They enslaved Native Americans but soon needed a new source of labor, taking Negroes from East Asia (Africa) as slaves and giving them Christianity, which functioned to make them "deaf, dumb and blind."[88] Christianity, Elijah Muhammad argued, continues to make black people deaf, dumb, and blind and to render black bodies in-place symbolically as ideologically white. He is thus suggesting that Christianity is an instrument of oppression.

This narrative, like other mythologies, attempts to explain the nature of the universe, metaphysics, theological anthropology, and certainly, evil and suffering that so-called Negroes have experienced for hundreds of years in America. At the same time, the epic reverses long-held notions about Africans and their descendants, especially in the United States and England—namely, that the hierarchical relationship between European Americans and African Americans, in which black people were subjugated, was a metaphysically fixed relationship that was/is characterized by binary oppositions such as good and evil, right and wrong, beautiful and grotesque, intelligent and bestial, subject and object, and so on.

In the scenario given to us by Master Fard Muhammad and Elijah Muhammad, it is the "white man" who is ontologically inferior, evil by nature, uncivilized, and deceptive; who utilizes Christianity to enslave and delude the "Original Man" so that he forgets who he is—Muslim and righteous by divine nature. He (the white man) is made, and because he is made rather than created, like the Lost-Found Tribe of Shabazz in the wilderness of North America, the devil, or the 666 beast of the Book of Revelation, he can do no righteousness with respect to the black nation.[89] The narrative ends with the fifth and final motif of retribution and regeneration when the Mother Plane, a UFO holding Master Fard (and later, Muhammad), returns to Earth to end the age of Yakub (i.e., the white race), ushering in a millennial era of peace. The devil's tricks and his deceptive religion are destined by God for destruction at the end of his six thousand-year rule for all of the murders and for systematically hoodwinking so-called Negroes into forgetting their divine nature and religion.[90] But ultimately it is Christianity that is the greatest ideological and conspiratorial force that is used to deceive black people and to whitenize black bodies.

The Science of Tricknology: Christianity and Black Bodies In-Place

Consistent with the mythology of Yakub, Muhammad maintained that black people are Muslim and righteous by nature. Christianity, which was used by the devil to enslave them, however, has led to a degeneration of culture and morality and given rise to a sort of retrograde amnesia about their true nature and identity.[91] As the discursive and ideological legacy of Yakub—who used its concepts, such as the belief in heaven, to destroy black babies and to make white people—Christianity is the religion of the devil, and Yakub is its God, since he was its originator. Christianity is the master signifier of "tricknology," a well-developed system of lies, a skillful and crafty science of deception that was used to enslave Africans and their African American descendants and is central to the perpetuation of their mental slavery. Muhammad states that "Christianity is a religion organized and backed by the devils for the purpose of making slaves of black mankind."[92] He also states, "Freedom, Justice, Equality; money, good homes, etc.—these Christianity cannot give us (not the Christianity that has been taught us). He (Allah) said that Christianity was organized by the white race and they placed the name Jesus on it being the founder and author to deceive black people into accepting it."[93] The very purpose of Christianity is to serve in the making of "slaves" of black people so that, for Muhammad, it is oxymoronic for a black person to be Christian. In the strongest possible terms, Christianity to him means "white," so black and "Christian" signifies having been whitenized symbolically.

This relationship between Christianity and black slavery is symbolized by John Hawkins, a frequently referenced English slave trader whom Muhammad names erroneously as solely responsible for enslaving millions of Africans and transporting them to America in 1555 in his slave ship *Jesus*.[94] Muhammad said, "When this ship was on its way back from another load of our people, our foreparents stared at the old slave ship as it departed and begged to be carried back, but to no avail, and they said that 'you can have this new Western world but give us the ship Jesus back to our people and country,' which now has become a song among our people, which goes something like this: 'You—can—have—all—the—world—but—give—me—Jesus.'"[95] The fact that the slave ship is named *Jesus* has vast implications for Muhammad. On the one hand, it represents Christianity's role in the transportation of Africans from their lands of origin to slavery in America. On the other hand, he seems to suggest that the longing for Jesus in black spiritual songs was really a desire to return to their home in Africa via the slave ship.

Christianity served to fix black bodies in-place, socially and symbolically, in a state of subjugation—"slavery." In other words, Christianity, as a religious discourse and a social philosophy, was a means by which the white race oppressed the black nation, perpetuating its social and economic dependence and control while promulgating its members' mental and spiritual inferiority. As a result, Elijah Muhammad hated Christianity; he saw it as demonic and as synonymous with whiteness, a trick of the devil writ large.[96] Thus, the Yakub myth is, among other things, intellectual resistance by African Americans to the totalizing and deterministic effects of a dominating and oppressive social system that functions to order and secure social relations between the "races." It seeks to disrupt, however inadequately, the perpetual reproduction of societies and institutions that terrorize and dehumanize black people.

African Americans, then, who were the promoters of the "devil's" religion, were the most deceived, the most ignorant, and the most whitenized—and, indeed, the worst traitors of their race, as they functioned in service of their own people's domination, too dumb to be aware that they were being used and tricked into doing so. Speaking in 1958 at a Saviour's Day, the NOI's national convention, which was also attended by a large contingency of four hundred African American Christians, Muhammad said:

> He uses the name Jesus, but you should be wise. The white man doesn't want to recognize no Black prophet, nor any Black angel, nor any God that is Black. He's got to be a white prophet. He's got to be a white angel. He's got to be a white God for him to recognize him. And he has you following that particular color, white. And he's indirectly made you to believe or think that when you go to heaven, you will be white like himself. Therefore that makes you always inclined to that particular color and desire to be that color instead of your own original color.[97]

Muhammad points out the apparent irony: white people would never recognize a black religion with a black pantheon, but African American Christians have to embrace the most pervasive ideology of white supremacy.

No class of people embodied the condition of having been whitenized more than African American Christian preachers. The "poor black clergy class" was the "worst," the most deluded by the white man's technology of tricks.[98] Whereas the divine nature of the true African American was black, Muslim, and righteous, the "Negro" preacher was the antithesis—"white," Christian, and "untrustworthy."[99] Although Muhammad viewed preachers as one group or "class," the Reverend Dr. Martin Luther King Jr., the civil rights leader of the 1950s and 1960s, was, for him, the worst of the worst:

> Reverend Martin Luther King, Jr., wants brotherhood with white America for himself and his followers. As reported here, the Nobel Peace Prize was conferred on him in Norway. Reverend King sharply warned in St. Paul's Cathedral that "A doctrine of black supremacy was as great a danger as one of white supremacy." . . . Of his own people he said, "We must not seek to rise from a position of disadvantage to one of advantage substituting injustice of one type for that of another." I have never heard of any such talk coming from a leader's mouth in all of my life. If a man is NOT going to rise from a position of disadvantage why is he preaching for the passage of the Civil Rights Bill for his people? . . . This kind of talk coming from a theological college graduate is almost unbelievable.[100]

Muhammad suggests that King's words erroneously indict the NOI as a reversal of supremacist ideologies and practices. Muhammad wants to show that this kind of rhetoric coming from a black Christian preacher exemplifies how far black embodiment had fallen from its divine state by accepting the Christian religion. He rightly ridicules the very idea that any such system of "black supremacy" that privileges white over black exists. Muhammad is even more astounded that someone as theologically educated as Dr. King could be so ignorant of the devil's tricknology, implying also that King was a hypocrite for advocating passage of the civil rights bill.

In Muhammad's view, since King represented the body politic of "reverends," he received the sharpest condemnation, but save for a few "acceptable" preachers, such as Congressman Adam Clayton Powell Jr., they were all the same.[101] These preachers were transformed by Christianity ideologically so that, for all intent and purposes, they functioned as though they were "white" vis-à-vis other black bodies. Subsequently, Muhammad leveled three basic critiques at them as rendered symbolically in-place by the devil's tricknology.

First, Muhammad critiqued them for their character, or lack of it. Preachers were anathema to him, and he appraised their whiteness and their symbolic in-placeness as castigating, violent, and personal. To Muhammad, black preachers were lazy, fearful, ignorant, and enemies of their own people.[102] He suggested that

> their mind and their heart is set upon the white man to be white. They want to be the children of white people. . . . They are a foolish people; they are the most ignorant and the foolish and frightened and the most dreadful leadership that I ever heard tell [sic] of in all the days of my life, it is the American so-called Negro preachers. He would not even look at you if he thought the white man didn't like you. He wouldn't mention your name in his [i.e., white people's] presence for nothing in the world only in the way of hate, scandal and disgrace.[103]

In Muhammad's view, not only did these preachers lack the fortitude and courage to confront white supremacy. They were also selfish and self-serving. For example, King's acceptance of the Nobel Peace Prize gave him a forum to address whites in a venue that had never before allowed a black person to speak. The accolades made sense to Muhammad, given that King preached only conciliatory messages that benefited him and the status quo for whites. Accordingly, Muhammad intimates that King would avoid even gazing on an African American whom white people did not like, all of which was in service of continued white domination of black people. He retorted, "No wonder he had the privilege of going into a cathedral where no so-called Negro had ever stood in the pulpit."[104] As a result of being whitenized by Christianity and serving as a good instrument of white control, Muhammad thought, King was rewarded with this recognition by whites. King demonstrated his self-interest, not only by accepting the award, which he should have denounced due to the injustice toward and inhumane treatment of black people, but also by accepting the substantial award money, which, at the time, was more than $50,000.[105] Even if King had refused the medal, Muhammad noted, "The money could have been accepted, since his people need it. Even if he did not need it himself, there are poor among his followers who really need financial help. He won neither peace nor justice for his people."[106]

Preachers were more than selfish. They were profoundly ignorant, even though, like King, they might have been college-educated. They still did not have the sense to recognize that they were being manipulated by the tricknology of the enemy. In fact, Muhammad thought, the Negro preacher was "blind, deaf and dumb."[107] He was too stupid to realize that he was a slave and being used to keep his people in bondage, having been blinded by his love for whites.[108] Yet Muhammad was not the first to criticize the black clergy class regarding their suspect character and education. Others in black communities had long been suspicious of African American preachers.

More than half a century earlier (1901), for instance, Booker T. Washington, considered by some the eminent black leader in the United States during the Reconstruction era of the late nineteenth and early twentieth centuries, was critical of black preachers. He was concerned about the paucity of education for the two dominant professions for black people who were recently emancipated—teaching and preaching—and suggested that many people took up these vocations as a racket, a hustle, to earn an easy living.[109] He did not reject preachers wholesale, as Muhammad did, however, for he affirmed that some preachers are "godly." Yet Washington's concern that many preachers were uninformed and opportunistic would find ample affirmation from Muhammad, for whom African American Christian ministers were "icemakers" because they froze the minds of people in ignorance.[110] In a nutshell, for Muhammad, the Negro preacher was a "hindrance to the truth of our people. . . . The preachers are afraid of the truth."[111] Their questionable character made them more susceptible to the tricknology of the enemy.

Second, along with commenting on their (lack of) character, Muhammad critiqued preachers for their beliefs in Christianity, the weapon of white hegemony.[112] Again, for him, Christianity was synonymous with whiteness in the mythology of Yakub, and Islam was the natural religion of the black race.[113] In other words, Christianity whitenized black people symbolically. Therefore, as a people who were ontologically Muslim, their Christian orientation defiled and polluted them, corrupted their god-given sensibilities, which were righteous and good. Thus, white religious ideology functioned to construct preachers—again, black bodies as *in-place* who were, in fact, untrustworthy sell-outs. This explained, for Muhammad, why preachers could cause disunity among black people or favor white people over their own communities.

What was really going on with preachers and so-called Negro Christians, Muhammad suggests, was that the religion of Yakub signified *trick-nology* in the ultimate sense of the word, for Christianity really veiled a worship of white people behind the veneration of religious ideas and symbols. Muhammad explains, "The only thing that will hold the Negro is his belief in whites as divinity. They hold to his religion which they [i.e., whites] use to deceive everyone they possibly can."[114] Muhammad saw evidence of this in many places—case in point, religious icons: "More than anyone else, those who worship his image (the so-called Negroes) are guilty of loving the white race and all that the race stands for. One can even find the pictures of white people on the walls, mantel, shelves, dressers and tables of their homes. Some carry them on their person. The so-called Negroes go to church and bow down to their statues under the name of Jesus and Mary and some under the name of Jesus' disciples, which are only the images of the white race, their arch-deceiver."[115] Indeed, he maintained, Christian belief had deleterious effects on black psyches and self-images, causing African Americans to become enamored by white physical features and "white" ideals. Accepting Christianity for African Americans, then, meant a total rejection of black self-respect and an uncritical embrace of everything "white." This devotion to whites and black symbolic in-placeness was so complete that some black people would even carry pictures of white religious icons with them. In fact, Muhammad blamed black erotic desire for whites squarely on Christian influence. Consequently, the slave master became an idol for African Americans, as did white women, he argued. They became the objects of intense desire and veneration, despite the fact that they were physically objectionable. Muhammad proclaims, "We worshipped the false beauty of the Slavemaster's [*sic*] leprous looking women."[116] Accordingly, the African American Christian longed for the day when the Christian "plurality (trinity) of white gods" would allow black people to "mix" (i.e., miscegenation) with white people.[117]

Yet again it was African American preachers such as King who exacerbated the problem of this asymmetrical "love" relationship between black and white peoples, in which the so-called Negroes were lovestruck and did not receive love in return from whites, who in reality regarded them with contempt. On the subject of this lopsided love affair, Muhammad suggests that African Americans who were symbolically in-place, like King, were intentionally complicit in manipulating black people:

> There are many of my poor black ignorant brothers and even preachers preaching the ignorant and lying stuff that you should love your enemy. What fool can love his enemy? Martin Luther calls himself a preacher and has written a book to try to fool you, to make you love the devil himself. How can Martin Luther, being the minister of God, he claims, teach his people to love their enemy, when God Himself said he had set a day to deal with his enemies. And he said himself, according to the Bible that Martin Luther reads, that there were two brothers—I loved one and hated the other. . . . Here comes the truth of the white man making you know that he cannot love—that he is the devil himself.[118]

Muhammad's remonstrance against Christianity was more than that it was loathsome to love one's enemies. He also argued against the evangelical and fundamentalist doctrines of the Trinity, the "brotherhood" of "man," the deity of Jesus, the virgin birth, the death of "white" Jesus for the redemption of humanity, the inerrancy of Scripture (whites tampered with it and altered it, making it a "poison book"), heaven, and the mystery and spirit existence of God.[119] All these doctrines indicated for him how far whitenized black people had fallen from their original state and the extent to which they had bought into a demonic ideology that, as Yakub's story indicates, was clearly used to kill and enslave black bodies. Christian preachers, then, were the worst type of "black" embodiment, not only because they had sold out and embraced Yakub's religion, but also because they became promulgators of it to their "own" people.

Muhammad was particularly aggressive in his assault on the Christian ideas of heaven and the incorporeality and immateriality of the Divine, which were an affront to Allah and to black bodies. Christianity was tricknology in that it served ideologically to support the mistreatment of black people, who were promised that heaven would be their reward for obedient service. Heaven was a lie. Rather, theology for Muhammad was largely but not exclusively earthbound and material. The notion of heaven was one that the slave master used to justify slavery, teaching that the slaves would get their reward in the afterlife while the slave-owning class received theirs in the here and now.[120] In reality, heaven and hell were right here—at least, heaven could be brought into existence on Earth. Hell was already here and now. Therefore, for Muhammad, the idea of heaven was connected with all of the deplorable and atrocious meanings that black bodies carry socially that resulted from the denigration and violence of slavery. For this reason, the Negro preacher who taught Christianity was vile because "he" participated in the deception and in the devaluation of black bodies.

Ironically, Muhammad's polemic against Christianity and its black preachers was self-serving, since he desired to prove his own eschatology—namely, that the prophecies of the Bible and the life and teachings of Jesus point to an actual, physical, bodily savior who came in the person of Master Fard Muhammad, "God in person."[121] As a result, Muhammad railed against any Christian teaching that would diminish the site of the black body as ultimate materiality and meaning—anything that would spiritualize and disembody Allah. He vehemently denounced the idea that God was a mystery or an incorporeal spirit—in his words, "a spook."[122] Once more, he connected this concept existentially to slavery and eschatologically to the bodily existence of Master Fard Muhammad, discussed earlier. For Fard Muhammad, God had to be a man (physically and in terms of gender) so people could recognize him.[123]

The implication was that Christians did not really know God, because if they did, they would know that God is a living, breathing, black human being just like them. Otherwise, "He" could not be their God and savior. God cannot be a mystery, because one would have no way of recognizing a god who did not have a body. Muhammad said explicitly that Christians *cannot* know God for this reason.[124]

According to Muhammad, the surest evidence that God is a man, contrary to the teaching of the Christian preachers, is that God speaks, and language is an embodied and material phenomenon. Muhammad explains, "They [the prophets] tell us that they heard God's voice speaking to them in their own language. Can a spirit speak a language while being and immaterial something? If God is not material, what pleasure would He get out of material beings and the material universe?"[125] The same reasoning holds for the materiality of the devil.[126] The devil is no spook either, and African American Muslims can recognize him. Unfortunately, Christians and preachers are still mentally dead, unable to see the devil for who and what he is.[127] Because of this, whitenized black bodies are bound to remain in-place symbolically and socially, for it is the nature of Christian teaching to keep their identity fixed and their activity and possibilities limited.

Finally, Muhammad critiqued preachers, African Americans whom he viewed as in-place, not only for their character and their beliefs but for their treasonous practices. It follows that, if he questioned the character of black preachers—believed them to be ignorant, untrustworthy, and fearful and believed that their Christian religion ensured that they would behave in ways that acquiesce to white supremacy—their social and religious practices would reflect their in-placeness as bodies that had been whitenized. Because these practices conflicted with essential elements of NOI praxis, Muhammad had little or no tolerance for the products of the devil's science of tricks.

Highest on the list of practices for which Muhammad expressed disdain was integration, which he thought was insanity. Who in their right mind would desire to live, go to school, and work with a devil who had enslaved them, lynched them, and raped their women? He saw the desire to integrate as indicative of a sick kind of love, a masochistic desire for the affection of whites and a literal continuation of slavery by choice: "The unwillingness of the slaves to leave their masters is due to their great love for the slave-masters. If America is unwilling to grant her 22 million ex-slaves freedom to go for self today, it is the same unwillingness of white America's forefathers in dealing with our parents less than 100 years ago. . . . As long as my people are the blind lovers of their enemies, they will seek to forever return to the bosom of their masters in no better status or position than that of a slave."[128] Preachers, then, were seen as being nostalgic for slavery and as emotionally dependent on their "slave-masters." In particular, Muhammad considered the civil rights preachers and Martin Luther King Jr. exceedingly appalling because they claimed to speak for God and to be leaders of the people in their quest for freedom, justice, and equality. To the contrary, Muhammad concluded, they were "leading" people into the "hell" from which they needed liberation. Muhammad saw King's efforts as futile because whites could not operate in ways that would benefit African Americans; it was against their nature.[129] King, he thought, was analogous to a dog who begged for food from its master. Most important, he saw King's focus on the racism of the southern United States as misguided, since white people in the South were connected to institutional power in America, such as those in Washington, DC; they were not distinct from it.

Rather, Muhammad maintained, separation is what black people needed—and a land of their own in which to live. While Edward Curtis, author of *Black Muslim Religion in the Nation of Islam, 1960–1975*, argues that Muhammad "rejected calls for blacks to return to Africa, since it was North American blacks that would lead other persons of color toward the restoration of black greatness," Muhammad's words on the subject are ambiguous.[130] He talks about going "back where we came from": "The American white man is not going to move out of his estate to give to the so-called Negroes. We are not asking you to do any such thing. No, only unless you prevent our going to our own. If you are going to prevent us from going to our own, or back where we came from, where you found us, then give us a place here for ourselves."[131] This could refer to Africa, since Muhammad seems to be referring to African Americans as going somewhere other than a separate land within the United States. He saw no evidence in history that integration made any sense, that white people could be trusted to do what was good and right for black people.[132] Again, it was against their nature to be good and peaceful, though civil rights preachers had believed they could be—that whites wanted integration and peace. Separation was the only solution to the race problem, but preachers were blinded by the ideology of Christianity, which had whitenized them. For that reason, Muhammad wanted the unfettered right to return to "where you found us" or land in the United States for a black nation in North America.

Because whites were violent and murderous by nature, according to the narrative of Yakub, Muhammad thought it was equally silly for the civil rights preachers to practice nonviolence as a method of social change. To some extent, he believed that the preachers were fearful and therefore lacked the fortitude to defend themselves against violent attacks. Whatever the case, nonviolence in the face of violence was inappropriate. He said that self-defense against dogs and police would be justified:

> The so-called Negroes of Birmingham, Alabama, would have been justified by the law of justice if they had killed every dog sicked [*sic*] upon them by the hired, tax-paid policemen, for the tax-payers did not hire dogs to police their lives and property. And if the policemen had fired upon those who defended themselves against the bites of savage dogs that the Police Department trained expressly for the purpose of attacking so-called Negroes, they would have been justified by God and the Divine law of self-defense to fight and defend themselves against such savage dog and human attack.[133]

But self-defense would not be without consequences. In the instance he cites, as soon as black people defended themselves against dogs and police by throwing rocks, the federal government called in the US Army, "not to help the so-called Negroes against the white southerners," but to support those who were abusing black citizens.[134]

Integration and nonviolence were not the only practices that Muhammad associated with black bodies in-place that had been whitenized by Christianity. He was strongly opposed to eating "traditional" African American foods, which he understood as slave food, and to wearing the slave masters' names.[135] I take up these two items in detail in the next chapter. For Muhammad, the consumption of slave food and the use of slave names signify debasement. Like the Christian preachers who practiced and advocated integration and nonviolence, such bodies had been duped by the devil's schemes—tricknology—that he used to ensure that black men and women would remain enslaved mentally and limited socially and economically.

Conclusion

Elijah Muhammad critiqued black bodies that had been whitenized by Christianity because they were antithetical to what he understood as the divine nature of black people: both Muslim and righteous. These whitenized bodies were black bodies in-place, fixed in identity symbolically and severely limited in social activity. Rooted in the myth of Yakub, Christianity was a religion that the slave master used to make black people slaves and to maintain the institution of slavery for hundreds of years. It was synonymous with white supremacy and Yakub's desire to dominate and destroy the original black people.

This story of Yakub connected Muhammad's followers to a theodicy and cosmology that gave them some basis for making sense of the world. It communicated to them that whites were violent because it was their nature and purpose as a grafted, "made," and "unlike kind" to be unruly and incorrigible. The story of Yakub was a source of secret knowledge about the universe, with its fanciful details of life on other planets and its notion of racial eugenics and genetic engineering. It was given legitimacy and consistency in Muhammad's life through his experiences of violence that seemed omnipresent and as much a part of his reality as the air he breathed. Racial violence, for him, was ubiquitous. More important, the mythology's cosmic reality "lifted" the meaning of black bodies from this Earth, where they had been dehumanized and disfigured, and connected them to a celestial reality that gave them new transcendent and ultimate meaning. Islam, too, became cosmic, and unlike Christianity, it was the religion of the universe, the one and true religion of the Original Man.

Therefore, embracing Christianity made African Americans untrustworthy, weak, and ineffective in the struggle for black equality—all while deceiving them about their true nature and about the savior, Master Fard Muhammad, Allah in the flesh, who had come to reconnect them to their divine heritage and birthright. In short, Christianity was tricknology, a science of deception that was so skillfully crafted that African Americans were often unaware that its doctrines rendered them perpetually obsequious. As such, it was the religion of Yakub.

The black purveyors of this religious ideology that functioned in service to white domination were the so-called Negro preachers, and Muhammad showed little mercy in his castigations of their character, beliefs, and practices—in part, Dennis Walker, the author of *Islam and the Search for African-American Nationhood*, notes, because African American clergy were accommodating the white American system and were accumulating property as a result. They were also impressing the masses to worship an otherworldly Jesus and to be patient in suffering, waiting for a better world to come. This undermined religious and political movements, such as the NOI, that were viewed as less accommodating.[136] The leader of these preachers who, for Muhammad, epitomized the need for mental resurrection was Martin Luther King Jr. Educated though he was, he remained ignorant of the Truth. Only Islam could bring freedom, justice, and equality to the black race, and Muhammad was intent on reimagining and remaking the race, including these black bodies in-place and those that had been symbolically whitenized by Christianity.

ELIJAH MUHAMMAD, TRANSCENDENT BLACKNESS, AND THE CONSTRUCTION OF IDEAL BLACK EMBODIMENT

2

The ideal or ultimate body for Elijah Muhammad was a religious body that privileged *symbolic* out-of-placeness over *social* out-of-placeness—that is, he was not necessarily interested in political engagement with an unjust system but was reclaiming and reforming bodies to prepare them for the world to come, a new world after the age of white domination that would disclose black bodies as sublime. As a religious leader, Muhammad was attempting, in all of his work, to break the hold of the meanings attached to black bodies in-place, or as defined by the racist social system in America.[1] The new bodies that he fashioned reflected a new social collectivity and cosmology: that of the Nation of Islam (NOI) and its own mythology and social organization.

This new and ideal symbolic body can be understood as being transcendently black and rooted in a tradition of racial uplift. The NOI did, however, make creative use of extant African American racial uplift ideologies in its attempt to reclaim and reform black bodies. In addition to its own religious mythology, at least three complimentary and inextricable streams of thought can be gleaned from its religious thought. The most prominent is the "politics of respectability," formulated and initiated by the Women's Convention of the National Baptist Convention in the early twentieth century (1900–1920) and given expression and named by Evelyn Brooks Higginbotham in *Righteous Discontent: The Women's Movement in the Black Church, 1880–1920*. In the politics of respectability, African American Baptist women sought to advance African Americans in the United States and in the eyes of white people by adopting Victorian notions of womanhood, thrift, self-help, and proper conduct, especially for poor and working black women.[2] The NOI taught these values through its Muslim Girls Training and General Course in Civilization (MGT-GCC), which I discuss later in this chapter.

Closely related to this is the second African American racial uplift motif: the notion of black industrialization, with its emphasis on self-help through participation in the trades and nonengagement or with agitation in the American political system. These ideas are most clearly found in the work and thought of Booker T. Washington and are given their most notable presentation in his biography, *Up from Slavery*, originally published in 1901.[3] Especially relevant is his 1895 address to the Cotton States and International Exposition in Atlanta—the famous "cast your bucket were you are" speech, which advocated that African Americans make their way in America at the turn of the century by taking advantage of the economic opportunities that whites made available in agriculture, mechanics, and domestic service.[4] It is widely known that Elijah Muhammad was an admirer of Washington.

The third important connection between the NOI and prominent racial uplift ideas is to be found in the work of E. Franklin Frazier. His *The Negro Family in the United States* was originally published in 1939.[5] An early sociologist from the University of Chicago school, Frazier analyzed black families during and subsequent to slavery. He argued that black social mobility was curtailed due to matrifocal families, in which men were absent, or to matriarchal ones, which lacked male labor and wage earnings. He was careful to lay blame in the hands of slavery, yet Frazier's interpreters, or Frazerians, suggested that the key to uplift was to retool black families and dislodge black women as their heads. Such ideas can be found explicitly in the Muhammad's and Louis Farrakhan's discourses on black uplift. Paulette Pierce and Brackette Williams note about "Frazerians" such as those in the NOI, that for them "the reform of the Black woman and the improvement of Black family life through creation of proper bourgeois domesticity was the *sine qua non* of racial redemption in U.S. society."[6] Elijah was famous for saying that a nation can rise no higher than its women.[7]

These ideas are significant to understanding the NOI. It is not enough simply to note that these three ideas existed and, as themes, were contemporaneous with the founding of the NOI, ostensibly on July 4, 1930. Nor it is sufficient to enumerate these three African American uplift motifs, for they cannot be understood separately. They are inextricable from one another, like a stool that has three legs: take one of the legs away and the stool will cease to function as a stool. In fact, it will no longer properly be a stool. As a whole, these three ideas constitute a racial uplift paradigm that I call a *perichoretic politics of racial uplift*.[8] All have whiteness as their object or respond to whiteness in attempts to render blackness acceptable. Two other aspects of this racial uplift ideology are crucially important. The first is that it is framed as a religious and Muslim discourse, not as secular; and second, it means that while my discussion revolves around four men, it is not androcentric, since the NOI's perichoretic politics of racial uplift necessitate black women's bodies as the vehicle of racial mobility, given that women were the major features in all three of the ideologies that the NOI adopted. That is, even when unspoken, African American Muslim women's embodiment and its reform is always the subtext for the NOI's racial reform project. This idea culminates in the epilogue, in which I discuss its implications for understanding the NOI and for future research.

In this ideology, blackness is a surplus category that encompasses the earthbound, extraterrestrial, and symbolic and not simply a racial category that designates people of African descent in the Americas, its received signification.[9] Furthermore, it is a semiotic embodiment that uncovers and discloses ultimate reality, which is cosmic and "extraterrestrial" even in its materiality.[10] Blackness is a signifier of a mythology that locates its origins in the cosmos, is ultimately defined by the Mother Plane, and discloses the hidden secrets of racial origins and history. Furthermore, bodies represent a social organization that privileges maleness and a particular black masculinity but is also a response to white hegemonic masculinity.

Muhammad used a variety of philosophical and theological resources and rituals in his endeavor to construct "beautiful" bodies with specific social and symbolic characteristics—in his words, "To shape a people for self respect and universal recognition."[11] The NOI rituals and ideas were the raw materials out of which the visionary Muhammad corporealized or embodied African American Muslims of the NOI, and they varied depending on whether Muhammad's concern was for the body as a biological reality or as symbol of the NOI collective and cosmology. The body was both material and metaphor, and Muhammad seemed aware that affecting the meaning of both aspects required distinct approaches.

In *Black Nationalism: A Search for an Identity in America*, E. U. Essien-Udom offers a basic classification that may assist us in entering the conversation about the foundational elements of embodiment—what he calls the "exoteric" and "esoteric" religious teachings of the NOI, or the practical and discursive elements it used in constructing and bestowing meaning on black bodies.[12] Exoteric forms, he writes,

> stem directly from Muhammad's attempt to cope with the social, cultural, and psychological environment in which the Negro finds himself [*sic*]. They offer the believer a set of incentives and a definite discipline which enable him to transcend the common plight and degradation of the Negro masses, and they impart to the movement an active, cohesive, and expanding existence. . . . Muhammad's exoteric teachings emphasize the techniques for attaining the good life in the "sweet here and now" and not in the "sweet bye and bye." Heaven and hell are thought to be "two conditions on earth which reflect one's state of mind, his moral conditions and actions."[13]

Out of concern for the existential and biological realities of black bodies, this regimen of practices allows African Americans not only to distinguish themselves from other black bodies but also to cope with the psychological and physical stressors, such as physical ailments, that are part of living a life that is characterized by oppression. Finally, and crucially, these codes applied to men and women differentially. I call these "exoteric praxis" to emphasize the ritual and practical nature of these more overt and public "teachings."

Exoteric and esoteric designations correspond roughly to the body as the material locus of the self and the body as a symbol of the collective, respectively. In other words, the nomenclature gives us a helpful way to conceptualize and frame the practices and discourses, which we can associate with Muhammad's particular bodily interest. Following the NOI's dietary rules would beautify the black body, and embracing the secret knowledge of Yakub and the Mother Plane would make the black body divine.

Exoteric Praxis and the Body as Material
Reality: Vibrancy, Health, and Cleanliness

DIETARY REGULATIONS

The ritual dietary codes of the NOI are significant both for the physical body and for the body as a symbol of the collective culture. This is clear in the influence of Muhammad's written work, including *How to Eat to Live, Book 1*, and *How to Eat to Live, Book 2*, which, some scholars argue, played an important part in the development of Black cultural nationalism, however limited cultural nationalism might be for framing the NOI. Indeed, in *How to Eat to Live*, Muhammad writes about "spiritual beauty," which "we achieve . . . through practicing or carrying into practice the spiritual laws."[14] But dietary codes are exoteric and symbolic because, although they are religious regulations that come from Allah, they are not necessarily private practices, and according to Muhammad, their primary purpose is to promote the health, beauty, and longevity of the physical body:

> There is no way for us to learn the right way to eat in order to live a long life, except through the guidance and teachings of Allah, Who came in the Person of Master Fard Muhammad. The Bible says that He will give us more life abundancy, but He demands strict obedience to His Will. There is no way of prolonging the life of human beings—or any other life—unless it begins with restrictions of the foods which sustain life: the right kinds of food and the proper time when it should be taken into our bodies.[15]

Muhammad maintains that knowledge of a diet that prolongs life could come only from Master Fard Muhammad, because as God the creator he would have indispensable and infallible information about such things as the workings and functions of the body. It follows that the only means of obtaining this beneficial knowledge is through strict adherence to the teachings and laws of the NOI, which, in his language, is obedience to Allah. Finally, the most significant laws begin with the physical body as a means of breaking social control previously exerted over black bodies through white domination and as a means of asserting his own ritual authority over such bodies.

The dietary laws regulate the types of food that NOI members can consume; when and how often they are to eat; how they are to prepare food; what they may not eat; and the appropriate times to eat and fast. The codes include dietary recommendations for extending one's life, health maintenance, weight loss and gain, market procurement of food, and even economic well-being, as proper attention to diet has the economic benefit of reducing medical issues and, therefore, health-related costs. The dietary laws constitute the strictest control of physical bodies in the NOI. Muhammad maintains: "Hereafter, I shall enforce restriction on my followers to eat as Allah bids us."[16] Elsewhere he states: "The eating regulations in this book are a 'must' with my followers. Begin at once—eat only one meal a day, regardless of the work you are doing."[17] But, as Edward Curtis points out, members adhered differentially to ritual control in the NOI, choosing for themselves which rituals to ignore and which to follow.[18] In this sense, Muhammad was naïve in his determination to "enforce restrictions" on his followers.

Of great interest in *How to Eat to Live, Books 1* and *2*, and *Message to the Blackman in America* are the foods that are prohibited: foods that Muhammad associated with slavery, such as collard and turnip greens, black-eyed peas, sweet potatoes, and pork (especially chitterlings or "chitlins").[19] Primary on this list is pork, or what Muhammad derogatorily calls "swine." Muhammad vociferously and repeatedly rails against the ingestion of pork more than any other food, suggesting: "The taking of the prohibited flesh of the swine as food is beyond righteous imagination."[20] The swine for him is a filthy animal that was grafted, or made by an artificial process, for medical purposes rather than for food. White people, according to Muhammad, introduced black people to the hog as food to make them immoral and weak, since a grafted animal or human is less strong and moral than the original.[21] Muhammad said, "Stay away from the hog, of which 10 ounces takes away from you, God has said, three one-hundredths per cent of beauty appearance."[22]

His concern for the beauty and longevity of the physical body extended to other foods, such as cornbread, chicken, grits, catfish, processed sugar, flour products, seafood, and more.[23] He suggested: "Eating the wrong food and eating it too often starts trouble in the physical body everywhere—from the sole of your feet to the crown of your head."[24] All of these foods were "slave foods," later reinscribed in African American culture as "soul food" as many black people moved into the middle classes and wanted to maintain a black identity.[25] An unspoken motivation for Muhammad's dietary interdictions, then, was to raise the status of black bodies from the grotesque, slave-oriented, and common to the differentiated and special. Muhammad was acutely aware of the relationship among food, status, and social class and therefore forbade the ingestion of any "filthy" or scavenger food that would work against the bodies he was trying to create.

Perhaps the most important reason for mandating this diet, as opposed to a vegan one, was that it differentiated NOI bodies from disgraceful black bodies in-place, epitomized by so-called Negro Christians:[26]

> The taking of the prohibited flesh of the swine as food is beyond righteous imagination. . . . They are so fond of swine flesh that they sacrifice it in the church, and then ask divine blessings upon it. They barbeque and cook it, and hold a feast in their places of worship and eat this slow-death poisonous animal—which God has forbidden—as though they had an option with God . . . Preachers and priests are working along with the enemy, or adversary, of God, teaching the people that it is all right to eat swine—their bellies stretched with the hog in them and saturated with the whiskey and wine. This is the type of religion under which you have been brought—Christianity and its preachers and priests. None of them have tried to prevent you from breaking this divine law by teaching you the consequences of such an act.[27]

It is clear that these people who are complicit with whites are indeed black clergy, that these "preachers and priests" work along with whites in advocating consumption of the hog—Muhammad thus caricatures black preachers as immoral and drunken buffoons whose bellies are "stretched with the hog in them and saturated with whiskey and wine." Note that Muhammad also implicates African American Catholic clergy—the "priests"—in this unholy conspiracy. He attempts to distinguish between the practices of Christians, whom he understands to be "white" and whom he condemns as "the enemy, or adversary of God," and those of his followers, whom he celebrates.

Additional aspects of food regulation offer details for attaining purity, cleanliness, and health of the physical body and include prohibitions against the use of alcohol, tobacco, and other drugs.[28] In a time when black life expectancy was considerably lower than that of whites, these practices were meant to prolong life—offering to do so by at least one hundred years and even to more than a thousand years.[29] In addition, these codes communicate that ideal black bodies are distinctive bodies, healthier in all ways than both white bodies and black bodies that tried to stay in-place.

Another means of distinguishing and valorizing black bodies was through the ritual practice of naming to mark people with new religious identities. Specifically, naming marks physical bodies as having undergone specific religious practices to become worthy members of the Nation of Islam. After writing a letter requesting membership in the NOI, undergoing a terse indoctrination and catechism in the form of required lessons and fulfilling other prerequisites, including regular attendance at temple services, new NOI members were given a new name. Essien-Udom wrote, "The member drops his last name and any middle initials. In place of these, the Messenger of Allah assigns to him a certain number of X or some other symbol."[30] Since African Americans were given slave names and lost their authentic African or Muslim names, this "X" (as in Malcolm X or Louis X, as Farrakhan was once known) stood for the unknown name just as in an algebraic equation X can represent an unidentified quantity.

Naming distinguished NOI members from other black bodies in the culture. According to Richard Brent Turner, author of *Islam in the African American Experience*, the practice was crucial to forming new black identities in America. Naming or self-signification was a form of resistance—a countermovement to the practice of stripping Africans of their cultural names and giving them the names of their European and American enslavers and endowing black bodies with the oppressive meanings of Western hegemony.[31] Muhammad proposes that "slave" names are part of the tripartite evil that keeps African Americans from authentic freedom: "Our first step is to give back to the white man his religion (Christianity), his church, and his names. These three are chains of slavery that hold us in bondage to them. We are free when we give up the above three."[32] Along the same lines, Muhammad advises that names have the power to keep black bodies enslaved "in the eyes of the civilized world today."[33] In this way, the NOI announces the reclamation of a body that once belonged physically, culturally, and ideologically to whites through slavery.[34]

Not only are new names a sign of bodies that have been reclaimed; they signify that these bodies now embrace a new cosmology and mythology, a new way of living in the world and new expectations for physical health and vibrancy. Renaming is efficacious for salvation and respect of the body. Muhammad often left ambiguous the nature of such salvation, stating simply that receiving the name of Allah "alone is enough to save

you."[35] Naming, however, implies that salvation comes through an enactment of the ritual life of the NOI.

As an example of these effects of renaming on black bodies, Muhammad cites Muhammad Ali (formerly Cassius Clay), one of his most famous
proselytes. He takes credit for Ali's success in boxing and his international
stature:

> The example was evident when I took Muhammad Ali (the World's
> Heavyweight Champion) out of the white man's name (the name that
> itself made him a servant and slave to the white man). All of Africa and
> Asia then acclaimed him as also being their champion. This shows you
> that all the previous black men of America who were bestowed with the
> title of world's heavyweight champion were only exalting the white man
> of America, Europe and Australia. . . . Just a change of name has given
> Brother Muhammad Ali a name of honor and a name of praise that will
> live forever (its meaning).[36]

Elijah Muhammad suggests that black men who were champions before Muhammad Ali were only giving glory to white men, whose names
they carried. This signifying denotes bodies that belong to a new order of
meaning—one that is beautiful and not associated with the nomenclature
that the dominant culture previously ascribed to them.

For Muhammad, naming is part of a larger project in the contest over
the identity of black bodies—which, accordingly, were not "colored"
or "Negro," as the dominant culture had designated them.[37] Thus, Master Fard's name itself is paradigmatic for Muslims in that he is God, and
his name designates beauty: "His name, Fard Muhammad [and 'Great
Mahdi'], is beautiful in its meaning."[38]

DRESS CODES

Like naming, the adornment of physical bodies identified some black
people as members of the NOI and black nation; in addition, Elijah Muhammad's NOI prescribed dress codes for male and female members.
Women were not allowed wear "immodest" clothing, just as they were not
allowed to use cosmetics or mechanically alter their hair using chemicals
or heat. Essien-Udom observes that NOI women "do not wear lipstick or
conspicuous cosmetics. The headtie is required for all Sisters."[39] Curtis also
notes that women "were to dress modestly and avoid makeup."[40] Dressing
modestly generally resulted in women wearing a head covering and long
dresses with long sleeves.[41] Muhammad notes, "We must stop our women,

at once, from imitating the white race, from trying to look other than their own kind, by bleaching, powdering, ironing and coloring their hair, painting their lips, cheeks, eyebrows, wearing shorts, going half-nude in public and going swimming on beaches with men."[42] As with dietary codes, Muhammad associates forbidden practices with white bodies, which the practice of cosmetology are meant to imitate. At the same time, he admonishes women, not men, against going half-naked in public.

Indeed, Muhammad's "we" were men of the NOI, whom he charged with policing women's bodies via these dress codes. It is conspicuous that he chastises only women although black men also made mechanical alterations to their bodies, such as bleaching their skin and chemically straightening their hair, arguably in imitation of white men. And men did not have to cover up their bodies for moral and social reasons. Instead, they generally wore dark business suits and sometimes bowties in formal activities of the NOI.[43] The suits were a way for the men in the Nation of Islam to distinguish themselves from other black men and signal their adherence to a set of normative values. The suit and bowties signified acceptance of so-called respectability politics, or the belief that dressing or behaving in a particular way said something about an individual's or a group's moral character. What the dress codes reveal, in many cases, is uneasiness about the female body and the idea that black women's bodies needed extra regulation, of the moral type, to control their behavior.

EDUCATION AND DISCIPLINE

The NOI also separately and differentially disciplines men's and women's bodies in education and training. The primary men's auxiliary was called the Fruit of Islam (FOI). There men were trained in martial arts, security, precision drill, proselytizing, physical and mental cleanliness, and "military" methods, including deference for the male power hierarchy.[44] As Elijah Muhammad defined the FOI:

> The Fruit of Islam means the first converts to Islam here in America and the first people to be cleaned and made fit to be called Muslims. And their training is on this basis, as being Muslims, to keep in practice, not just say in their faith or belief. You must put into practice the principles of Islam that you believe in and serve as an example for others who would accept Islam. They take physical training and exercises in many ways to keep physically fit and healthy and to try to get away from many of the physical ailments that they have suffered long before coming into the knowledge of Islam.[45]

Muhammad saw the physical exercising of men in the FOI as an important aspect of NOI religion and as a means of inculcating discipline. In addition, the FOI represented the eminence of men in the religion and, conversely, the subjugated status of women. Men were first, meaning that Islam was primarily a religion of men and for men. At this point, we see Muhammad's continued concern for aesthetics and beauty in that healthy, masculine, and disciplined bodies are of utmost importance.

But despite the fact that the auxiliaries were, ironically, homosocial— and, like fraternities and sororities, arguably homoerotic—the NOI did not tolerate homosexuality (actual same-sex or same-gender loving romantic relationships). In the NOI's view, homosexuality precluded the cleanliness and discipline that it was advocating. In fact, Muhammad vociferously condemned gay and lesbian relationships as "filthy" practices that indicated criminality. Moreover, he held that such relationships and practices were induced by the lack of discipline in schools:

> The freedom of uncleanliness [in America] is granted and is worshiped. The percentage of sexual worship of the same sex is greater than in any other government on the face of the earth. Little children are being taught sex almost from the cradle, making the whole nation, as one man put it 90 per cent freaks of nature. On the streets of any metropolitan city in America, it is common to see men sweethearting with men and women sweethearting with women. Little boys with boys and little girls with girls. It is so common that a decent family is puzzled as to where to send their children for schooling. They are all-girls schools of sweethearts. The same sex falling upon their own. Boys' colleges are breeding such filthy practices, the jails, prisons, and the Federal Penitentiaries are breeding dens of homosexuals.[46]

To Muhammad's mind, the lack of discipline—in part characterized by integration—results in such filth as homosexuality, and it was worshiped by many. These practices were "unclean" and, as with the Sodomites, would lead to plagues of death and famines.[47] Such "filth" and "uncleanliness" was, in part, a result of so-called freedom in America, which, Muhammad tacitly suggested, would not be the case with his members, whom he sought to control in a much stricter manner.[48]

This is especially curious, given that Muhammad was most critical of schools structured by gender in the same ways that NOI educational and disciplinary groups were organized. Emphasis was placed on the proper conduct, discipline, and order of men and women. For men, strict adherence to male leadership was required. Hence, the FOI leader of individual temples is called the captain, and the national security leader is the supreme captain, a title that connotes authority and discipline.[49] One of the most powerful positions in the NOI, the supreme captain had the power to impose ritual disciplinary measures on members.[50] The ritualized nature of the FOI practices gave it religious importance, as Curtis observes. Auxiliary members often wore uniforms, fezzes, and dark suits and were made to salute and march with military precision. In short, FOI education, dress, and discipline were meant to make "men out of boys" in the sense that they emphasized masculinity, power, discipline, and domination.[51]

Muhammad contended that the FOI functioned primarily to discipline bodies and secondarily for self-defense and security.[52] Yet it seems fairly clear that masculinity was constructed over and against women's bodies. Most notably, professed "protection" of black "womanhood" was part of the ideology and practice of the FOI.[53]

The corresponding organization for women and girls in which womanhood was constructed was the Muslim Girls Training and General Course in Civilization.[54] To a great extent, the MGT-GCC reinforced male dominance in the domestic and obsequious nature of its disciplines. As Muhammad writes: "The Muslim girls of our Nation should spare no effort to learn their special duties and responsibilities as future wives and mothers. The University of Islam in Chicago and Detroit are both equipped to give them the finest training in their special fields. Those who are unable to attend one of these schools should take advantage of the instruction available in the Temple of Islam M.G.T. (Muslim Girls' Training) classes."[55] The MGT-GCC was organized along the same lines as the FOI, except, as noted earlier, the education and training relegated women primarily to domestic roles. For instance, women and girls learned how to cook, rear children, take care of their husbands, sew, keep tidy homes, and keep their bodies clean.[56]

PRAYER

An additional ritual significant for the body as material reality is the prayer service, which emphasizes bodily comportment, including cleanliness, posture, and language.[57]

Indeed, the prayer service is a religious ceremony in which participants engage in various public and private practices. Its private aspects are meant to develop one's inner self, suggests Muhammad.[58] The public aspect is performed in a congregation, preferably in a mosque.[59] As part of the prayer service, members perform an ablution ritual in which they wash parts of their bodies in preparation for prayer: "We see him turning himself to Allah to recite the prayer of the righteous. . . . We see him washing his hands and all the exposed parts of his body. We see him washing his face, his eyes, his ears, mouth and nose and even those wet hands go over his head to clean the very scalp. . . . He is now ready for the prayer service of the Nation of Islam and to recite the oft-repeated prayer."[60] While understood as a religious obligation, these acts are morally based and suggest a desire for the literal cleanliness of the body in the life of the worshiper.[61] Of course, "Many believers associated Islamic religion with what might be called proper etiquette, clean living, and the care of one's body."[62] Bodily cleanliness is analogous to religious purity. Bodily posture is also meant to communicate something positive about the body and the spiritual life of the believer. Standing in the act of prayer signifies moral righteousness: "The prayer is recited standing erect with face towards the east with hands raised declaring to the one God, Allah, that he has turned himself to Allah (God) the originator of the heavens and earth. This prayer and positions are especially designed and worded for those lost sheep (the so-called Negroes) who have been lost from the knowledge of their God and people and now declare that they are turned again to their God, Allah, and are upright to him."[63]

But even in the prayer rituals, special consideration had to be given to women if they were to receive the full benefits of the positive meaning that prayer afforded black bodies. In an extension of the dress code, women had to cover themselves in prayer. As Muhammad explains, "Allah accepts not the prayers of a woman arrived at puberty unless she covers her head as well as her whole body."[64] Muhammad does not elaborate or suggest why this covering is necessary for women. One can only conjecture that the covering marks a woman's body as inferior in status to men and the need for men to protect women represents their own sexual anxieties.

WOMEN'S BODIES

All of this came together in response to the NOI's masculine insecurity under white supremacy as women's bodies were brought under the ultimate control of men in issues of childbirth, birth control, and child nursing.[65] All these regulations also dislodged women from symbolically and "spiritually" superior positions.[66] That is, not only were men in the NOI concerned about white supremacy; they were also unconsciously faced with the dilemma of what to do about the problem that women posed to their masculinity: women could be closer to a God, who was male, in a cosmology that recognized intimate relationships as appropriate only between men and women. Addressing monotheism—in particular, Judaism and its many traditions—the Jewish scholar Howard Eilberg-Schwartz sought to explore a similar problem in *God's Phallus and Other Problems for Men and Monotheism*.[67] What I offer here is a nuanced view of the NOI that goes beyond the purview of Eilberg-Schwartz's study, since the NOI was countering immediate matters that rendered black bodies in jeopardy.

Moreover, Muhammad said, black women's bodies had to be "regulated" in the NOI, though not without their consent and enthusiasm, to protect black men and the reproduction of the black nation through them: "It is a disgrace upon us black people of America to permit ourselves and our future generations to be cut off and destroyed by ignorant, foolish, pleasure-seeking girls and women of our own who do not know what they are doing when they swallow the birth control pill. I repeat: If you accept Allah (God) and follow me and if you give birth to 100 children, each of you girls and women is [*sic*] considered more blessed and right in the eyes of Allah (God) than those who try to kill the birth seed."[68] Muhammad makes similar statements about birth control and the control of black women's bodies in *Message to the Blackman in America*.[69] Often, this bodily control is advocated under the guise of "protecting" and "elevating" black women, since "our women have been and still are being used by the devil white race, ever since we were first brought here to these States as slaves. They cannot go around without being winked at, whistled at, yelled at, slapped, patted. . . . You do nothing about it, nor do you even protest. You cannot control or protect your women."[70]

The white man is thus constructed as a lustful rival who desires the bodies of black women. Mohammad argues: "He [the white man] stands before the so-called Negro woman to deceive her by feigning love and love-making with her; give the so-called Negro woman preference over her husband or brother in hiring. . . . In some cities, the Negro woman receives much higher salary than the so-called Negro man. The devil takes the so-called Negro woman and puts his hands and arms around her body."[71] Again, Muhammad speaks about women on behalf of the men ("people") who should control them. Indeed, the bodies of black women are not their own; rather, they are sites of contestation between black and white men. White men, he argues, pretend to love black women to have sexual intercourse with them. As a reward or an incentive, he suggests, white men, whom he sees in dominant corporate positions, offer black women jobs that are superior to those of African American men, circumventing what Muhammad viewed as the natural order of gendered relations that privileges men. He goes on to suggest that the behavior of white men and black women is threatening to black men because it is an "outright destruction of the moral principles of the black man."[72] Black women's bodies are an extension of black men; women's bodies are not their own but belong to their husbands or men in authority over them. If black men see black women as extensions of their own bodies or as their property, the idea of white men having sexual intercourse with black women could elicit anxiety about homosexuality or about black men being dominated and entered sexually by white men. Some of this concern for controlling women's bodies may stem from the perception that the social and biological reproduction of African American communities was at risk due to the rise in the social status of black women and their resulting close proximity to white men.

In response, black (male) bodies had to be strong and able to withstand and repel the sexual advances of white men, in part through strict control of black women. This also helps to explain the importance of black women working as homemakers in the NOI rather than as domestics in white households, where they might be subjected to advances by whites and other men. Certainly, it was related to dietary laws and other rituals by which Muhammad established bodily and social control over his members.

Ultimately, as Mary Douglas argues, concern with ingestion (as in the NOI dietary regulations) and bodily purity represent the ideal theocracy.[73] Bodies represent social systems—in this case, the ideals of the NOI collective that are an attempt to disrupt America's social control of black bodies. Ultimately, the rituals all have a theologically aesthetic function, as Muhammad indicates, and his ideals parallel Douglas's interpretation that bodies mirror society: "A well-educated, cultured and courteous people make a beautiful society when it is spiritual."[74]

Esoteric Principles and the Body as a Symbol of the Collective: Yakub, the Mother Plane, and Transcendent Blackness

Muhammad privileged the symbolic aspects of NOI religion over the material ones and the physical body—that is, he was concerned with bodies constructed in accordance with the theological, cosmological, and mythological foundations of the religious assembly. The ideal black body in the NOI gained its ultimate meaning and importance not in praxis but in the discursive aspects of the religion. In short, discourses such as the Yakub myth and the Mother Plane revealed the black body's true nature as cosmic, mystical-esoteric, and ultimate—as transcendent.

Through a notion of transcendence, the NOI was able to construct bodies whose meanings were not of this evil and racist world or time, despite their materiality. In addition to its transhistorical and trans-geographical implications, transcendence signifies the idea that the ultimate significance and meaning of this world will be revealed by, and is tied to, entities that exist beyond earthly bounds. This is a strategic move. It is "out there" that defines black bodies, not simply local and earthly discourses of blackness infected by white supremacy. When the Mother Plane returns, at the end of the age, the true nature of black bodies will be unveiled.

This apocalyptic denouement will end the present age (indicated by the Arabic term *ad-dunya*) and reveal the truth. This does not pose a conflict with the NOI's earthbound theology, however. Rather, transcendence through cosmic and esoteric ideas gives coherence to an earthly existence that otherwise would be absurd, mundane, and terrifying. Similar to the aesthetics of Frank Burch Brown's notion of "immanent transcendence," in which the Divine is seen to be near a person and present in him or her, NOI esoteric religion is earthbound and material as the Divine lived among them in the person of Master Fard Muhammad. In a sense, NOI bodies are themselves divine and cosmic—apotheosized.[75] By the early 1970s, indeed, Karl Evanzz notes, "The Messenger [Elijah Muhammad] had also began to move more toward Sufism and the notion that each man [*sic*] has the potential to be a god."[76] But such mystical dimensions do not represent a later turn in Muhammad's theology: they were present from the beginning, as seen in the narrative of Yakub. The notion of ideal, sublime bodies was the ultimate means by which black bodies become beautiful in earthly circumstances that otherwise render them grotesque, the least beautiful bodies on Earth.

Esotericism, which deals with secretive and hidden ideas and practices that posit correspondences between this world and the unseen world, is helpful in making sense of the NOI.[77] Modern esotericism (mid-nineteenth century) is a response to the increasing secularization of nature and the rise of mechanistic worldviews, an attempt to reenchant the world by seeing it as alive and active. Esotericism, according to Wouter Hanegraaf, professor of History of Hermetic Philosophy at the University of Amsterdam, is an alternate view of the world as "organic" and "a science based on religious assumptions."[78]

In "Africana Esoteric Studies and Western Intellectual Hegemony: A Continuing Conversation with Western Esotericism," Biko Mandela Gray, Hugh R. Page Jr., and I discuss the merits and shortcomings of Western esotericism (WE). We argue that the discipline explores and explains what some scholars consider "rejected knowledge." We state that the hidden discourses and related "practices in the 'Western world'" offer alternative epistemologies, the religious ways of knowing that are structured out of and excluded from mainstream intellectual thought through various discursive schemes that privilege materialist, "scientific," and historically Christian modalities of praxis.[79] We further argue that WE is primarily an area of study of white European and American scholars.

The article takes on the implications of the overwhelming presence of European and American scholars in WE. We note, for example, that the "extent to which such esoteric epistemologies and practices within African and African diasporic settings have received scholarly attention has been limited."[80] Fortunately, my work and the work of others in *Esotericism in African American Religious Experience* addresses this limitation. We lay "the groundwork, push for a decentering of Europe and whiteness, implied in and by the signifier 'Western.'"[81] This work calls for a more nuanced approach that recognizes the existence and validity of "esotericisms" in the Africana world (and, hence, globally) that are neither dependent exclusively on nor wholly derivative from Western esoteric exemplars, which enables scholars to better and more fully understand groups such as the NOI.

As seen in the mythology of Yakub, esotericism endeavors to unite science and religion.[82] Curtis points out that it also includes mystical teachings, resulting in a unitary view of the universe, adding, "In the NOI's schools, some students became master esotericists, offering their own interpretations of Elijah Muhammad's cryptic teachings, especially on the nature of time."[83]

A key influence on NOI esotericism was theosophy ("divine wisdom"), a philosophical movement that was largely responsible for importing occultism and esotericism from Europe to America and that therefore played an important role in Western esoteric thought. Parenthetically, Evanzz claims that the NOI's founder, W. D. Fard Muhammad, was a member of the Theosophical Society, among many other religious and nationalistic organizations, while he resided in San Francisco; he says that Fard joined under the alias "George Farr."[84] Moreover, esotericism is often syncretic in nature.[85] Other strong influences on NOI thought include elements of, among others, Marcus Garvey's Universal Negro Improvement Association, black nationalism, African American Christianity, Freemasonry, Noble Drew Ali's Moorish Science Temple (which itself originated in Freemasonry), the Watchtower Bible and Tract Society (Jehovah's Witnesses), scientific cosmology, and mathematics.[86] After the death of Noble Drew Ali, the founder of the Moorish Science Temple in 1929, Master Fard Muhammad claimed to be his reincarnation.[87] As Dennis Walker contends in *Islam and the Search for African-American Nationhood: Elijah Muhammad, Louis Farrakhan and the Nation of Islam*, the NOI was built "by many hands."[88] In Claude Lévi-Strauss's term, the NOI is a *bricolage*.[89]

An important aspect of esotericism is gnosis, or secret knowledge that challenges received and accepted truth in the world, to which only the adepts connected to hidden and mystical sources have access. Curtis intimates that many NOI members believed that Elijah Muhammad had such access to esoteric knowledge, "a kind of gnosis that paved the way for a perfect understanding of the universe."[90] Muhammad himself claimed to have access to esoteric knowledge regarding the nature of reality (i.e., metaphysics), God, and race, and that African Americans had access to it through him. He said only that it came from his relationship with Master Fard, the Great Mahdi, who taught him: "The secret of who God is and who is the devil has been a mystery to the average one of mankind, to be revealed in all of its clearness to one who was so ignorant that he know [*sic*] not even himself—born blind, deaf and dumb. All praise is due to the Great Mahdi, who was to come and has come, the sole master of the worlds. I ask myself at times, 'What can I do to repay Allah (the Great Mahdi, Fard Muhammad) for his coming, wisdom, and knowledge and understanding?'"[91] Muhammad seems tacitly self-conscious about his own lack of formal education, and he expresses gratitude for the gift of secret knowledge that Fard transmitted to him. In fact, he argues, Fard himself is hidden away in occultation, like the expected Mahdi of Shi'ite Islam, until the time of his unveiling and judgment on the world: "Since His work is to destroy the wicked, He must remain hidden from the eyes of the world until the time is ripe (the end), for the two (God and devil) cannot rule together."[92] Simultaneously, the secret knowledge of Master Fard Muhammad is cloaked in the symbols of Freemasonry.[93] Claiming to have been a Mason and to have studied the science of Masonry in the Congressional Library in Washington, DC, Muhammad alleges that the white Masons do not understand the real truth of masonry.[94]

Along this line of reasoning, he proclaims that the Masonic symbols on the Masons' attire point to the so-called Negro: "The fez represents the universe," he retorts. "The Blackman made this fez. What I mean, the Sun, Moon and Star. . . . We are the Square, and we are the Star, and we are the Moon. . . . The white man knows nothing about the creation of such planets. This is why I teach you the theology of it."[95]

Muhammad establishes an ambiguous link between the FOI, secret knowledge, and Freemasonry: "The brothers, the Fruit of Islam (FOI) are men who have learned more about Masonry that you [i.e., white masons]. Your masonry [FOI/NOI] has included the history of your slavery, but you don't know it. Your first three degrees there, they are the answer to your slavery, if you understand. But not understanding them, as the white man would not teach you the theology inside of it, it makes you dumb to even that which you actually own."[96] As in Masonry, access to this secret knowledge appears to be gendered, given that Muhammad's references are directed exclusively toward men. Men, such as the FOI, are privy to the symbolic and religious wisdom revealed in Masonic forms. Muhammad also acknowledges the relationship between Islam in America and Freemasonry, stating: "Islam has been practiced in secrecy called Higher Masonry, Shriner, that is a small degree of knowledge of Islam is taught in secrecy by that society. You don't need to join Masonry to be a Muslim."[97] Also interesting is that the fez was a regular part of the NOI attire, particularly for the FOI.[98]

Hidden in the symbols and language of Masonry, then, is the nature and origin of the cosmos, the "supreme wisdom" of which is the identity of Allah and the divine genesis of the black race.[99] To that end, Muhammad proclaims, "The Original Man, Allah has declared, is none other than the black man. He is the first and last, and maker and owner of the universe; from him come all—brown, yellow, red and white."[100] Therefore, the knowledge that is embedded in Masonry is most likely the disclosure of the history and origin of the black race, which is given discursive expression by Muhammad in the many disjunctive discourses on Yakub. This source, albeit concealed, suggests that all human life on the planet comes from the black race and that the black body therefore is the source and standard for humanity, not the lowest form.

Moreover, black bodies in the NOI are cosmic, according to the Yakub mythology. Their origin is interstellar, and they are related to beings on other planets. *How to Eat to Live, Book 2*, conflates the dietary codes and people on Mars with beautiful bodies: "WE ARE A LONG WAY off from the life of the people on Mars, Who Allah in the Person of Master Fard Muhammad, to Whom Praise is due forever, taught me, lived an average life of the equivalent of 1200 years of our earth calendar. This in fact has been the Original Nation's calendar year ever since God created the Heavens and the Earth, so teaches the Holy Qur'an. If you want a beautiful appearance, eat the proper food and eat one meal a day."[101] The term *Original Nation* connects the people on Mars with the NOI, the Lost-Found Tribe of Shabazz, whose origins are the same.[102] Muhammad also indicates that the sense of time has been distorted on Earth as it currently exists. In other words, one year for the Original People, prior to the "fall" or rebellion of Yakub, used to equal what is now 1,200 Earth years. The bodies of the black beings on Mars are physically superior and provide a model for what black bodies on Earth can be.

Recall that Muhammad relished the idea of being related to "black" people on other planets, especially Mars. This is one of the important distinctions between the origins of black people and the *made* "white man." White people are a small, limited group, while the black race is cosmic: "That's the truth. You have people on Mars! Think how great you are. Ask the white man if he has any out there. We have life on other planets, but he don't."[103] Therefore, black identity cannot be solely or properly constructed out of the experiences and racist discourses of the West. The true identity and meaning of black bodies lies in trillions of years of history prior to the existence of Europeans and Americans.

Still, although the people on Mars grow to be seven to nine feet tall and live for a thousand years or more, they are intellectually inferior black people in the universe, says Muhammad. African Americans "are the most intelligent beings in the universe."[104] Locating superior intelligence in black bodies of Earth rather than Mars, again, suggests the eminence of the symbolic over the social for Muhammad. In this case, the black Martians offer an example of superior physical bodies, but he is well aware of the Western attacks on the black intellect as inferior. As a counter to that, he locates the superior consciousness here on Earth. Accordingly, blackness is constituted as transcendent in NOI mythology since it is connected to the origin of the universe by way of the "Black God," who created the cosmos.[105]

A second aspect of the Yakub narrative that is noteworthy for the construction of ideal black bodies is the "racial" mythology of Master Fard Muhammad's (Allah's) identity. Master Fard has been described as phenotypically "white."[106] While NOI mythology deems him literally and physically "black," though "light color," some question his ambiguous racial background and wonder if he is "black" at all.[107] The August 15, 1959, edition of the *Chicago New Crusader* printed a picture of Master Fard on its front page, with a headline in bold red letters: "White Man Is God for Cult of Islam."[108] Indeed, for Essien-Udom, Fard's ethnic identity, apparently accurately indicated by this "embarrassing expose," seems a foregone conclusion: "We have noted already that Master Muhammad is by all standards a white person."[109] Likewise, Claude A. Clegg III describes Fard as "a short, fair-skinned man with dark, straight hair" who presented himself as a "mulatto"; the "Islamic instructor was difficult to distinguish from a white man yet appeared comfortable among large crowds of Detroit blacks."[110] Regardless of whether one could definitively establish Fard's racial identity, the problem of his light complexion and "Caucasoid" features seemingly posed a problem for the NOI.

Elijah Muhammad (and Fard, who reportedly narrated the story to him) contended that Fard was strategically and intentionally of mixed black and white ancestry:

> Who is His father if God is not His Father? God is His Father, but the Father is also a man. You have heard of old that God prepared a body, or the expected Son of Man; Jesus is a specially prepared man to do a work of redeeming the lost sheep (the so-called Negro). He [Fard Muhammad] had to have a body that would be part of each side (black and white), half and half. Therefore, being born or made from both people, He is able to go among both black and white without being discovered or recognized. This He has done in the person of Master W. F. Muhammad, the man who was made by His Father to go and search for the lost members of the Tribe of Shabazz.[111]

Given his racial ambiguity, Fard Muhammad would be able to mingle among white people to gather counterintelligence. Elijah Muhammad never asks the obvious question: Does being born half-white make Allah half devil, since devils, by nature, "have no good in them?"[112] And how might this affect his divinity or power? Nor does Muhammad adequately explain how, being God, Master Fard was "born" of a "father" after being self-created and having created the cosmos. Rather, he simply appeals to traditional Christology, confident that, by appealing to the analogy of Jesus, he can placate his NOI audience of former Christians, who understand that Jesus could be man and God and yet "born" without serious challenge.[113]

The story maintains that Fard's mother was a white woman from the Caucasus Mountains named Baby Gee.[114] In a 1958 speech, Muhammad locates the devil nature in Master Fard's mother, proclaiming: "The God cleaned her. Is that right? He stripped her of the devil and made her fit to give birth to a child, that he intends to use to go after his people to redeem that people from her people."[115] Elsewhere, Muhammad elaborates:

It goes on also for the Mahdi being born out of His nation. But the man that produced the child, that she gave birth to was of us, Black man. He married her to get an unlike child so that he could send that child among our people and his people to produce a ruler of us who were lost among the unlike people. The man he made from among his people, and the enemy, was and is the God of judgment and destruction of the unlike people, who has attracted us for these last 6,000 years to follow them.[116]

This aspect of the narrative bespeaks a concern for the issues of both complexion and gender in an apparent attempt to maintain the integrity of Fard's identity and divinity (Moses is also half-white) and how whiteness has attracted black people. Muhammad emphasizes that Fard was black and "was of us," despite the obvious issues with his appearance.

The final phase of the Yakub story—in fact, the culmination of the narrative—will bring into full realization the significance of black bodies: the arrival of the Mother Plane, which will destroy this present world order and establish the new millennium in which black bodies will exist in their intended state in peace. Muhammad suggests that some people will not only survive the judgment long enough to see the destruction that the Mother Plane brings on the old world, they will escape destruction altogether:

Allah has warned us of how He would (one day) destroy the world with bombs, poison gas, and finally fire that would consume and destroy everything of the present world. Not anything of it (the present white mankind) would be left. Those escaping the destruction would not be allowed to take anything of it out with them. . . . Ezekiel saw it [the Mother Plane] a long time ago. It was built for the purpose of destroying the present world. Allah has also hinted at plaguing the world with rain, snow, hail and earthquakes.[117]

To whom will black bodies be revealed in all their glory? The texts are somewhat ambiguous on this point. On the one hand, bombs, fire, and gas will destroy the present world seemingly in an instant. On the other hand, many whites will witness the judgment, since rain, snow, hail, and earthquakes probably would not destroy the world immediately. That enemy witnesses would survive to see the glory of the truth of black bodies is indicated in Muhammad's suggestion that some will escape destruction. Muhammad does point out that his desire is for whites to recognize the uniqueness and ultimacy of black bodies. He suggests that black bodies will take on new meaning when the New World comes into being and that whites will learn the truth of the religion of Allah, pointing to the continued existence of an undefined representation of them:

> The so-called Negroes will be the beneficiaries (of the New World), for they, too, will be made "New" by Allah. They will take on new growth— spiritual as well as physical—and will become the most beautiful, the most wise, the most powerful and the most progressive people that ever lived! . . . The White Christians think that they and their religion will be the rulers in the New World. Followers of other religions think the same. But they will be greatly surprised and disappointed, for Allah has rejected all religions except Islam.[118]

Muhammad announces that black bodies—as both biological and religious symbols of the collective—will be changed and unveiled as the greatest and most beautiful, powerful, and intelligent bodies ever to exist and stipulates that whites will behold this revelation, much to their chagrin, as they expected Christianity to be the religion of the new millennium.

The Mother Plane, variously called the Mother Ship and the Mother Wheel, is of utmost importance, revealing the ideal black body in all its glory. It brings the black body to fruition and imbues it with all of its cosmic, transcendent, and divine meaning. Muhammad's idea of the Mother Plane is derived from a literal reading of Ezekiel 1, in which the prophet experienced a *visio Dei* in the form of a "space" vehicle, described as a wheel within a wheel.[119] According to Muhammad, the Mother Plane is a military weapon. The dimensions of the Wheel are one-half mile by one-half mile.[120] In fact, though human-made, the Mother Plane is a small planet that can remain in outer space for a year without descending into the Earth's atmosphere to take on oxygen and hydrogen.[121]

As a metaphor for beautiful black bodies, the Mother Plane discloses the racial genius of the black race—a brilliance that heretofore has been suppressed and hidden from the world in the service of white domination and oppression. It is gendered as feminine because it carries in its core other planes: "The Wheel, the Mother Ship, is one of the greatest wonders of man in making military weapons. The Black Scientists knew at the time that they built the Mother Ship, that the Mother Ship and its well-trained crew would have to fight with her and the other Nations of the earth. . . . Actually, the Wheel, the Mother Ship, serves as a carrier for 1,500 deadly prepared planes with which to visit mankind [sic] on Planet Earth."[122] The Mother Plane is evidence of the aesthetic, mathematical, and technical wizardry of the black nation. It indicates the astounding intellect of black people—that black bodies are not devoid of consciousness and intellect, as some Western philosophies have argued. On the contrary: "The finest [black] brains were used to build it."[123] The Wheel is a wonder even to Muhammad, who is overwhelmed by its majesty: "The Wheel is so wonderful that even the prophet had to declare it in these words, 'O Wheel, O Wheel' meaning that he is admiring his vision that he was receiving from Allah (God). The Wheel is the most wonderful and the most miraculous mechanical building of plane [sic] that has ever been imagined by man. The planes on this Wheel will be sent down, earthward, and are capable of destroying the world almost at once."[124]

Indeed, the Mother Plane is a vehicle of justice that will not only destroy the devil and the evil present world; it will usher in a millennial reign and peace on the Earth for the black nation (i.e., black, brown, red, yellow), whose bodies will be transformed into their perfect state.[125] As Muhammad elaborates, "There will be such a charge in the general atmosphere of the earth (in the Hereafter) that people will think it is a new earth. It will be the heaven of righteousness forever; no sickness, no hospitals, no insane asylums, no gambling, no cursing or swearing will be heard in that life. . . . You will be clothed in silk, interwoven with gold, and eat the best food that you desire. This is the time when you enter such life, for your God is here in Person."[126] In preparation for this millennial existence and as evidence of its possibility, Muhammad demands that his followers adopt a moral and courageous lifestyle immediately: "All fear, grief and sorrow will stop on this side as a proof."[127] In short, he desires an ethic of proper conduct that signifies on the NOI dietary and dress codes.

In *Children of Ezekiel: Aliens, UFOs, the Crisis of Race, and the Advent of the End Time*, Michael Lieb surveys fictional literature, religious ideas, and scientific technology that engages and uses Ezekiel's vision as a model or guide and those who view it as a literal ancient visitation by a divine being or space aliens. He argues that Ezekiel's vision provides an aesthetic archetype that expresses the human desire to technologize and mechanize the ineffable, the inexpressible, and the unknowable—to render it intelligible and mundane in order to master it.[128] One such technological machine, he contends, is the unidentified flying object (UFO).[129] Using Heideggerian language, Lieb affirms that the Mother Plane, a type of UFO ontotechnology, represents the mechanism through which the being of a thing is revealed, brought forth, disclosed, unconcealed—in this case, the true nature of the black race.[130] This disclosure or bringing forth is an aesthetic endeavor in that the highest form of *technē*, skill, and know-how, *poiesis*, is the artistic meaningful uncovering.[131] Richard Rojcewicz, author of *The Gods and Technology: A Reading of Heidegger*, contends that Heidegger's sense of bringing forth something out of concealment to show itself in its unconcealed state means not that it is creating something but, instead, that it is uncovering something that already exists for witnesses to behold.[132] Accordingly, this technology of epistemology denotes Muhammad's longing to transform the otherness of the divine and secret knowledge and the unknown into an essence that can be appropriated and "placed in service of those who are no longer human but tantamount to gods," often as compensation for their relative powerlessness.[133] The Mother Plane can be read, then, as a divine vehicle, a chariot of work (*ma'aseh merkabah*), that discloses the truth (*alētheia*), previous gnosis, of black bodies in all their splendor—cosmic, transcendent, ultimate, divine, and destroying the evil reign of oppression—and that establishes a new order that discloses once and for all the nature of those who were once the most despised people on the planet.[134]

Muhammad intimates that the world has had glimpses of the Mother Plane. These "sightings" are epistemological misrecognitions of the Mother Plane as ordinary UFOs, due to the temporal limitations of the knowledge and intellect of whites, who have had only six thousand years of experience on this Earth since their making. [135] The black race's knowledge, by contrast, is cumulative and cosmic, reflecting trillions of years of data of sublime proportions.[136] This gnosis signifies that black bodies are much more complex than other bodies on the planet, and they are capable of unrivaled intellectual capacity of cosmic proportions that will be brought to fruition at the arrival of the Mother Plane. In addition, their misrecognition is due to their own perverse intentions and behavior, according to Lieb. Charles Long, author of *Significations: Signs, Symbols, and Images in the Interpretation of Religion*, means something similar when he talks about America's violent past with respect to Native Americans and Africans—its *arche*. That is, the failure to deal with the genesis of its own existence as such has led to self-concealment, a difficulty in assigning proper language to reality, and to the misinterpretation of such.[137] Muhammad says that Allah will use the Mother Plane to judge America and the world for its horrific treatment, lynching, and enslavement of black people:[138]

> But America brought this woe upon herself, by not doing Justice to her Black slaves. . . . Allah (God) wants to pay America for her injustice to we, the poor Black man in America, the Black slave! . . . America has not received much woe yet, for how she killed outright, the poor Black man in the south (GA). America has hated her Black slave worse than she hates rattlesnakes. America has given her Black slave every evil and indecent name that she could think of while yet her Black slave has been her safety ground.[139]

Nevertheless, whites have some limited knowledge of the Mother Plane and the impending judgment of Master Fard Muhammad upon them. This is the real reason for the American space program (i.e., NASA), says Muhammad. American space technology is conspiratorial in nature. Its real intent is to escape destruction or to attempt to launch a defensive counterattack from the Moon, Mars, or Venus. Even this, he says, will not work: "You cannot live on the Moon, only just so long as your oxygen and hydrogen last you. The moon is about the closest platform that I know of, that you could probably use. Venus and Mars. . . . [Y]ou cannot use Venus and Mars. The people on Mars will not let you light (land) on Mars. If they do let you land on Mars; they will be silly to do so."[140] Black people on Mars and Venus will thus participate in the thwarting of any attempts by NASA or other white space technologies that seek to delay or prevent the Mother Plane from destroying the present world and upsetting global white supremacy by revealing black bodies as cosmic. These agencies may try to attack the Mother Plane, but their technology is too limited.

In a demonstration of black intellectual and psychic abilities, however, Muhammad proposes that African Americans, who are connected psychically to one another and to the Mother Plane, can detect the Mother Plane through telepathic clairvoyance: "You can do it [read the thoughts of others] yourself if you will take the time, clear your mind, and then go some place where no one will disturb you, and concentrate on that Wheel or that Brother After a while you what the Brother is saying to himself. Maybe you can hear the motors going in one of the wheels."[141] Even before the Mother Plane arrives, Muhammad points to the potential of black intellect by suggesting black bodies are imbued with extrasensory perceptions and abilities that are not earthbound. Lieb likens this to a form of meditative transcendence similar to Merkabah mysticism, in which the adherent connects to a source or form of power not readily available materially.[142]

Conclusion

Elijah Muhammad's project was the meaningful making and unveiling of ideal black bodies. In this endeavor, he used a variety of ritual, theological, and philosophical sources to reimagine and re-present the race. While he was concerned with physical and religious-symbolic bodies, practices varied depending on which body was his concern. For bodies as material and biological, he was concerned with ritual practices that improved the physical appearance, health, and cleanliness; for black bodies as symbols of the NOI collective that resisted being totalized and defined by the social system at large, the sources were much more discursive—mythological, theological. Muhammad privileged the religious over the sociopolitical. His ideal bodies were out-of-place symbolically rather than socially, since Muhammad was rarely if ever interested in his members' engaging oppressive government and social structures. His interest was in teaching them more accurately who they were and imparting esoteric knowledge that revealed their ultimate place in the cosmos. Reflecting the mythological, cosmological, and theological discourses that located the origins of blackness extraterrestrially, and their ultimate meaning having been disclosed and unconcealed by the Mother Plane, black bodies signal transcendence. That is, they pointed "out there" for their significance even though they were material and earthbound.

The NOI black body is an ideal black body that was differentiated by critiquing certain unappealing black bodies and through its own religious system, which constituted a distinct black embodied economy as Muslim, male, masculine, healthy, adult, "middle class," heterosexual, mystical-esoteric, light-complexioned, and gifted/intelligent. Martha Lee concludes, as I do here, that "all of these set Muslims apart from other Blacks" and gave them cohesiveness and identity. [143] What gets effectively eschewed and marginalized is a body constituted by any combination of features from the default "lower-class" black embodied economy—namely, Christian, female, effeminate male, "homosexual," dark-complexioned, political/"integrationist," working class/poor, disabled, and so on.

The discourses of Yakub and the Mother Plane critiqued and challenged discourses of white superiority; ideal black bodies were *dangerous* to the dominant culture because they were symbolically out-of-place. They resisted being rendered inferior. These were healthy and vibrant bodies superior to any other bodies in existence on Earth, and they were more gifted intellectually than any in the universe. They were the most beautiful and the most righteous religious bodies, and because of this attitude about who they were, the NOI was not afraid to transgress symbolic boundaries by critiquing white supremacy as a farce, an illusion. Therefore, even though Muhammad never advised his members to engage social structures of oppression or harm white Americans in any way, this symbolic out-of-placeness was, nevertheless, a threat to the social order. Muhammad was a religious leader rather than a black nationalist, and his primary goals were to construct ideal black bodies that would be prepared for the New World and the greatness that was to come at its arrival.

MALCOLM X AND THE POLITICS OF RESISTANCE
VISIBLE BODIES, LANGUAGE, AND THE IMPLIED CRITIQUE OF ELIJAH MUHAMMAD

Although much fascination and lore has been devoted to Malcolm X's "conversion" to Sunni Islam, little attention has been given to his religious life prior to leaving the Nation of Islam (NOI) in 1964 and to his struggle with the mythology and theology of Elijah Muhammad. The millenarian and apocalyptic orientation of the Yakub narrative made direct political agitation irrelevant in a world in which "evil white devils" would ultimately be destroyed and in which a new world would be constituted as the perfect black utopia; at the coming of the Mother Plane, black bodies in the NOI would be unveiled and constituted as physically and symbolically sublime and ultimate. Such an orientation makes the NOI untenable for black nationalists, since there is no need to set up a nation-state when the Mother Plane will return at the end of the age to destroy this evil world and institute a millennial kingdom on Earth. But Malcolm longed to be engaged socially and bodily in the struggle for justice, not just symbolically as a distant critic.

The image of "Malcolm" has been reified as a paragon of masculinity, which obfuscates his frailties, his personal relationships, and his religious life. The frequent response to racism is to foreground black figures, generally male, as examples of heroic geniuses who contradict the assumptions of white supremacy and the stereotypes of black inferiority. Speaking after Malcolm's assassination in 1965, the Reverend Albert B. Cleage (a.k.a. Jaramogi Abebe Agyeman, the Holy Patriarch of the Pan-African Orthodox Christian Church) said, "Brother Malcolm has become a symbol, a dream, a hope, a nostalgia for the past, a mystique, a shadow sometimes without substance, 'our shining black prince,' to whom we do obeisance, about whom we write heroic poems. But I think Brother Malcolm the man is in danger of being lost in a vast tissue of distortions which now constitute Malcolm the myth."[1] He was right: Malcolm had become a legend, an image, that had little to do with the complicated life of the man. Cleage goes on to dispel the myths that Malcolm became an integrationist, that he accepted "Islam" uncritically after he made the hajj, and that, after this pilgrimage, race was no longer important to him.[2] Michael Eric Dyson's *Making Malcolm: The Myth and Meaning of Malcolm X* and Manning Marable's *Living Black History: How Reimagining the African American Past Can Remake America's Racial Future* concur.[3] The authors rail against the social, economic, and "intellectual" forces that intentionally give inadequate attention to Malcolm's life and work in service of constructing a symbol that can serve as the impetus for political and disciplinary projects. Dyson contends that critical studies of Malcolm, to the contrary, must offer the "thickest description" of his life and career possible, including his achievements and failures, without resorting to a biographical reductionism that obscures the complexities of his life. He concludes: "Judging by these standards, the literature on Malcolm X has often missed the mark. . . . Much writing about Malcolm has either lost its way in the murky waters of psychology dissolved from history or simply substituted defensive praise for critical appraisal. At times, insights on Malcolm have been tarnished by insular ideological arguments that neither illuminate nor surprise."[4] Indeed, Dyson has in mind many critical appraisals of Malcolm but, in particular, *The Autobiography of Malcolm X*, much of which reflects Alex Haley's ideological commitments and literary intentions.[5] Hence, many studies, Dyson and Marable maintain, offer only limited views that are constrained by a desire either to deify or to demonize Malcolm X for political purposes. Fixing Malcolm's image as static does violence to his creative genius as a man whose hallmark, Marable declares in *Malcolm X:*

A Life of Reinvention, was his ability to improvise and remake himself in challenging situations.[6]

A telling example of such conventional constructs and reifications is the poem "A Poem for Black Hearts," by Amiri Baraka, which appears in his book *Eulogies*.[7] It idolizes Malcolm as a "black god" who was martyred because of his love for black people:

> For Malcolm's heart,
> raising us above our filthy cities,
> for his stride, and his beat, and his address
> to the grey monsters of the world, For Malcolm's
> pleas for your dignity, black man, for your life,
> black man, for the filling of your minds
> with righteousness, For all of him dead and
> gone and vanished from us, and all of him, . . .
> and all of yourself, look up, . . .
> black man, quit whining and stooping, for all of him,
> For Great Malcolm a prince of the earth, let nothing in us rest
> until we avenge ourselves for his death, stupid animals
> that killed him, let us never breathe a pure breath
> if we fail, and white men call us faggots till the end of
> the earth.[8]

Here, Malcolm is a masculine messiah "prince" who raised "us [black men] above our filthy cities." Disturbingly, obvious sexism and blatant homophobia get conflated with Malcolm's image. The vengeful anger in this poem is curious but comprehensible, an attempt, seemingly, to express the anxiety and feeling of being dominated by white supremacy; it may assist in veiling the homoerotic overtones in the longing for and nostalgic devotion to Malcolm.[9] Similarly, discursively and culturally violent themes surface, particularly in the writings of cultural nationalists and African American radicals, apparently without any trepidation that they may not be wholly consistent with Malcolm's life and thought.

More generally, mythic constructions like these of Malcolm are favorable bodily constructions that deflect or refute racist depictions of African Americans. They are the response of black communities to white representations of black embodiment—in this case, Malcolm's black body—as socially and symbolically in-place, as inferior, in what Victor Anderson calls "ontological blackness."[10] As Marable and other scholars note, such reifications and prominent counter-significations of white supremacist notions often jettison complexity, contradiction, and any aspects that seem to complicate refutation of racist narratives. I would add that, in particular, they make it hard to see that Malcolm was a deeply religious and theological person *during* his tenure in the NOI. Many works on Malcolm's life and thought focus narrowly on his "black nationalist," social, and political thought and ignore his theological commitments.[11]

Louis DeCaro's *On the Side of My People: A Religious Life of Malcolm X* attempts to examine Malcolm's religious life in a way that I find unhelpful.[12] DeCaro frames his interpretation of Malcolm's religious life in terms of "cult" and "orthodoxy." He contends, *"On the Side of My People* is also a religious study and therefore requires religious terminology. The terminology that seems most appropriate to me is that of orthodoxy versus cult."[13] The "cult" aspect of Malcolm was, of course, his life in the NOI, and "orthodoxy," a term that is almost as fraught with problems as "cult," represents the flourishing Malcolm who embraced Sunni Islam, although it is never clear exactly what these terms mean conceptually. The term "cult" has little usefulness in the study of religion. Some religions are small, new, or enclavist or by their very nature will never be "mainstream." Casting the NOI as a cult sets up a false binary that renders Malcolm's former life in the NOI—a new and emerging religion rather than a cult—as problematic and his life as an "orthodox Muslim" as a space of flourishing, as positive, and so on. This is an exceedingly troubling methodology. What is required is a close examination and interpretation of Malcolm's religious life—for my purposes—primarily while he was in the NOI.

Malcolm was a flourishing thinker while he was a member of the NOI, not simply afterward, though he didn't always agree with Elijah Muhammad. Thus, a look at Malcolm's struggle with the NOI mythology disrupts static constructions of his life and deepens critiques of those constructions. Malcolm was initially deeply committed to the mythology, theology, and ideals of the Nation of Islam. In short, he shared Muhammad's ideals and his concerns for black bodies until about 1959. While he was still a member of the NOI, Malcolm appropriated its religious teachings in creative ways.

Malcolm X and the Theology and Thought of Elijah Muhammad: Consonance and Consent

Initially, Malcolm was deeply committed to the mythology, theology, and ideals of the NOI.[14] He shared Muhammad's ideals and his concerns for black bodies for many years. But Malcolm seemed to reflect either disagreement with Muhammad or a shift in Muhammad's thought with respect to Free-masonry and devilish white people. For Malcolm (and perhaps for Mu-hammad), the Masons and the Jehovah's Witnesses were ideological and theological opponents of the NOI.[15] This is, of course, peculiar, since the NOI has its genealogical roots in Freemasonry and borrowed heavily both from it and from the Watchtower Bible and Tract Society's Charles "Taze" Russell and Joseph Franklin "Judge" Rutherford. Yet Muhammad is re-ported to have stated the following in a Saviour's Day address delivered on February 26, 1958: "We are the true witnesses of God. You have a gang of devils around here calling themselves Jehovah's Witnesses. Talking about they are the witness of Jehovah, when did a devil become a witness of Je-hovah?"[16] A few pages later in the same publication, Muhammad offers a remonstrance against the Freemasons and how they fail to treat "Negroes" as equals, no matter how high they rise through the degrees of the secret order.[17] Malcolm's introduction into the dogma of the NOI will include the theme of race and Masonry.

Indeed, Malcolm's early catechism into NOI doctrine by his brother Reginald included an extremely rationalistic notion of God, which equated God with epistemology. "Who would be a man who knows every-thing," his brother asked him. Malcolm replied "God."[18] That is, God *is* knowledge—not only information but, literally, geometrical, mathemati-cal, philosophical, and theological gnosis embodied. While God was 360 degrees of knowledge, the devil was knowledge of only 33 degrees, which signifies the highest degree in American Masonry. "The white man is the devil," Reginald retorted, "especially Masons."[19] Malcolm suggested that this idea was consistent with his life as he reflected on it and was a revela-tion of truth.[20] This idea points further to his perspective as highly empiri-cal and rational, which on the surface seems to concur with the perspective of Muhammad that black bodies are largely, but not exclusively material.

It is not wholly clear whether the views of Freemasonry (and of the Jehovah's Witnesses) in the *Autobiography* reflect an evolution in Mu-hammad's thought, Reginald's views, or Malcolm's perspective (in retro-spect).[21] If it is Malcolm's perspective, however, it is somewhat of a diver-gence and a contradiction, because in that for Muhammad, Masonry was not the master signifier of the devil. In fact, embedded in the symbols and secret knowledge of Masonry was the truth of the black race: that they were the original people of the universe and that Allah was a black god. Furthermore, such a perspective as Malcolm's would conflict with Muham-mad's, given that it (i.e., whites as Masonic) would seem to render white bodies esoteric, mystical, and gnostic, making them not characteristically and categorically different from black bodies, since the knowledge within Freemasonry reflected the deepest and ultimate esoteric knowledge of the universe.

Muhammad privileged the symbolic over the social—that black bodies were the recipients and carriers of religious meanings by way of discourses such as Yakub myth that valorized them. This meant, among other things, that these bodies were clandestine and detached from mainstream public life—and, indeed, the NOI was an enclavist religious organization. Since the Mother Plane was the vehicle by which the world would be destroyed and by which the new peaceful world would be generated, the NOI did not require its members to engage corrupt social systems bodily (i.e., socially). Quite the contrary: Muhammad forbade his members to vote (until late in his life) and to participate in activist groups and severely limited their interaction with whites and civic groups. Muhammad taught that Allah would take action in the world, at the return of the Mother Plane, and refused to allow Malcolm to involve the NOI in the politics of the civil rights movement; he ignored white people who were violent to black people and the NOI, while at the same time, the NOI apportioned inordinately violent retaliation against other black bodies, especially against people who left the Nation of Islam.[22] Responses to white violence directed at black bodies was met with measured symbolic gestures in the form of "verbal retaliation" that were theological in nature.

Three areas, in particular, are important to a discussion of the consonance between Malcolm and Muhammad on black bodies: the Yakub/ Mother Plane discourse, the evil of white people, and the centrality of bodies to black liberation.

The Yakub story appealed to Malcolm in part because he already had a materialist and "scientific" perspective on the world; the largely earthbound theology of the narrative helped to give further coherence to that perspective. Malcolm agreed that God could not be a spirit or "spook"; that heaven did not exist; and that hell was on Earth, not some celestial reality.[23] His discourse sounds like the astrophysical and geographical notions embedded in the Yakub narrative when he talks about the origins of the races not as epochal but as historical and scientific. As late as December 1962 and early 1963, Malcolm continued to teach the Yakub narrative in great detail.[24] In the lecture "Black Man's History," given in a December 1962, Malcolm connects NOI cosmology and mythology to the numerical distances of the planets in the solar system to communicate the scientific nature of Yakub:

The Honorable Elijah Muhammad teaches us that sixty-six trillion years ago—trillion, how much is trillion? Not hundreds, nor thousands, nor millions, nor billions, but sixty-six trillion years ago—the black man was here. We have the sun which is the center of the universe; 36,000,000 miles from the sun is the planet Mercury, and 67,200,000 miles from the sun is the planet called Venus, and 93,000,000 miles from the sun is the planet that you and I live on called Earth, 141,500,000 miles out here is a planet called Mars, and 483,000,000 miles from the sun is a planet called Jupiter. . . . So right here this planet that you and I live on called Earth, that rotates around the sun. The Honorable Elijah Muhammad teaches us that sixty-six trillion years ago our people were living on this planet: the black man was living on this planet.[25]

This was not mythology for Malcolm. The implications of this notion are that black bodies are concrete and material and that their activity may perhaps be better focused on the here and now, since heaven does not exist as a transcendent reality. This was especially poignant given the formerly Christian NOI audience to which he was speaking.

Likewise, Malcolm embraced Muhammad's and Fard's idea that white people were devils, as the Yakub story detailed.[26] As he pondered his life in the *Autobiography*, his experience seemed to confirm this.[27] For example, only one of his father's many brothers died of natural causes. Nearly all of the others died at the hands of whites:

Among the many reasons my father had decided to risk and dedicate his life to help disseminate this [black nationalist, Garveyite] philosophy among his people was that he had seen four of his six brothers die by violence, three of them killed by white men, including one by lynching. What my father could not know is that of the remaining three, including himself, only one, my Uncle Jim, would die in bed, of natural causes. Northern white police were later to shoot my Uncle Oscar, and my father was finally himself to die by the white man's hands.[28]

His father was killed by a group of violent racists called the Black Legion, who laid him on a railway track in front of a streetcar. According to Malcolm, his father was almost cut in half and his skull was crushed.[29] Malcolm enumerates these events in the *Autobiography* to explain why, for him, America was a nightmare. Because of his experiences, Malcolm was unable to see any good in the racist American system, and the story of Yakub, as the creator of the devil, resonated.

In keeping with this interpretation, Cleage suggests that naming whites as the enemies of African Americans was the basic truth that was the foundation for everything that Malcolm said and did, and that he, Muhammad, and Malcolm all agreed on this teaching.[30] Cleage states it this way: "The white man [sic] is your enemy. That is a basic principle, we can't forget it."[31] This principle was encapsulated in Malcolm's famous address, "Message to the Grass Roots," at the Detroit Northern Negro Grass Roots Leadership Conference, held at the King Solomon Baptist Church in 1963. Malcolm asserted:

> America's problem is us. We're her problem. . . . When we come together, we don't come together as Baptists and Methodists. You don't catch hell because you're a Methodist. You don't catch hell because you're a Methodist or Baptist, you don't catch hell because you're a Democrat or Republican, you don't catch hell because you're a Mason or an Elk, and you sure don't catch hell because you're an American. You catch hell because you're a black man [sic]. You catch hell, all of us catch hell for the same reason.[32]

Malcolm stated this same basic position in the 1964 speech "The Ballot or the Bullet"—that is, even after Muhammad had "silenced" him for his comments on John F. Kennedy's assassination.[33]

Moreover, Malcolm's use of the words "black, brown, red, yellow" to refer to colonized people indicates a basic conservation of Muhammad's metaphysics of world order as a black-and-nonblack (i.e., white) binary. Stated differently, even his reference to "black, brown, red, and yellow" was rooted in Muhammad's notion of black—in my understanding as a surplus category that is also metaphysical—that was expressed in the Yakub saga. There, Muhammad understood the Black Nation to be characterized by people, who, again, were "black, brown, red, [and] yellow." Malcolm seems to retain this way of organizing the world in racial terms at least as a strategic approach to combating white supremacy. His contention is that whites have positioned themselves violently over and against black people and people of color and that the recognition of whites as a common enemy who reduces all black people to an externalized and racialized epidermis is a necessary precondition for a liberating consciousness and strategy.[34]

Cleage saw revolutionary insight in Malcolm's words, recognizing the necessity, as Malcolm argued, to name the enemy and understand how white supremacy functioned. The violence and domination of white supremacy was not predicated on black cultural differences or on religious and social affiliations. Cleage concludes, "We can be discriminated against because our physical characteristics make us recognizable and enable the white group which holds power to keep us separate, powerless, and stigmatized as 'inferior.' We are oppressed as members of a group, not as individuals. We suffer as individuals and we are humiliated as individuals, but only because we belong to the Black group."[35] He tacitly approves of Malcolm's coalition building by reminding his audience of the veracity of Malcolm's claim that African Americans are discriminated against, not because of social class, education, or religion, but because of their phenotype and, in particular, their skin color. But again, this basic position is rooted in Muhammad's and Fard's Yakub myth.

The most significant way in which Malcolm agreed with Muhammad and was influenced by him, even after leaving the NOI, was in his recognition of the centrality of the body—understood both as biological and as a symbol of a given social collectivity—in the struggle for African American liberation and selfhood.[36] Race (and, we see later, gender), for Malcolm, was attached to the body in real and concrete ways. Indeed, race was biological and social. That he viewed race as biological reality can be seen in numerous instances in which Malcolm referred to the body by way of appeal to the senses. For example, he reflected on how, as children, he and his siblings noticed that white bodies smelled different.[37] Similarly, he recalled that, while as a youth in a Mason, Michigan, reform school, he observed this again and that whites had a different sense of taste: "I noticed again how white people smelled differently from us, and how their food tasted differently, not seasoned like Negro cooking."[38] A highly simplistic and reductionistic trope holds that such notions somehow point to an alleged "black supremacist" system of black power in relation to whites. But Malcolm creatively and subversively signifies on white supremacist notions of taste as a marker of civility and human development in white cultured subjects—for them, African American foods indicated black inferiority—and points them back at whites as a critique.

Malcolm, again, may have been unconsciously following Muhammad in his ruminations on white smell and taste. Muhammad—for whom race was biological and ontological and the differences between black bodies and white ones were qualitative and metaphysical—connected the sense of taste to the deterioration of the white race. Speaking of how, having been newly made by Yakub, whites were degenerated culturally after deceiving the original (black) people for six months, Muhammad includes food as a critical detail: "They were punished by being deprived of divine guidance for 2000 years which brought them almost into the family of wild beasts—going upon all fours; eating raw and unseasoned, uncooked food; living in caves and tree tops, climbing and jumping from one tree to the other."[39] Muhammad describes early whites as evolutionarily regressed, almost to a state of animality in which their behavior was erratic and their sense of taste was dulled. Tied to the story of Yakub, the aesthetics of taste further demonstrate why white people are so violent toward people of color: they are not as humanly developed as they suppose themselves to be. Malcolm's earlier reference to unseasoned food may also refer to his sense of the debasement of whites, even though he is popularly depicted as having moved away from notions of race after his religious experience of the hajj.

Malcolm also communicates his views of race as a biological reality and the body as central to liberation in discussions of consanguinity. In his essentialist notions of black nationalism and Pan-Africanism, Malcolm regarded all "black" people or people of African descent as related to him.[40] In his words, "I considered all Negroes to be my blood brothers."[41] His position was influenced by Marcus M. Garvey, whose writings, Malcolm suggested, the nascent Organization for Afro-American Unity (June 28, 1964) should follow.[42] Most immediately, his position was based on the religion of his former mentor, Elijah Muhammad, who Malcolm credits with a viable long-term project to return African Americans to the continent of Africa. He claims that "Elijah Muhammad's solution is the best one . . . our people going back home, to our African homeland."[43] This idea of African emigration was popularly called "black to Africa." As late as November 1963, Malcolm seems to conceive race as a metaphysical notion, holding that many different kinds of nonwhite people are "black" biologically and socially. "And every time you look at yourself," he exclaims, "be you black, brown, red or yellow, a so-called Negro, you represent a person who poses such a serious problem for America because you're not wanted."[44] Africans, Latinos, Asians, and Native Americans are all subsumed under the category "so-called Negro," which, again, was a term with roots in the Moorish Science Temple of America, a prominent religious antecedent of the NOI. "What you and I need to do is learn to forget our differences," Malcolm recommended, "so we're all black people, so-called Negroes, second-class citizens, ex-slaves."[45]

The context seems clear. Malcolm was speaking at a black Baptist church (King Solomon's Baptist Church) in Detroit to an audience that was "almost all black and with non-Muslims in the great majority."[46] This was one of the last speeches Malcolm would deliver before being suspended from the NOI by Muhammad. It is not completely astonishing that he held this position. But what was beginning to appear in his active public speaking is a subtle signal that he was moving away from Muhammad's enclavist institutional orientation. In other words, through his lectures and appearances, even as he espoused ideals that were closely tied to Muhammad, Malcolm implied that NOI black bodies were more active and less sectarian, given that many of his most significant speeches prior to leaving the NOI expressed much more appreciation for African American Christians.[47]

The idea that black people constitute a nation is deeply engrained, engendered from Malcolm's relationship with Muhammad. In fact, Muhammad argued that the term "race" should be applied not to African Americans but to white people, given that they were made. Black people were not a race or subclass of humanity. Rather, they were the Original People, constituting a nation, not a race: "The race is a made race. This is why you should not accept calling [sic] a 'race.' YOU ARE A NATION! Not to think over a Negro or a Colored people."[48] Important here is the idea that nationalism presupposes an essentialized notion of race, but the nomenclature, "nation," profoundly influenced Malcolm, even after his departure from the NOI. He proclaimed: "Our gospel is black nationalism. We're not trying to threaten the existence of any organization, but we're spreading the gospel of black nationalism. Anywhere there's a church that is also preaching and practicing the gospel of black nationalism, join that church. If NAACP [the National Association for the Advancement of Colored People] is preaching and practicing the gospel of black nationalism, join the NAACP. If CORE [the Congress of Racial Equality] is spreading and practicing the gospel of black nationalism, join CORE. Join any organization that has a gospel that's for the uplift of the black man."[49]

Malcolm's views of the solution to the race problem were increasingly less parochial, but he still understood bodies as biological and race as a determinative factor that defined black bodies and tied them together. It could be argued that at this point in his life—after leaving the NOI and prior to his excursion to Africa and the Middle East—race was his religion. In other words, his convoluted notion of religion was located in black bodies, which for him may have been the only things that were concrete, stable, and quantifiable. His material and empirical outlook on life, gained from Muhammad, remained his measuring rod for knowledge, truth, and authority.

Likewise, Malcolm inherited this notion of nationhood through blood from Muhammad and maintained it as an important part of his political program throughout his life. After his international travels, he dealt openly and honestly with the fact that the idea needed explicit reappraisal and, perhaps, broadening explicitly to include "Africans" on the continent, who might not be "black" in ways that were understood in America.[50] Dean E. Robinson, who wrote *Black Nationalism in American Politics and Thought*, argues that Muhammad established a template for 1960s black nationalism and that Malcolm broadened its applicability and secularized it in the Organization of Afro-American Unity (OAAU) platform.[51] What Robinson misses is that such an idea was not "secularized." Religious nationalism—rather than black nationalism—was always part of Malcolm's religious inheritance from Muhammad and therefore was not new, although Malcolm may have repackaged the idea of race for a new international audience and program.

A second example of Malcolm's thinking about consanguinity, indicating a physical biological ontology of race and the body as biological, can be read in his struggle with his own mixed ancestry. He reported that his maternal grandmother had been raped by a slave owner, thus "polluting" his blood—an invasion into his body that he detested: "If I could drain away *his* blood that pollutes *my* body, and pollutes my complexion, I'd do it! Because I hate every drop of that rapist's blood that's in me!"[52] Malcolm talked openly and ambivalently about how he believed his light complexion gave him a sort of "privilege" in his life. Such a complexion, in Muhammad's ideal black bodily economy, was one of the many factors in his rise and subsequent fall in the NOI, as Malcolm approximated these religious ideals in and on his own body.

"Blood" also determined certain behavioral characteristics for Malcolm, as with Muhammad. For instance, Malcolm differentially embraced racial stereotypes of black bodies, depending on whether or not he considered them harmful to black selfhood. In yet another indication that he regarded race as something biological, he intimated that "whites are correct in thinking that black people are natural dancers."[53] Conversely, having white ancestry and a light complexion seemed to carry adverse meaning that had destructive consequences for African Americans. Along this line, Muhammad reported that his paternal great-grandmother was half-white, "and she acted like it"—thus equating the presence of "white blood" with negative activity.[54]

Malcolm was affected by this stereotype, even within his own family. His wife, Betty Shabazz, tells a story about him as a father: "At first it bothered him that Attallah was so light (Malcolm didn't want any light children) and we both wondered what in the world we'd done wrong for this little girl to come out looking like that."[55] It disturbed Malcolm that his daughter was born light-complexioned, as if she bore the emblem of a violent and oppressive people and the evidence of rape. In fact, Attallah's skin color, Betty indicates, did conjure Malcolm's reflexive anxieties. He suggested that Betty be strict in raising their daughter because he saw the "wildness" in her that was also in him.[56]

More generally, Malcolm critiqued black bodies that reflected the social system—that is, the racist culture of America—such as the black bodies in-place that Muhammad saw as ideologically "whitenized." In the last year of his life, Malcolm still believed, like Muhammad, that Christianity functioned ideologically to render black embodiment symbolically in-place—that is, "to brainwash the Black man. It has taught him to look for his heaven in the hereafter while the white man enjoys his heaven on earth. I chose to be a Black Muslim and a realist. The American whites talk but do not practice brotherhood; therefore it is my duty to fight this evil. You see, you can't write up on some freedom, you must fight up on some freedom."[57] The point is significant, in part, because the *Autobiography* may leave one with the impression that the ideological break with Muhammad was much more significant than it appears to be. Yet this critique also implicates Muhammad, who talks about Christians but fails to "fight."

Two metaphors, both of which had the body as their references, further characterize Malcolm's critique of black bodies that mirrored the racist social system and functioned in service of its maintenance. The first of these metaphors was "black bodies with white heads."[58] He used this pejorative particularly for "Negro leaders," who for him were "black" physically but ideologically acted in accordance and complicity with white supremacy:

> Today's Uncle Tom doesn't wear a handkerchief on his head. This modern, twentieth-century Uncle Thomas now often wears a top hat. He's usually well-dressed and well-educated. He's often the personification of culture and refinement. The twentieth-century Uncle Thomas sometimes speaks with a Yale or Harvard accent. Sometimes he is known as Professor, Doctor, Judge, and Reverend, even Right Reverend Doctor. . . . Never before in America had these hand-picked so-called "leaders" been publicly blasted in this way. They reacted to the truth about themselves even more hotly than the devilish white man. . . . "Black bodies with white heads!" I called them what they were. Every one of those "Negro progress" organizations had the same composition. Black "leaders" were

out in the public eye—to be seen by the Negroes for whom they were supposed to be fighting the white man. But obscurely, behind the scenes, was a white boss—a president, or board chairman, or some other title, pulling the real strings.[59]

These black bodies reflected the mentality of the white-dominated system, with little or no self-conscious agency of their own. Malcolm was extremely critical of those, including African American Christians, whom he saw as acting in the interest of the continued domination by whites. These people may have been black, but they had been co-opted by the system in ways that made them ineffective as "leaders." In fact, they were not leaders at all, according to him; they were "puppets."[60] While Muhammad's primary criticism was of Negro Christians, Malcolm included African Americans in the academy. He clearly was not being anti-intellectual in this; rather, he seemed to suggest that the knowledge of the "black . . . Ph.D. 'house' and 'yard' Negroes" was invalid because they were handpicked by whites to oppose the NOI and keep black people in-place.[61]

Martin Luther King Jr. was the epitome of "black bodies with white heads," given his popularity, his relationship to whites and goal of integrating with them, his education, and his public criticism of the NOI that, at times, was inaccurate and meant to placate whites. King said of the NOI, for example, "The Black Muslims are a quasi-religious, sociopolitical movement that has appealed to some Negroes who formerly were Christians. What this appeal actually represents was an indictment of Christian failures to live up to Christianity's precepts."[62] King closely follows C. Eric Lincoln here. In fairness to King, who was speaking in 1965, Lincoln's *The Black Muslims in America* was the first, and more popular, of only two book-length academic works on the Nation of Islam at this time, and very few reliable works interpreted the religious dimensions of the NOI.[63] Likewise, it was Lincoln's conclusion that the NOI was a sociopolitical group and not a religious group (which was also E. U. Essien-Udom's conclusion in the book that followed Lincoln's).[64] Lincoln would later correct this position. Nonetheless, the most obvious chauvinism in King's statement was the denial of anything legitimate about the NOI, the contention that it existed only because of the failures of Christianity. To an extent, Malcolm, like Muhammad, was responding to these caricatures of NOI religion.

The second metaphor that signified black bodies in-place that had been "whitenized" ideologically by the social system was that of the "conk." The conk was a process by which black men straightened their hair to resemble white men's hair that Malcolm associated with lower-class African Americans in the early 1940s. He noticed the style in the Boston ghetto as a teenager, after he had moved from Michigan to Boston to live with his sister Ella; he was attracted to the style in part because he did not like his natural hair, which he referred to depreciatively as "kinky."[65] He wrote, "The sharp-dressed young 'cats' who hung on the corners and in the poolrooms, bars, and restaurants, and who obviously didn't work anywhere, completely entranced me. I couldn't get over marveling at how their hair was straight and shiny like white men's hair; Ella told me this was called a 'conk.'" [66] Conking was a "painful" process that required the use of Red Devil lye, two eggs, two medium-size white potatoes, and Vaseline.[67] Malcolm was willing to endure the pain of applying this concoction because, as he reported, he had internalized white standards of beauty, the ideal of which is represented by blond hair and blue eyes—what Cornel West called the "normative gaze."[68] Malcolm looked back critically at his younger self:

> How ridiculous I was! Stupid enough to stand there simply lost in admiration of my hair now looking "white" reflected in the mirror in Shorty's room. I vowed that I'd never again be without a conk, and I never was for many years. . . . It was my first real step toward self-degradation: when I endured all that pain, literally burning my flesh to have it look like a white man's hair. I had joined that multitude of Negro men and women in America who are brainwashed into believing that black people are "inferior" and that white people are "superior"—that they will even violate and mutilate their God-created bodies to try to look "pretty" by white standards. . . . Conk—the emblem of shame that he is black.[69]

He came to understand the conk, then, as a symbol that African American men had totally sold out to the system—completely bought into the notion that they were inferior. Malcolm's emphasis on the pain of the process is emblematic of the deep-rooted injury to the black psyche vis-à-vis whiteness that the conk represents: the white aesthetic was so pervasive in black communities that one would be willing to endure physical agony to achieve acceptability.

The cultural equivalent of the conk for black women, Malcolm suggests, was the wearing of blond wigs, in particular, and the loud and extravagant colors of platinum, pink, red, and purple.[70] But the ultimate parallel and cultural extension of this injury was the adoration of a blond-haired, blue-eyed Jesus—for Malcolm, the pinnacle of brainwashing. Malcolm gave an example of the type of remonstrance he would offer Negro Christians when he went "fishing," or engaged in proselytizing them:

> Brothers and sisters, the white man has brainwashed us black people to fashion our gaze upon a blond-haired, blue-eyed Jesus! We're worshiping a Jesus that doesn't even *look* like us! Oh, yes! Now just bear with me, listen to the teachings of the Messenger of Allah, The Honorable Elijah Muhammad. Now, just think of this. The blond-haired, blue-eyed white man has taught you and me to worship a *white* Jesus, and to shout and sing and pray to this God that's *his* God, the white man's God. The white man has taught us to shout and sing and pray until we *die*, to wait until *death*, for some dreamy heaven-in-the-hereafter, when we're *dead*, while this white man has milk and honey in the streets paved with golden dollars right here on *this* earth![71]

This type of polemic was meant to make an absurdity out of the white Christian ideology that "brainwashed" millions of African Americans into inferiority complexes.

In other words, the embedded racial codes in the worship of a white Jesus, as well as the conk, functioned in service of white domination and to give it ultimate significance (at least, in the case of the white Jesus). Malcolm suggested that this was an intentional machination that had everyday consequences: "Look at not only how *you* live, but look at how anybody that you *know* lives—that way, you'll be sure that you're not just a bad-luck accident. And when you get through looking at where *you* live, then you take a walk down across Central Park, and start to look what this white God has brought to the white man. I mean take yourself a look down there at how the white man is living!"[72] Malcolm tried to show his audience how whiteness functioned surreptitiously and was manifested—embodied in the ocular sense—as a gaze on Jesus and literally as a mechanical alteration of black bodies in the form of conking. Worshiping a white Jesus and conking resulted from the same self-denial and assimilation of white supremacy. He also reaffirmed his conflicting class-consciousnesses. Though he denied identifying with middle-class African Americans, he was, like Muhammad, critical of the values and behavior of the working classes, insisting that he respected "upper-class Negroes," who never conked their hair.[73]

Malcolm's later thinking on black features and hair, in relation to a cultural context that viewed them as devalued, is consistent with the colorism and negative issues with black features that runs throughout his thought.

In 1962, he still evidenced the internalized residual effects of the Western acculturation that also characterizes Muhammad's narrative on Yakub.[74] For example, in his lecture "Black Man's History," he says: "Our people were soft; they were black *but* soft and delicate, fine. They had straight hair. Right here on this Earth you find some of them look like that today. They are black as night, but their hair is like silk, and originally *all* our people had that kind of hair. But Africa, and living in the open, living a jungle life, eating all kinds of food had an effect on the appearance of our people."[75] Malcolm goes on to say that "nappy hair" is a result of "living in a rough climate" and that the remnants of this primordial hair can be seen in the eyebrows of black people, which are straight-haired.[76] Also, contrast the use of the phrase "black as night," a negative image, to describe some African American complexions, with the use of the term "silk", a designation of wealth, status, and privilege, to depict hair that was "Caucasoid" (remember, for Malcolm the conk resembles white people's hair). Moreover, he describes typical black hair as a degradation of original black features, using the derogatory appellation "nappy" in doing so.

The issue of mechanical hair alterations and the conk, in particular, symbolized African Americans' deep indoctrination into the values and aesthetics of white Americans. Both of these metaphors—black bodies with white heads and the conk—were discourses that created apertures for the exercise of Malcolm's own agency and recalcitrance. This resistance was made necessary by the cultural limitations placed on black existence generally and, more specifically, by the religious restrictions and interdictions of the Honorable Elijah Muhammad, his leader and spiritual guide.[77]

Malcolm X on the Religion and Praxis of Elijah Muhammad: Conflict and Critique

Malcolm expressed growing frustration about the constraints on his agency—indeed, the power and control over his body—exerted by Muhammad and the NOI. In particular, as David Howard-Pitney concludes, Malcolm began to "chafe under Muhammad's strict prohibitions against his followers engaging in any protest against white authorities."[78] By 1963, Malcolm wished to engage actively and bodily in the civil rights movement. At its most basic level, Malcolm's desire to join the movement and his resentment of Muhammad's failure to engage whites bodily implied a critique of the theology and apolitical posture of Muhammad and the NOI.

Malcolm grew restless with what we have called Muhammad's religious and symbolic out-of-placeness.

Malcolm struggled for his own bodily agency while with the Nation of Islam. He also understood the nature of agential black bodies characteristically differently from Muhammad, and that in both of these was an implied but pronounced critique of the basic beliefs and practices of the organization that he held so dear.

Malcolm believed that the NOI should be involved with advocating for civil rights *physically*, by way of protest, voting, and political activities—and, if need be, defense of black communities. He recognized that these activities would be socially out-of-place and that, as a result, he would be considered *dangerous*. In a letter from Cairo dated August 29, 1964, he explains to the leadership of the Organization of Afro-American Unity and Muslim Mosque, Inc., "What I am trying to do is very dangerous, because it is a direct threat to the entire international system of racist exploitation. It is a threat to discrimination in all its international forms"[79] He was aware of how the social system sought to control recalcitrant black bodies to maintain the system of privileges: "Therefore, if I die or am killed before I make it back to the States, you can rest assured that what I've already set in motion will never be stopped."[80] What he must have been referring to in this letter was his work on behalf of the primary goal of the OAAU: to bring to the floor of the United Nations human rights violations charges against the United States for its violent and inhumane treatment of African Americans.[81] Malcolm thought that Muhammad and the NOI had enormous potential to affect the civil rights movement and the international fight for justice positively. But they were too interested in enclavist religious matters.

Furthermore, Malcolm thought that the NOI should act on its cosmology to challenge the socially constructed boundaries of acceptable black activity with aggressive responses and protests. "Even Malcolm found Muhammad's claim that God would punish the white man for his evil deeds difficult to accept and to explain to others," maintains James H. Cone.[82] Malcolm thought that Muhammad and the NOI were inordinately heavy-handed in their treatment of rival and "apostate" African Americans and showed undue restraint with whites, often justifying the inactivity and "nonengagement policy" with claims that suggested Allah would deal with them later. He also became aware of and embarrassed by remarks of black communities on the disparate responses of the NOI to white people and to black people.

Malcolm believed that the NOI should defend itself and retaliate for acts of violence against it. His mounting frustration with the NOI—while he was still a member of the group—was a passive-aggressive critique of Muhammad's millenarianism. He no longer found satisfaction in the apocalyptic pronouncements that the cataclysmic end of the age of the white man was coming and that the glory of the black race would be realized at the appearance of the Mother Plane. He admitted this dissatisfaction to other ministers within the NOI and to the public.[83]

The "initial fissure" between Malcolm and Muhammad came when Malcolm decided in 1963 to investigate independently rumors of Muhammad's sexual liaisons and extramarital children, Michael A. Gomez argues in *Black Crescent: The Experience and Legacy of African Muslims in the Americas*: "His very decision to investigate the rumors by interviewing several secretaries rather than first going to Mr. Muhammad is instructive in that it represents an initial fissure in his faith in Mr. Muhammad."[84] But Malcolm's many questions of Muhammad's judgment and theology denote not only an ideological and theological shift in his thinking; more important, they signify an affective rupture in the psychic bond between him and his mentor. That is, despite his overt loyalty, Malcolm had begun to exhibit emotional distance from Muhammad well before this "investigation." Moreover, it seems to me that Malcolm probably knew about Muhammad's infidelities as early as 1955.[85] It is likely that the more pressing issue in the fissure may have been contestation over female love interests.

Malcolm grew so impatient with such a philosophy that it became difficult for him to conceal his feelings.[86] His dissatisfaction with Muhammad's decisions was no mere triviality. The very presence of his discontentment signaled doubt about the core beliefs of the Nation of Islam (i.e., Yakub) and about their relevance to the African American struggle. In other words, his longing to join the active protest for justice and equality suggested at least a nascent disbelief in the Yakub–Mother Plane/Mothership discourse.[87]

While he was a member of the Nation of Islam, Malcolm's progressive disenchantment was tenuously ameliorated by his prominent stature, which afforded him the opportunity for existential transcendence, even if only temporarily. He was able to find meaning by countering the limitations placed on him by Muhammad in two areas. These practices had direct bearing on black bodies in the NOI, including his body. First, Malcolm X made black bodies in the NOI visible through his tireless proselytic work. It was he who was responsible for the growth of the NOI after he joined the movement in the early 1950s, ultimately making the group known to the general public.[88] One scholar suggests that Muhammad had forty temples and four hundred members when Malcolm joined the Nation of Islam in 1952. Primarily due to Malcolm's charisma and efforts, NOI temples may have numbered one hundred, and the membership may have swelled to forty thousand by 1964.[89] Malcolm gained visibility in his role as missionary and temple planter and studied the evangelist Billy Graham's techniques and emulated his method of supporting churches through evangelism, according to DeCaro's *Malcolm and the Cross: The Nation of Islam, Malcolm X, and Christianity*.[90]

That Malcolm may have seen himself as the Muslim counterpart to Billy Graham also says something about his self-consciousness—that he thrived off his sense of freedom and agency and that he was the most successful and fulfilled when he was able to function with a degree of freedom, as he did with temple planting. This image of himself also may have pointed to a desire on his part for the prominence and recognition that Graham's type of missionization afforded him. Having been directly involved in all or nearly all of the temple or mosques that had been established since 1952 gave him a "virtual omnipresence"; even in his absence, his generative presence, his creative finger, loomed large.[91] Dean Robinson notes that "Malcolm X figures prominently because without him the Nation of Islam would have never have achieved its status—in terms of membership or influence."[92]

The second practice that allowed Malcolm to transcend his bodily constrictions was his use of the language of remonstrance. In his "Message to the Grass Roots" speech, he challenged the parochialism of Muhammad, intentionally or not, by advocating a broadened international and national coalition of people, who were not Muslims, who could combat oppression.[93] He addressed his words to America's people of color and suggested that the colonized world (i.e., "black, brown, red, yellow")—especially black people—needed to come together to confront white supremacy. [94]

Malcolm's use of language to transcend his circumstances was especially strong regarding his criticism of the civil rights movement. Through the materiality of language and desire—that is, language as embodied and material—he was able to create a social world and an identity in which he was an *active* participant in the struggle for justice and equality, even though his overt language of critique would seem merely symbolic.[95] That is, language (*nommo*) is creative and generative. Following George Yancy, Geneva Smitherman, and Judith Butler, we know that language does more than just *say* something.[96] It *does* something—that is, it performs some-thing and represents it as already constituted.[97] So Malcolm was not simply "saying something" when he spoke about civil rights. He was "there," effecting change.

In fact, one could argue that his vociferous, often circumlocutious, pronouncements in opposition to many of the practices of the civil rights movement, such as its commitment to nonviolence, partly expressed Malcolm's desire to insert himself into social activities as a theorist and agent of change, which was otherwise constricted by the jurisdiction of Muhammad's NOI. Malcolm also used written language in his newspaper columns and in *Muhammad Speaks*, a periodical of the NOI that he founded and to which he was a major contributor.

Malcolm desired to be present bodily in the political process, and language (as a material extension of his physical body) allowed him to transcend his constraints and to be "present" bodily in the struggle for jus-tice. His speech "God's Judgment of White America (The Chickens Are Coming Home to Roost)," delivered on December 4, 1963, offers useful illustrations:

> Among whites here in America, the political teams are no longer divided into Democrats and Republicans. The whites who are now struggling for control of the American political throne are divided into "liberal" and "conservative" camps. The white liberals from both parties cross party lines to work together toward the same goals, and white conservatives from both parties do likewise. The white liberal differs from the white conservative only in one way: the liberal is more deceitful than the con-servative. The liberal is more hypocritical than the conservative. Both want power, but the white liberal is the one who has perfected the art of posing as the Negro's friend and benefactor.[98]

Here Malcolm inserted himself directly into the milieu of American public life through political commentary about the shift in the nature of Ameri-can politics of affiliation vis-à-vis race and African Americans. He sug-gests that both Republicans and Democrats are part of the same system but that the "new" nomenclatures "conservative" (Republicans) and "lib-eral" (Democrats) are deceptive. Malcolm seemed to respect the conserva-tives more because they were more forthcoming about who they were and what they wanted, while liberals played a "game," making African Ameri-cans feel that they served their interests while concealing the fact that black people were really "pawn[s]" as whites pursued their own self-interest.[99]

Ultimately, he made his body visible through these rhetorical acts and his longing for direct confrontation with the system, and he implicitly critiqued and demarcated the distinction between his view of the world and that of his mentor, Elijah Muhammad.

Malcolm's use of language was a departure from that of his spiritual leader. Even through his critique of black bodies in-place, Muhammad seemed to have no overt desire to affect the direction of the movement or to join it. Furthermore, Muhammad's pronouncements about Christianity and culture may have served as a psychological factor for his followers in that it could give them a sense of security—that they were indeed in the right religious organization. More important, through his criticism, Muhammad was performing "Messengership," for lack of a better word, demonstrating to his followers that he alone embodied the truth of God. Malcolm's use of language, by contrast, was a means of affecting and effectively participating surreptitiously in the civil rights movement and American politics. To that end, this was yet another implied critique of Muhammad that spoke to the core (at times unconscious) doubt that he had regarding the most central precepts of the NOI eschatology and by extension—and contrary to other accounts—the divine inspiration of his mentor.

Unable to reconcile his commitment to the NOI and his belief that it could be a great political force in America with his growing desire for active participation in political activities, Malcolm grew increasingly disgruntled.[100] He began to see the NOI as a force that worked against his bodily agency. Malcolm attempted to employ his own form of recalcitrance while in the Nation of Islam (Muhammad did let him critique Martin Luther King Jr. and the civil rights movement in a limited sense), but when such exercises were seen as crossing the constraining boundaries of the NOI, they were summarily prohibited. Malcolm was "censored and isolated, thus forced to withdraw into himself as he had done in early adolescence."[101]

The tension between Malcolm's ostensible agreement with Muhammad's religious teachings and his visceral reactions and political desires while still a member of the NOI was a strong ambivalence, at best, and at worst, subtle and implied disbelief with which he wrestled for several years. His growing desire to be an active participant in the civil rights movement was an implied critique of Muhammad's most fundamental precepts. Ultimately, it was impossible to reconcile that desire, that sense of calling and belonging, with the Yakub–Mothership (UFO) discourse. The way in which he saw black bodies as most recalcitrant and "black"—that is, through direct, aggressive sociopolitical activity and self-defense—could thrive only outside Muhammad's project. Malcolm was thus frustrated with Elijah Muhammad and the Nation of Islam, which, he said, never made an effort to create a nation-state and never actually advocated a separate black state (i.e., that they were never black nationalists).[102]

Conclusion

The clearest evidence of Malcolm's fundamental disagreement with and critique of Muhammad's orientation toward black bodies (i.e., privileging of symbolic out-of-placeness) can be seen in the many things he said (and did) immediately after he withdrew from the NOI officially in 1964.[103] He made his critique explicit after he left, saying, "Elijah believes that God is going to come and straighten things out. I believe that too. But whereas Elijah is willing to sit and wait, I'm not willing to sit and wait on God to come. If he doesn't come soon, it will be too late. I believe in religion, but a religion that includes political, economic, and social action designed to eliminate some of these things, and make a paradise here on earth while we're waiting on the other."[104] Malcolm suggested that he believed conceptually in a God who would attend eschatologically to social and political inequalities and the injustices that African Americans and colonized people had experienced. He insisted that his form of belief, unlike Muhammad's, did not lead to a quietism that made sociopolitical engagement irrelevant due to the belief that human activity would be immaterial since God ultimately would handle these matters. Malcolm's words also indicated a subtle doubt in God's immanent engagement of the world—that God might not eradicate racism or, at least, might not do so in time. (Qualitatively, there is no difference between the two.) Moreover, he reinforced the priority of social out-of-placeness—that religious black bodies should stand up to and face the exigencies of their day. In a *New York Times* interview that appeared on February 22, 1965, the day after his death, Malcolm proclaimed, "I feel like a man who has been asleep somewhat and under someone else's control. I feel that what I'm thinking and saying is now for myself. Before it was for and by the guidance of Elijah Muhammad. Now I think with my own mind, sir!"[105] While what happened after Malcolm's defection from the NOI is somewhat outside the purview of this chapter, that he advocated voting, self-defense, and coalition building indicates his immediate response to Muhammad and reveals convictions that he held prior to leaving the NOI.

As he became much more public in his prophetic and intellectual activity, Malcolm shifted away from the view of whites as ontologically evil.

After leaving the NOI, he revised Muhammad's position, says Cleage, to one that viewed white people as "beasts" because of how they treated black people. Likewise, a beast is lower than a human, and in some ways this notion reproduces Muhammad's human (black) and nonhuman (white) dichotomy by signifying on white notions of humanity as quintessentially white, even though the distinction is behavioral (i.e., existential) and not ontological.[106] Malcolm would suggest in 1965 (again, after leaving the NOI) that the American system nourished whites psychologically to act in evil and violent ways; that it was the culture and social system of America that was to blame for the behavior of whites, not that they were qualitatively different in nature from African Americans or people of color generally.[107] Of course, the flaw in this logic is that people constitute the "system," and social institutions function in service of those who are in power. So while Malcolm may effectively have rejected the specific mythological, ahistorical, and nonscientific content of the Yakub narrative, he nevertheless retained the ultimate meaning of the epic: the identification and naming of the enemy of the black race.

Malcolm's project was a cultural critical and activist program whose resulting meaning, like Muhammad's ideal, would have been seen as black bodies out-of-place socially and symbolically. But unlike Muhammad, Malcolm was not satisfied with symbolic out-of-placeness or with being the member of an enclavist religious group that did not engage in overt civil rights and human rights agitation. Malcolm's social critique created a space and justification for his social endeavor, a divergence from the ideology of Elijah Muhammad. He makes this discrepancy very clear when he was asked about the distinction between his social thought and Muhammad's that might have led to his departure from the NOI. He explains his rationale:

> I didn't break [with the NOI], there was a split. The split came about primarily because they put me out, and they put me out because of my uncompromising approach to problems I thought should be solved and the movement could solve. I felt the movement was dragging its feet in many areas. It didn't involve itself in the civil or civic or political struggles our people were confronted by. All it did was stress the importance of moral reformation—don't drink, don't smoke, don't permit fornication and adultery.... So the only way it could function and be meaningful in the community was to take part in political and economic facets of the Negro struggle. And the organization wouldn't do that because the stand

it would have to take would have been too militant, uncompromising, and activist, and the hierarchy had gotten too conservative.[108]

Malcolm is direct: he did not leave the Nation of Islam; he was expelled, "put out," because of his perspective that the NOI should be involved in direct, bodily, confrontational activities that pertained to the liberation of black people from oppression.[109] He is critical of the NOI's hypocrisy for preaching moral purity but failing to practice it. Given its empty moral pronouncements, the group could have remained meaningful to the black struggle only by engaging in political and economic activities that would benefit all black people, not simply the NOI. Malcolm also tacitly admits here that Muhammad was a "religious" leader and, as such, emphasized moral behavior but remained on the sidelines socially.

Physical black bodies as active, socially engaged, unruly, and agential entities were the carriers of meaning that signified their full humanity. They gained such meaning as they participated in their own liberation struggle. Freedom-producing activity—whether it was voting and political engagement or self-defense of black communities—is when black bodies came into realization as religious and as human.[110] They did not do so strictly through moral discourse or enclavist sensibilities.[111] Yet again, this did not negate Malcolm's knowledge that black bodies were important carriers of meaning—that is, that they were symbols. It only exemplified that black bodies that could be apprehended as socially out-of-place were crucially important for him.

Malcolm X and Wallace Muhammad (later, Warith Deen Mohammed) were close during their time in the Nation of Islam and often confided in each other. Collage created for the author by David Metcalfe.

WARITH DEEN MOHAMMED AND THE NATION OF ISLAM

RACE AND BLACK EMBODIMENT IN "ISLAMIC" FORM

Warith Deen Mohammed (a.k.a. Wallace D. Muhammad) appropriated Sunni Islam for the Nation of Islam (NOI), constructing black ("Islamic") bodies in ways that engaged with but critiqued both Elijah Muhammad and Malcolm X.[1] His incessant attention to race in his early years indicates his privileging, like his father, Elijah Muhammad, of the symbolic over the social. He disagreed with his father, however, in finding Islam concrete and fixed (e.g., the Five Pillars) and not esoteric and "spooky."[2] Furthermore, religion was not something private and exclusive for him, as it was for Muhammad. It was universal. But this Sunni notion of the universality (*ummah*) of religion also posed problems for Mohammed, who recognized the particular (*asabiya*) effects of racism on African Americans.[3] At the same time, like Malcolm, at least, he recognized the importance of the social—that is, of physical bodies engaging in activities, encroaching on spaces that cross or approach boundaries and thus could be considered threatening. Therefore, he recast black embodiment *symbolically*, seeing

African Americans "cultured" through and in Islam to dislodge them from the negative meanings of inferiority attached to them by the racist social system. Mohammed sought to symbolically disrupt that system's reproduction of black bodies in-place; moreover, his emphasis on diet, proper attire, and clean living, as well as on voting and participation in social activism and the political process, carried out his concern for black (physical) bodies *socially*. In doing so, however, Mohammed also critiqued Malcolm X, who viewed religion and social responsibility as somewhat separate.

Subsequently, Mohammed embraced a distinctive tradition within African American Islam and the NOI—actually consistent with the ideas of both Muhammad and Malcolm X—that held the ostensible universal (Islam) in tension with the obvious particular (i.e., race). The body and the significance of race remained his central focus as he shifted to a manner of religion more closely related to international Sunni Islam.

But Mohammed was not the obvious or easy successor to his father as leader of the NOI. His ascension to the leadership position was something of a coup. Louis Farrakhan had positioned himself to be the next chief minister of the Nation of Islam prior to Muhammad's death on February 25, 1975.[4] He seemingly held the credentials that would allow him to move smoothly into the lead role. Like Malcolm X, who had been expected to succeed Muhammad until he was expelled from the Nation of Islam and then assassinated, he was Muhammad's national representative. In addition, he was the minister of Harlem's Temple No. 7, the most prestigious post in the NOI, second in importance only to Chicago's Temple No. 2, the international headquarters—a sure sign that he was the next in line to lead the Nation of Islam. How Mohammed ascended to the top position instead would play an important theological role in the direction he would take the NOI.

Mohammed was named the successor to Elijah Muhammad's NOI on February 26, 1975, and he renamed the group the World Community of al-Islam in the West (WCIW) on October 18, 1976.[5] However, he maintained that it remained the NOI in spite of these changes in leadership and in name. In fact, he claimed to conceive of the WCIW as the resurrection of the NOI, which had fallen from its cultural foundation when he took it over.[6] This chapter is concerned mostly with the years from 1975, when Elijah Muhammad died and his son Mohammed assumed leadership, to 1978, when Mohammed "excommunicated" Farrakhan from his NOI, or WCIW, and Farrakhan began his own Nation of Islam that claimed to be the authentic legacy of his teachers, Elijah Muhammad and Master

Fard Muhammad.[7] In his later years, Mohammed, who died in 2008, was one of the most important Muslim leaders in America and one of the more significant in the world. He certainly would not have been considered socially or symbolically *out*-of-place during this period of his life. But in this first decade after his father's death, he was maligned by immigrant Sunni Muslims, who accused him of teaching the same doctrines as his father and Fard. In fact, Mohammed resisted and refuted such criticisms and his critics' attempts to police African American Muslim practices and beliefs. He did so precisely by suggesting the importance of his social, historical, and cultural (i.e., "racial") situatedness and by declaring that this particularity necessitated a specific appropriation of Islam.

Concurrently, Mohammed continued to move the wciw toward a more globally acceptable form of Islam until he resigned from the presidency on September 10, 1978, and appointed a council of imams to run the group.[8] Still, Mohammed continued to consider his group the noi and embraced this legacy throughout the 1980s, locating all of his teachings in the theology and program of Master Fard Muhammad and his own father, the Honorable Elijah Muhammad.[9]

Unfortunately, Mohammed's work in the Nation of Islam has received far less scholarly attention than that of the other noi leaders.[10] Because of the paucity of primary literature during this limited period, as well, I use principal sources that Mohammed published in the 1980s, many of which reproduce speeches, lectures, and homilies from the mid- to late 1970s, in which he offers his perspective on these transitional years.[11] In addition, the chapter employs sources that draw on the noi publication *Muhammad Speaks* (later, *Bilalian News*), which recorded some of the doctrinal and political issues of the period.[12]

Warith Deen Mohammed: Allah's Final Messenger?

Elijah Muhammad's demise put the Nation of Islam in an awkward position of having to determine the succession of a man who was supposedly Allah's final messenger, not unlike Sunni interpretations of the Prophet Muhammad Ibn-Abdullah as the Seal of the Prophets (*khatm*), or the final prophet who fulfills the meaning or is the final revelation of all those who came before him.

The sociology of religion scholar Lawrence Mamiya has pointed out how similar Farrakhan was to Malcolm X in ways that made him a likely successor to Elijah Muhammad. "If anyone in the Muslim movement closely resembles Malcolm X in career and style it is Minister Louis Farrakhan."[13] Both were "fair-skinned," an important factor to the group; both were born to Caribbean mothers. As I indicated earlier, they were both ministers of the Harlem temple, and they both started newspapers for the NOI. Like Malcolm X, Farrakhan approximated Muhammad's ideal black bodily economy: he was male, heterosexual, masculine, "middle-class," light-complexioned, mystical-esoteric, intelligent, and healthy. Other important features included rhetorical and leadership abilities and charisma. These characteristics were also more or less equal between Mohammed and Farrakhan. So the factor determining succession was how successfully each manipulated power, though this might not have been immediately obvious.

Members of the NOI found reasons that made it convenient, if not expedient, to appoint Mohammed the leader of the movement. For example, numerology and mystical thinking played a part in the decision to appoint him. Mohammed had been his father's seventh-born child, which was thought to signify something special about him. Moreover, Mohammed was the only child born after the arrival of the founder of the NOI. Finally, he (Wallace Deen Muhammad) was named after the founder, Wallace D. Fard Muhammad. Mohammed was cognizant of these factors: "The power of mystery. The other children were already born when Fard Muhammad came. I was the only child born during his stay with us. I was chosen because a new baby, new birth—they wanted a Christ figure, someone with a mystery about [him]. There was this newborn baby predicted by Fard Muhammad to be a male and so it happened the guess was right. I say a 'guess' not to laugh at our religion. I say 'guess' because that's the language the Honorable Elijah Muhammad used."[14] Mattias Gardell, a European scholar of the NOI, agrees that numerology and legend in the NOI pointed to a divine purpose of Mohammed's birth, especially as indicated by the number seven, which symbolized the reestablishment of "black world leadership," perfection, and masculinity. Indeed, Master Fard was said to have written in chalk the name of the child to be—"Wallace"—on the back door of the home of Elijah Muhammad and to have foretold that he would be the leader of the NOI.[15]

The numerological significance of Mohammed's birth and the prophetic acts of Master Fard initiated and contributed to the aura that encircled him throughout his life. This mystery surrounding him, Mohammed seems to suggest, outweighed the fact that his relationship with his father was volatile and that he was "excommunicated" from the Nation of Islam on several occasions for being critical of Muhammad's theology and practice.[16] In fact, one of the episodes of estrangement lasted until the year before his father's death in 1975:

> The longest period of my suspension was between the years of 1964 and 1969. During that time I was stripped of all minister's privileges. In 1966, early 1967 all support—even family relations were denied me. I couldn't even socialize with family members. . . . In '69 things began to warm up. In 1970 I was admitted back. Once right after Malcolm's assassination I was admitted back, but that didn't last very long. I was right back out. I was admitted back in 1970 again. I stay [sic] in the good graces of Elijah Muhammad until now. . . . It was back in 1974 that the Honorable Elijah Muhammad accepted me back into the ministry.[17]

Again, in a sense, it seems odd that Mohammed became the leader of the Nation of Islam, since he was constantly in trouble due to his theological and political differences with Muhammad; but maybe his insight was acute when he suggested that he became the successor partly due to people's desire for an "heir" (pun intended) of mystery and prophecy. Linking his leadership of the NOI to prophesy was a strategic move, that allowed him later to couch his new Sunni teachings in the theology of Muhammad and to argue that, ultimately, Sunni Islam was the logical and natural fulfillment of his father's work and Master Fard Muhammad's intentions.

But perhaps Mohammed was not being wholly forthcoming by locating his rise to prominence in the mystery and prophecy of his predecessors, thereby obfuscating any political moves or power plays that he may have made. For example, Edward Curtis, who also considers it remarkable that Mohammed became the overseer, notes a more political power move: "Wallace flatly told National Secretary Abass Rassoull and National Spokesman Louis Farrakhan that he would succeed his father and specifically warned Farrakhan not to interfere."[18]

Perhaps becoming the leader was not so "mysterious," then.

In fact, it appears that, despite the very different trajectory and theological commitments of the NOI to his own, Mohammed coveted the post and employed strong-arm tactics and manipulation of his paternal relationship to position himself for a successful takeover of the NOI. For example, Farrakhan claims that Mohammed threatened him to stay out of his takeover of the nation. Without such strategic maneuvers, Mohammed might well have suspected that Farrakhan, his chief rival, would be the next man to command the group—hence, his stern warning to him to watch his step. Interestingly enough, Mohammed may have had some assistance from the Federal Bureau of Investigation (FBI) in gaining the leadership position; he sought protection from the organization when he felt his life was in danger after one of his excommunications, and the FBI believed that he would be the most desirable leader, for its purposes, to head the NOI.[19]

Once Mohammed gained the leadership, he made the NOI a Sunni Muslim organization in an effort to bridge the old with the new:

> We decided that we were ready, we have the dedication. We've been in the habit too long to give it up; we have the moral strength to accept the job ahead of us, and we have the courage to act on that moral strength. So the Nation of Islam is not going out of business. We said we're going to stay in business until we can evolve it up a little higher. And that's what we did. We used the Divine principle of evolving into a society. We translated language and put it in words that would lift the dead matter of 1975 up to another living level. . . . [H]ere is a way for us to keep our identity in the old life and come into a new life.[20]

Mohammed described the transition as a "metamorphosis," a natural process in the evolution of life from one stage to another, which allows the organism to maintain its identity but to grow and mature into a fuller existence.[21] This is how he understood the NOI and its relationship to the subsequent incarnations. The sentence "We translated the language" speaks to the method by which the NOI made the transition and maintained coherence between its origins and the new directions in which it was going. It is a reference, it seems, to the practice of reinterpreting the language and mythology of Fard and Muhammad and giving it a literal meaning that pointed prophetically to their Nation of Islam's new course.

For example, Mohammed saw in the Yakub mythology symbolic language that enabled him to make sense of the trajectory of the NOI.[22] Couched in the language and symbolic teachings of Muhammad and Fard were data that pointed to Sunni Islam and the NOI's current path. In this way, Mohammed was able to connect the prophecy surrounding his birth to the prophetic reinterpretation of the theology and mythology of Fard and Muhammad, what he called the "dark symbolism of mathematical theology" and, hence, to demythologize—or per Martha Lee, to "de-eschatologize"—the teachings.[23] He indicated gratitude that he was able to make sense of how the earlier teachings had concrete application in the current program.

It was important personally and politically that Mohammed was able to signify for his congregation that he was taking them in the direction that Fard and Muhammad wanted them to go and that they were the fulfillment of the esoteric teachings of the NOI leaders. Furthermore, he thought that Fard and the story of Yakub that he taught helped to explain African Americans' feeling of psychological inferiority.[24] To this end, in fact, he claimed that many of Fard's teachings, including the catechism, introduced them to the Qur'an and made them desire it.[25] He was aware that the teachings did not line up absolutely with so-called orthodoxy, but like Abdul Basit Naeem, a Pakistani Muslim and NOI supporter in the 1950s, he believed that the teachings were meant for their particular situation and that the NOI would grow in "Islamic" knowledge as time progressed.[26]

Finally, Mohammed was careful to point to the NOI and the WCIW as the same organization. He did not desire to compartmentalize or to see the movement as disjunctive. Rather, as stated earlier, he wanted to see it as a coherent fulfillment of the prophetic symbolism of his predecessors, and whether he actually believed it or not, he intended to communicate this idea to his listeners. When asked about the history of the WCIW in February 1979, he offered one history: "The organization began in the early 1930s, the historical date in our records is July 4, 1930. The organization was established under the name Lost Found Nation of Islam in America. The purpose of that organization was to separate blacks and whites. More importantly, the purpose was to regenerate the spiritual and the moral life of people who were living poor and ignorant lives."[27] Mohammed did not offer a separate history for the WCIW. Instead, he indicated the purpose of the organization and explicitly described the movement as continuous.

What this "continuity" meant for black bodies is complicated, however. One the one hand, Mohammed wanted black bodies to be seen in concrete terms of Islam, which he understood as established, true, historical, and cultured. That is, Islam is a "fact." Furthermore, the manner in which he gained power (instead of Farrakhan) suggests that he understood in very concrete and material terms that power is pursued and seized and that competition is eliminated, overpowered, or outwitted. On the other hand, putting his Islam in terms of contiguity with Fard and Muhammad meant that some meanings attached to their bodies, such as their esoteric, mystical, and enclavist orientations, would persist. This was strategic for Mohammed, who used such an orientation to justify his leadership and the direction that he was going, arguing for symbolic and allegorical interpretations of Fard and Mohammed. Simultaneously, this presented somewhat of a conflict and contradiction in that he wanted black bodies to be seen as concrete, historical, cultured, and religious and not as mystical or "spooky." Yet, it's precisely the "spooky" that he used to his advantage as a strategic dissemblance or an outright manipulation of the language and symbols of the NOI to effectuate his desire for the direction of the movement.

Race and Islam: Mohammed's Nation and Islamic Black Bodies (Doubly) Out-of-Place

Race was the critical lens through which Warith Deen Mohammed deployed Sunni Islam for his NOI constituents. This, I argue, is an enduring legacy that characterized his Islamic praxis through the various morphologies of his religious groups, well after the NOI that he led ceased to exist as such.[28] These Islamic black bodies were out-of-place in two ways: in relation to whiteness in America and in relation to immigrant Muslims in America. Just as important, in his understanding of what it meant to be Muslim, the social aspects of religion (i.e., political involvement, social service, uplift, etc.) were commensurate with the symbolic tenets (i.e., doctrine, purity of Islamic observances, etc.). Hence, the identity of black bodies in Islam were shaped by both symbolic and social facets of religion, although the symbolic were more important. Mohammed described the unique features of his new organization and connected the teachings of the NOI in the 1930s to the socioeconomic conditions that African Americans faced and, by extension, to the efforts of the WCIW:

> I think the present community thinking in the World Community of al-Islam in the West is a result of the earlier teachings. We find many Islamic organizations but I don't believe there is one to be found like ours. I don't know of a single Islamic organization in America or outside that is really like ours. We put emphasis on the application of the religion in one's daily life and involvement in outer community. In the East, Muslims do apply their religion to their daily lives because that's what it's for. But few of them who live in America practice their religion that way.[29]

Mohammed made a qualitative distinction between other Islamic organizations and the WCIW, giving priority to his own group because of its emphasis on practicing Islam in a manner that impacted the culture directly. He also indicated implicitly that perhaps something about America morphed the religion of Islam so it became less socially relevant than Islam in the East, which he seemed to valorize as the standard.

THE BODY AS A SOCIAL SYSTEM

Mohammed used the body as a metaphor to demonstrate that religion was to be both material and otherworldly, which is to say, oriented toward social ideas and religious discourses. *As the Light Shineth from the East* is by far his most significant work—indeed, his magnum opus, due to its connection to his life in the NOI, the range of topics it covers, the relation between the theology and themes of the early NOI and the WCIW, and the early date of some of its writings and vignettes (1970s). In it he says that the body is a social system that points to the divine importance of social action.[30] "The balance is between the religious life and the material existence," he writes. "The anatomy of society should be the anatomy of the human being. You have a heart in the center, and that heart is pumping blood throughout the whole body. You have the vision before you and the ears divinely placed to catch the sound in the front, on the sides, behind and all around."[31] He continues by making the link between the body as a sort of divinely created socioreligious institution and the epistemological nature of the body that holds the key to understanding religion as eminently social: "God has built a great edifice in the human structure, and we should pay some attention to God's handiwork in those things that operate between the skies and earth. If we take heed of His hints in His creation, the hints that are in His designs, I'm sure we will get a sign to uplift humanity much greater than the world has seen yet."[32] For Mohammed, the physical body was a divine signifier of the importance of the relationship between the spiritual and the material, the heavenly and the earthly. He argued that embedded in the body is the knowledge and insight of how societies should function.

Through reflection on the body, suggested Mohammed, one should gain a greater sense of the urgency of the need for human uplift. Though he used terms of the human body that are universal, it can be inferred from the fact that his audience was African American that he wanted them to note, in particular, that their bodies were carriers of divine meaning.

Mohammed spoke of the literal head of the physical body as signifying divine intentionality. In this case, the head pertains to the need of human beings to be governed: "God in structuring our human bodies, has hinted to us the need to grow into government. He put a head on our body. And in the head, messages are received from all parts of the body."[33] He continually used the term *hint* in various contexts, indicating that the meanings of the body were neither made explicit nor public and that such insight was of a special, most likely private and esoteric, nature.[34] And while his use of *head* as a metaphor for government could indicate the intellect and vision needed to govern, as such, it probably indicated a hierarchical notion of leadership that would seem to be in conflict with his later steps to decentralize the NOI and with his own subsequent explanation. In short, the body is semiotic in that its members symbolize social realities.

Mohammed concludes that, through the body, "God is telling us" that leadership and government are "natural," but a government that rules over people is not, since "we exist by having government in ourselves."[35] Although he failed to elucidate what he meant by this notion of internal government, he pointed to a religiously taught morality that one internalized, thus circumventing the need for formal social government. With "natural" government, he could be making another reference to religious morality (i.e., governing/policing the body) that he essentialized.

In other words, he may have been claiming that the problems of a society are a result of behaviors that involve the body or center on the body that are unnatural (e.g., sexual immorality, illicit drug use, etc.). Mohammed says elsewhere in *As the Light Shineth from the East*, for instance: "If a member in our society begins to abuse their body we punish that member by bringing them before the congregation and showing the crazy thing to the congregation to shame him out of his crazy ways. We will put him in a restricted class. We deny him the full membership activity. Limit his voice and restrict his activities in the community."[36] Sounding similar to the ritual discipline of the Fruit of Islam (FOI), this notion that the community polices the body is in part a function of the body representing the social system (in this case, a religious collectivity); preventing corruption of an individual's body is an attempt to maintain the "purity" of the group. In addition, it indicates that as a physical body has many members that belong to it, so, too, does a social system. Hence, individuals have no rights or absolute agency outside of the religious group: "Your body doesn't belong to you. . . . What gives you the right to think that you have a special right to do what you want with your body? . . . Because we know that if he treats himself [i.e., his body] like that, some ignorant grown-up or some little child may be influenced by his conduct; and pretty soon this independent germ who claims an independence that never belong [*sic*] to any individual will corrupt the whole society. You don't have any rights to do what you want with yourself."[37] Thus, in the scheme of Mohammed's social order, bodily agency was limited, though individuals could act in ways that threatened the sanctity of the group. Indeed, left to their own hedonistic initiative, human beings might act in a manner that harmed the collective: "You've just got to have a sensational charge. So-called civilized people, Bilalians too. A trio having sex. Two males and one female. Sometimes the whole pig sty of males and females having sex. Nothing is bad. We have been conditioned, programmed to believe that nothing should be denied a human being—if it's not harming people. Whatever he wants to do with his own life is his business."[38]

This is why Mohammed advocated bodily control. Individuals should not have the right to pursue whatever bodily pleasures they chose; human agency should be monitored and regulated. Reminiscent of Elijah Muhammad, he used the term *so-called* to call into question the claim of civility that was made by people who engaged in hedonistic practices. He is clear that he was concerned primarily about "homosexuality" and polyamorous heterosexuality, both of which he considered deviant and lacking morality. Mohammed suggests African Americans identify as "Bilalians." The term *Bilalians too* indicates that African Americans are not the primary object of the judgment that he is making about society, but that they have been co-opted by these values. It is evident that Mohammed disagreed with assertions of human freedom that locate ultimate agency in the individual body. Accordingly, one's body belongs to the collective and is expected to function in service of the group.

In sum, Islam, in Mohammed's conception, was concerned with both the symbolic and the social. To be sure, the symbolic and the social were intertwined and both expressed authentic religion, and he used the body to illustrate this contention. The body signified Allah's attention to social matters, including the ways in which societies were organized and governed. Mohammed wanted to appreciate the body—or, at least, certain bodies—as religious and as the purveyors of divine intent and order. In the end, such bodies were signifiers of divine activity.

Despite Mohammed's pronouncements about the universality of Islam and Islamic identity, he gave a great deal of attention to the subject of *race*—discussing its problems, addressing African American identity and culture, and speaking to the particularities of African American existence.[39] Race, it seems, was the most contentious subject, the most mired in conflict, yet apparently the area that concerned him the most when he addressed black believers in Islam.[40] His focus on African American conditions of existence seems to have arisen out of both his desire for Sunni Islam to be relevant to that existence and his upbringing in the NOI that engendered in him a perspective that made black bodies central in his understanding of the world.

Mohammed attempted to balance the two, since to embrace the one might be to deny the other. The notion that Islam is universal is problematic, at best, given that it also becomes a totalizing metanarrative that governs and determines values and behavior for every aspect of human life. Mohammed maintained, for instance, that Islam "determines for the believer good manners, good thinking, everything."[41] At the same time, he expressed his desire to see everyone converted to Islam, claiming that the "desire of the true believer [is] to see everybody in his religion."[42] How, then, does one mediate the particular if the universal is unmitigated?

Mohammed was tactical in managing the problematic and perennial issue of Arab Muslim enslavement of Africans, which might challenge the notion of the universality of Islam. For instance, he attempted to circumvent the issue by attributing racism and enslavement to undefined influences that entered Islam after the Prophet Muhammad.[43] He said, "There is no excuse for any racism or any color consciousness in the Muslim world. If any of our people have it, they got it from new kinds of racist influences that have been brought about since the mission and words of the Prophet Muhammad. They have no excuse for it."[44] This philosophical move attempts to relieve Muslims and Islam of the responsibility for racism and to preserve the notion of universality. Ronald Segal, the author of *Islam's Black Slaves: The Other Black Diaspora*, however, ties the institution of slavery—indeed, black slavery—to the very inception of Islam in the seventh century. It is an institution that, according to Segal, endures in the present. Likewise, Sylviane A. Diouf's *Servants of Allah: African Muslims Enslaved in the Americas* gives little attention to the Muslim role in the slave trade, focusing instead on the European Christian transatlantic trade and valorizing African Muslim attempts to maintain their religion in America and in slavery. Diouf says, for example, "Islam was also the first revealed religion freely followed—as opposed to imposed Christianity by the Africans who were transported to the New World."[45] But such a statement reveals a bias toward valorizing Islam that, at the same time, obfuscates Arab and African Muslim slavery and compulsory religion via jihads and reformers (*mujadid*) and therefore overemphasizes the role of Christianity.

Both Islam and Christianity (and, to an extent, Judaism) were culpable and at times brutal and inhumane toward Africans. John Hunwick and Eve Trout Powell contend in *The African Diaspora in the Mediterranean Lands of Islam* that this tendency to give greater attention to the transatlantic slave trade and very little to Muslim slavery and the forced migration of Africans to the lands of the Mediterranean is a pervasive practice in Islamic discourse.[46] Mohammed, either naïvely or grossly inaccurately, or both, claimed that racism did not exist in Islam: "You cannot be a racist and call yourself a Muslim."[47] Nearly four decade earlier, his father had made the same factual error, stating, "The Arabs are said to have slaves. The Arabs will answer for themselves, but I do know that no Muslim will enslave another Muslim."[48]

Furthermore, Mohammed strategically circumvented the question of enslavement through appeal to reason, suggesting that one should not throw the baby out with the bathwater: not only did he minimize Islam's role, but he suggested that the benefits of Islam far outweighed the minor and aberrant part that Muslims might have played in slavery: "Do you think an intelligent man—even if he knew for certain that some Arabs were in the slave trade business—would separate himself from the great past, from his great history and dignity in al-Islam simply because some Arabs had a part in the slave trade? No intelligent man would do that kind of foolish thing."[49] This is an astounding claim, given the enormity of genocide and the enduring black holocaust that was and is connected to slavery.

Mohammed continued his Islamic apology by excusing the behavior of some and, in a contradictory manner, claimed that his Islamic apology did not change the nature of the religion for him: "So, if history shows me that an Arab or some Arabs or hundreds of thousands of Arabs were involved in the slave traffic, that would not change my faith. That would not make me walk any slower toward my Arab brother who is a Muslim. I will keep my same love and appreciation for my Muslim Arab brother. I will keep my same devotion to Allah. I will keep my eyes and my whole self turned toward the ka'abah at Mecca. I don't care what the Arabs did or what they do."[50] His conclusion and his insistence that what Arab Muslims did or do with respect to Africans is curious, given that he was constantly critical of whites and their practice of slavery.[51] Accordingly, he implicitly blamed white Christians for the criticism of Islam's role in the slave trade while simultaneously defending Arab Muslims, suggesting:

> No Arab could ever do those things and come out with the Holy Qur'an in his arms. Question those who told you that the Arabs did those things. Question their history and see the evil things that they did with the Bible in their arms. There are pictures right now of them standing having parties, smoking, drinking, laughing and celebrating at the sight of a poor Bilalian [i.e., an African American] being burned up at the stake or lynched on the tree. And there are pictures right now of some preachers in their midst holding a Bible under his [sic] arm. I'm not trying to say that Christian is bad, but I'm saying you shouldn't throw stones if you live in glass houses.[52]

In this statement, Mohammed is much more explicit in his attack on racism and the particularities of African American experience. That Muslims could not do violence to Africans and African Americans and "come out with the Holy Qur'an in his arms" is blatantly false and contrary to historical evidence. Here, in an attempt to maintain the integrity of Islam, he lashes out at white Christians, whom he perceives are the ones making the claim that Islam is associated with enslaving black people. He accuses them of hypocrisy—of challenging the universality of Islam by invoking the trope of slavery in particular lynching—while failing to come to grips with their own brutal treatment of African Americans. His language is intentionally inflammatory: he indicts white Christianity for its ideological and practical conflicts, and he amplifies this contention by appealing to traditional conservative moral taboos. He suggests that these same Christians who would charge Muslims with racism say nothing about the Christians who are violent racists; moreover, they have parties, smoke, and drink alcohol.

Mohammed took the tension between the universal (symbolic) and the particular (social) a step further, suggesting that African Americans had to have an ideology and method that was universal if they were to push against and beyond the barriers that had kept them oppressed. In effect, he suggested that the symbolic and the social had to come together if they were to overcome some of the lingering effects of racism and slavery.[53] He insisted, "If you are going to establish yourself as a Race, as an ethnic group, that can best be done upon the Universal Plan." Presumably this universal plan is Islam, the "universal groove," to which he maintained black people must be connected.[54]

Mohammed makes his claim for the primacy of Islam for African Americans explicit in *An African American Genesis*, where he argues that Islam is the remedy for the problems of African Americans and that a sincere religious morality can ennoble them and reconnect them to their historical Islamic roots. He argues that in Islam, African Americans can establish a meaningful group identity.[55] According to this school of thought, black people can be revitalized and made anew if their ways of being in the world are "infuse[d]" with an Islamic ethos.[56] His concern for race, racism, and Islam reflected his desire to valorize black bodies and to distance them from their historical association with race and racism, all of which were negative to Mohammed. His desire to disrupt black bodies symbolically from continuing to carry such negative meanings (black bodies in-place) or to reproduce the effects of racism can be clearly seen in how far he was willing to go to advocate for Islam, which, for him, was the apex of culture and dignity.

In the mid-1970s, Mohammed made one of his more controversial remarks, declaring that African Americans would be better off by abandoning Christianity and embracing Islam: "It would be better if our people left the church and came into the mosque. It would give them a level of dignity in this country that they never enjoyed before."[57] One of the benefits of Islam is that it does not allow anthropomorphism, which in context implies that it offers no space for the perpetuation of a privileged status for some and subjugation for others based on imaging the Divine in their own form—for example, as "white images of heaven, God, angels . . . Jesus."[58] Islam's denial of imaging the Divine in human form and its universality—and, thus, its lack of racial hierarchy—would allow African Americans more opportunity to find equality. Again, he ignored strains of Arab supremacy and nationalism and many other issues when he preferentially invited black people to trade one set of problems for another.

Moreover, it is in *An African American Genesis* that he ultimately privileges particularity over universality and signals that race shapes the hermeneutic through which he deploys Islam. Contrary to his rhetoric suggesting a color-blind religion, he engages here in some of the most stirring race talk. Mohammed claims that, because Islam is a religion of peace, it offers "no radical teachings on race."[59] But he then proceeds to connect radical claims of race-consciousness and black self-respect regarding the black body to the teachings of Islam and the Qur'an: "When I hear or read that God has created my form beautiful, there is nothing anyone can tell me to discourage me, to make me feel inferior and make me think that nappy hair, a wide nose, black skin or thick lips are ugly."[60] At the same time, Mohammed's language reproduces stereotypes when he describes his hair as "nappy," his nose as "wide," and his lips as "thick"—negative terms for black body parts that are necessary only over and against the assumption of a white normative gaze.

He explicitly, if not directly, acknowledges the precarious condition of African Americans that required attention to the specific experiences they had in America: "Our [black] behavior is the result of or the effects of the peculiar experience behind us."[61] It is this "peculiar" experience of white supremacy that moved him to read, or reread, Sunni Islam for African American people, despite his insistence throughout his corpus that Islam is basically the Five Pillars, the oneness of humanity, which comes from the "pure concepts" in the Qur'an; the divine law, or "Shar'ee"; and clean moral living.[62] Curiously, Mohammed found something divinely providential and special about the deleterious experiences of African Americans in the United States that sounds suspiciously like the valorization of suffering: "I believe with all of my heart, and with every fiber of my being that God has blessed us as a people by putting us into this situation."[63] At the same time, he pushed against "this situation" in a move reminiscent of Martin Luther King's advocating of a "temporary segregation" for African Americans, Elijah Muhammad's "go for self," and the black nationalism that Mohammed himself so often criticized: he advocated a "strategic withdrawal" from "the whiteman."[64]

According to Mohammed, pervasive white supremacy exemplified in slavery had had pernicious effects on the black psyche and destroyed black culture, history, and religion (i.e., Islam). The drastic solution would be physical separation from whites: "We need to set up camp in a desirable climate for six months, or a year, even longer if necessary. We need to stay together until we come out with what we need."[65] African Americans also needed their own ideology and group identity, he suggested (though this conflicted with his claim of universality). Oddly enough, he located this idea in the thought of W. E. B. Du Bois, Benjamin Mays, Franz Fanon, and Carter G. Woodson, asserting that "they all headed in this direction."[66] That is, rather than appealing to Islam alone as the ultimate source in his justification for radical race-inspired and therapeutic separation to remediate the black condition, he cited black critical, social, and race theorists.

At this juncture (we return to this idea later), we should also note that Mohammed contends that white supremacy and slavery upset the natural order of things that God had established in black families, particularly the role of women.[67] Consistent with this claim, he declared that the subjugated status of women—indeed, the gendered social order—was ontological, established by God, and supported by the Qur'an.[68] In a sense, while he blamed racism for the pathology in black communities, he also stated that black women had been unwittingly and passively complicit: "This world has frightened the woman out of her domain. In her home domain is the fortress for protection of the life of society. And it has been the deterioration of home life that has resulted in bringing down the race."[69] Only God can give black men the power to correct the problems that racism has caused in the black family, he maintained.[70] Mohammed, then, reinforced the notion that domestic spaces were the domain of black women and that black women were ontologically subservient to black men, who alone have the power to disrupt the constraints of white supremacy.

Mohammed seemed aware of the negative trappings of the notion of "race," though he obviously did not always avoid them. Simultaneously, he was ever conscious of the ways in which black bodies in-place carried negative meaning due to racialization.[71] Hollywood and the media, he argued, had had negative effects on the black self-image and the representation of black bodies. A decade earlier, in the 1960s, African Americans were proud. They marched and raised black fists in protest of injustices. They were real men. African Americans had more substantive internal activities and self-consciousness. Mohammed pointed to slogans that signified political and cultural aspects of black life in support of his charges: Stokely Carmichael's (Kwame Ture's) shout of, and demand for, "black power," and James Brown's melodic but political song "Say It Loud—I'm Black and I'm Proud." But, Mohammed claimed, Hollywood and television had turned black men into "dressed-up peacock sissy pimps in long chinchilla coats . . . a bunch of pampered sissies."[72] The result, he said, in line with stereotypical and inaccurate tropes that are common to this day, is that African Americans became a "welfare class."[73] The connection between the depreciation in black culture and television and movies, however, is unsubstantiated. Mohammed framed the derogation of black life in male terms, citing the "pimp"—exaggerated, colorful, opulent, and feminine—as proof that whites viewed black identity as a caricature and that the meaning of blackness in America was undeniably destructive.

BILAL AND BLACK EMBODIMENT

Mohammed sought to redeem black bodies from such vulnerability to decrepit depictions and miserable meanings. He desired to dissociate them from being in-place—that is, from inferiority and lack of culture and history that such terms indicate—as did his father. He focused on African American identity in addition to culture as a strategy to evade the social and psychological ramifications of race-based nomenclatures such as "black" and "African American." The term *black*, he maintained, had no history; rather, it was only a geographical identity (though he did not indicate what geography the category signified).[74] Instead, he proposed that African Americans call themselves "Bilalians" after the seventh-century African slave and Muslim convert Bilal ibn Rabah, who was the first prayer caller (*mu'adhdhin*) in Islam.[75] This was not his own creative and original idea. Rather, Mohammed follows his father in valorizing Bilal. As early as November 1966, Elijah Muhammad had shown a film on Bilal to members of the NOI and suggested that Bilal was the first black man to embrace Islam, contradicting his own notion that African Americans were Muslim ontologically.[76] His son echoed: "I think it's [*sic*] more dignity in identifying with an ancestor than in identifying with skin color. When I say I am a Bilalian, I'm saying that I am a man like Bilal. When I say I am black, I'm saying I am a man like black skinned people and black skinned are not only in the Bilalian ethnic family; they are also in the Indian ethnic family. So, I should ask you if you're black, which black?"[77] Therefore, Mohammed's goal was to associate African Americans with a "racial" nomenclature and symbol that indicates culture, history, and dignity. It is also clear that for him, "black," while problematic, held some diversity of meaning—"which black?"—that "Bilal" did not hold. It was a term that, for him, was all-encompassing for people heretofore referred to as "black."

Mohammed seems to have embraced some of the positive aspects of this notion, despite his objection to *race*, in his constant attention to pernicious African American experiences and the effects of *racism* (white supremacy), particularly enslavement. This seems clear in his desire to bind black people to Bilal ibn Rabah and in his instituting Ethnic Survival Week in 1978 as a replacement for Saviour's Day, in which the NOI historically celebrated the "birthday" of God, Master Fard Muhammad. The inaugural Ethnic Survival Week addresses (plus an address delivered to the American Academy of Religion) are published as his magnum opus, *As the Light Shineth from the East.*[78] He dedicates the lectures to "great Bilalian (African American) leaders," including Omar ibn Said, Nat Turner, Samuel E. Cornish, Benjamin Banneker, Clara Muhammad, Frederick Douglass, Noble Drew Ali, John Brown, Dr. Fard Muhammad, Elijah Muhammad, Booker T. Washington, Malcolm X, Martin Luther King Jr., Harriet Tubman, George Washington Carver, Marcus Garvey, and many others—a litany of "race" heroes.[79]

In reconceptualizing race (while glorifying African American culture and history) to reimagine black embodiment—and in imposing Bilal as the paradigmatic figure who represents all African Americans, all black people—Mohammed reified black history, culture, religious orientation, gender, time, and diversity.[80] That is to say, he compressed complexity into sameness and anachronism (again, what Victor Anderson calls "ontological blackness"). Mohammed theologized all of these factors until, in the end, "Bilal," as a symbol, became transcendental and mystical in its scope to signify all realities of all black people.

Mohammed was evidently aware of some objections to the use of Bilal as the quintessential symbol of blackness:

> As I said earlier, some of you don't like the term Bilalian—it's okay with me. If you like the term "Afro-American" then we can still talk. But you know, even the term Afro-American was a compromise. Afro-American—why cut the word short? Because niggers weren't ready to say "African." They were afraid to identity with Africa. Marcus Garvey said, Afro-American; that's like cutting the word short. That's like an Irish-American calling himself, "Ir-American." The Irish-American is not afraid to use the whole name—"Irish-American." And I'm telling you, until we get that same kind of respect, get rid of that old fear in us—an unnecessary fear, an uncalled for fear in 1978. We have to get the courage and appreciation for reality, for truth to say, "African-American," because that's what we are. Now I don't like the term "African" because the Caucasians gave the continent that name. I like the term "Bilalian." What's wrong with the term "Bilalian?"[81]

Lawrence Mamiya argues that the use of Bilal as a symbol of black people is related to the history of African American identification with Ethiopia, especially in nineteenth-century black religious and nationalist thought.[82] In addition, Bilal's appeal—perhaps his real appeal for Mohammed—is the fact that he was a significant Muslim who happened to be Ethiopian.

Four factors drive the identification. The first is Bilal's uniqueness as the first prayer caller, or muezzin (*mu'adhdhin*), who offered the litany (*adhan*) that signaled to Muslims that it was time to pray.[83] The second, and perhaps most powerful for Mohammed, was Bilal's identity as a slave who, when free, asserted his right to remain free to serve God. According to Muhammad Abdul-Rauf's *Bilāl Ibn Rabāh: A Leading Companion of the Prophet Muhammad*, the "narrative" regarding the conversation between Bilal and Abu Bakr, who purchased his freedom, proceeds this way: "Abu Bakr! *If you have purchased me to be your slave, keep me in your possession; but if you have paid my price for the sake of God, let me be free to serve God.* I have been looking for this moment to see you restored fully to your liberty, Abu Bakr responded. You are as free as you can be."[84]

I use the term *narrative* here because it is not clear from my reading of the texts on Bilal that they are historical. The texts, indeed, read as if they were constructed as a legendary account to support certain doctrinal and theological positions in Islam (e.g., slavery, succession after the Prophet Muhammad, racial inclusion, etc.)—that is, the text is apologetic. Mohammed mistakenly read the narrative of Bilal as historical fact. It is also clear that Abdul-Rauf's account, published in 1977, may have been the primary source for Mohammed and his movement. The preface appears to substantiate my claim: "This book has been written in response to a request made by one of my dear brothers, Karim Abdul Aziz, a leading figure in the energetic movement of the Nation of Islam in North America. After a little reflection, I realized the tremendous value of such a book to us, the members of the Muslim community in America. This is not only because Bilal shared his African roots with a large segment of our community, but his life and noble virtues can be a tremendous source of inspiration to Muslims all over the world."[85] Mohammed seems to have been familiar with this narrative because he alludes it when he, again, argues for why Bilal should be the paragon of black identification: "Study the history of Bilal, and if you don't see a prophetic figure resembling us—the whole people—a figure speaking to our problems and to our beautiful destiny, that *we are not free to be possessed again by those who freed us. We are free to go independently for ourselves as other people are free to do.*"[86]

Mohammed perhaps saw this account as particularly piercing in its relation to African Americans, but the reference in context points to Bilal's desire to practice the nascent rituals of Islam rather than return to the brutality and limited existence of slavery. This might be especially meaningful for African Americans who are Muslim. Note the similarities in the italicized passages—one by Abdul-Rauf; the other by Mohammed. It is difficult to imagine that Mohammed is not alluding to Bilal's alleged statement to Abu Bakr about remaining free to serve God rather than being possessed by emancipators.

The third factor in play that might have influenced identification with Bilal is the extended remonstrance that he apparently makes concerning Islam and slavery.[87] Bilal reportedly argues that Islam has actually helped "the slave" and that sudden emancipation would hurt the slave and the master because the institution of slavery in Islam protected human rights for the enslaved.[88] The implication is that such dissolution of the institution would injure Muslim masters, given the (obvious) loss of benefits that he leaves unarticulated.[89] Abdul-Rauf also uses Bilal's dialogue on slavery as a means to demonstrate that Islam is better for the slave than Christianity or Judaism. Bilal allegedly reports: "'To help the slave, Islam has done what no other system and no other religion did or could do,' Bilal answered. 'The Torah enjoined slavery, and Christianity was silent about it. But Islam has left no chance except that it urged the emancipation of slaves, (as a mandatory obligation or as a recommended action). It promises great rewards for emancipating a slave; and makes this emancipation one of the foremost duties incumbent upon a believer as a manifestation of his gratitude for the blessings of God.'"[90] This doctrinal statement regarding slavery is an important addendum that may lend to the appeal of Bilal to people of African descent whose ancestors were slaves, especially for those who were Muslim. Moreover, Bilal goes on to imply that embedded in the foundation of Islam is the potential that the slaves, who are apparently due a portion of the obligatory alms (*zakat*), can be and are empowered eventually to purchase their own freedom with funds they have saved.[91]

The fourth and final factor influencing the selection of Bilal as "black" exemplar supreme is the potential that the figure offers for centering black people in the drama of prophetic succession in Islam. In other words, the issue of who was to succeed the Prophet Muhammad as the leader of Muslims (*Khalifa/Amir al-Mu'minina*) plays out in the life of Bilal as the central character. This is particularly decisive for Muslims such as Mohammed, who identify as Sunni, as they trace authentic succession through Abu Bakr, in contrast with the Shi'ites, who see Ali, the prophet's younger cousin, as the rightful heir. As the story goes, when the Prophet Muhammad was so gravely ill that he could not respond to Bilal's invitation to lead the congregation in prayer, as he normally did, the Prophet appointed Abu Bakr to lead the prayers.[92] When Abu Bakr could not be located, Bilal requested that Umar stand in—that is, until Abu Bakr was located. Hence, after the Prophet died (632 CE/11 AH), succession of the caliphate was interpreted as proceeding to Abu Bakr, rather than Ali, and then to Umar. But it was Abu Bakr who apparently paid the "ransom money" for Bilal, said Mohammed.[93]

Mohammed observed, intentionally, that the man who paid the price for Bilal's freedom to worship God became the caliph, or leader of the religious community. He used the narrow instance of Abu Bakr paying the "ransom money" for Bilal as a metonym for Islam and the emancipation of black people from slavery. The authority for this movement seems to reside in the fact that Bilal, who prior to the Prophet's death would not say the *adhan* for anyone but him, offered it for Abu Bakr and later for Umar.[94]

It seems unmistakable that religious commitment, rather than a concern for Bilal's universally "black" ideal, was the impetus for selecting him as the archetype for black bodies.[95] For Mohammed, Bilal gave African Americans a historical and cultural genealogy that made black bodies beautiful in terms of their meaning, and like Elijah Muhammad, he was attempting to create distance from and deflect the negative meanings black bodies carried as a result of slavery, lynching, and racist discourses. Mohammed treated the notion of *race* as if it was mutually exclusive and diametrically opposed to *culture*, which he sought to reinstitute in black life.

Culture, as such, was the key to black bodies' being seen as civilized, refined, and human. Mohammed was explicit in his aspiration to bring sophistication back to African Americans. He reflected nostalgically, "'A people without a culture are bare as a tree.' . . . The Bilalians used to really repeat this quote from the Bible, especially when they were thinking about their problem of trying to get equality and opportunity in America."[96] African Americans had lost this consciousness of culture that once characterized them, however, and the NOI specifically had fallen from the civility and style that, Mohammed thought, once characterized it. Using the caricature of the NOI "super-fly" ministers who were wearing "diamond rings" and "chinchilla coats," he stated bluntly that they were "wearing pimp's clothes and preaching nation building."[97] The pimp aesthetic, to which he also referred elsewhere in his writing and speeches, was symptomatic evidence of the loss of cultural ethos about which Mohammed was melancholy. Embodied in Bilal, he saw the cultural redemption of a people whose culture and history had been marred with pain: "We share one painful history [with Bilal], and one glorious rise from that history . . . and yet stand up as human beings to tell the inhuman racist his shame."[98] "Black," he maintained, did not imply culture and civilization. Only "Bilalian" captured it.[99]

Mohammed's goal for black people in this manner remained consistent with the goals of Elijah Muhammad and Fard Muhammad (and Malcolm X and Farrakhan, for that matter): to raise the status of black people as they were seen by the world, to shape their image, to have more control over the behavior of those who would be detrimental to their respectability, and to engender respectability and cultural values in black communities:

> We can't rise up in the eyes of the world as a civilized Community, and productive people while carrying chinchilla coats, Super-Fly pimps, sissies, dope peddlers, wine drunkards and vulgar talkers who are just satisfied to stand on the corner and talk nasty for 16 hours, go home and sleep eight hours, get up and get right back on the job and talk nasty for another 16 hours. . . . How are we going to rise? We can't rise until we strip off this kind of self-inflicting ignorance and filth that we have on us that's maming [sic] us physically, morally and spiritually. We first have to dump this stuff to move on. We have to go back. We can't solve 1975. Go back to the teaching of Dr. Fard Muhammad that tells us that civilization means culture, refinement, happiness, peace, and love, and that the duty of the civilized person is to teach that to the uncivilized. We have to go back to that. We have to reform ourselves in the intelligent dignified image.[100]

Mohammed not only sounds like Elijah Muhammad and Master Fard, he locates the solution to the black plight in black people's ethos and program. Consistent with his father's, his tone is moralistic, and his interdictions are puritanical, espousing the same conservative values and lifestyle that was the hallmark of the NOI for nearly fifty years. He calls for the reform of African Americans who are in the "mud" (though he does not use the term here)—those who are poor and whose mores and behavior reflect those who have internalized the values of the dominant culture and have bought into stereotypes and images of black bodies as buffoons and street hustlers. "Go[ing] back" means embracing the core values of the movement and immersing oneself in the ethos and aesthetic that gave them a sense of somebodiness, pride, and respectability. In short, he tells his audience, "We must have culture, dear people."[101]

Mohammed's longing for the culture of the NOI's past would not let him mourn and move forward, for he was certain that the teachings and practices of the NOI held an essential truth about beautifying black bodies: that the culture of the NOI's past rested in the elegance and aesthetics that Master Fard Muhammad brought to black people. In his words, Fard gave them "righteousness," "refinement," and "culture."[102] Note that Mohammed also deflects attention away from Fard's notion of racial separation, emphasizing that the NOI's founder taught corporate responsibility and civility. Out of respect for what Fard gave the Nation of Islam, Mohammed calls him "Wali," the honorific title for a holy man or saint in the religion of Islam, the "master" who gave his followers independence and authenticity.

"And I Am Not White Either": Mohammed and the "Foreigner" as a Negative Trope of Purity and Authenticity

The opposite of Bilal was the figure of the foreigner. Mohammed used the term *foreigner* and its variations as the negative trope of purity and authenticity—that is, over against things and people who were not African American and "black." Mohammed marked himself as an (sometimes *the*) authoritative, undefiled, and bona fide leader of African Americans and Muslims who embodied the best values and morality needed to reform black communities. Operating in the background of this consciousness regarding things foreign is a puritanical morality that grounds his sense of authenticity in an idealized notion of the black body that is pure and uncontaminated by worldly and depraved behavior. He contended that *his body* corresponded analogically to his desire for an African American community whose culture and lifestyle was self-regulating, autonomous, and beautiful. This awareness of foreigners functioned discursively vis-à-vis whites and immigrant Muslims to create a space in which black people could construct their own reality and religion.

Mohammed was critical of the political, economic, and psychological influences that white people had on African Americans—an influence that even led to the founding of the NOI because, according to him, Master Fard Muhammad was a white man and a foreigner: "I don't know how many of you had it, but I know I had it and many of my friends had it—the picture of Dr. Fard himself. That man didn't look like an original black man in terms of pigmentation. He looked like a Georgia Caucasian white."[103] Had Fard not been a white man, he contended, black people would not have listened to him and considered him authoritative. He explained:

> It was easy for him to be a substitute or take the place of Christ in our minds and hearts because he was, himself, resembling Caucasian people. I don't believe he would have been a success if he had big thick lips, a flat nose, kinky hair and black skin. I don't believe that we would have listened

to him. The self-image was so hated and so rejected by us because of the brainwashing and the lies that we were given by the Caucasian in America of our origin as a people.[104]

Mohammed points out the deep-seated difficulty that African Americans had with their image of their own bodies in relation to whiteness and, ironically, again made his points using pejorative terms to describe black features. He believed that racism had so ingrained black self-hatred in African Americans that they would have rejected a black messiah figure because he was "black." It was only because Fard was white, or looked white, he thought, that black people had embraced him as a religious leader and as God. Consequently, Mohammaed wanted to break this reliance on whites as a symbolic presence in the mentalities of African Americans and break the sociopolitical and religious hold that whites had on black communities. He lamented the Du Boisian double consciousness of many African Americans: "Blacks who see with the eyes of white Americans [sic]. No vision of their own. Most of them don't have the courage to step outside the mold that the European, the Westerner created."[105] Referring to Fard, he warned, "We are in these traps and predicaments not because of our doing, but because of foreign people have dictated to us where we should go."[106] According to Mohammed, it was not Elijah Muhammad who originated Yakub and the idea that white people were devils, the FOI, the Muslim Girls Training and General Course in Civilization, or the University of Islam, for example. Fard gave him all of that, and, Mohammed implied, it was corrupting: "It came from a foreigner. And that's why it was unsuccessful."[107]

Mohammed attributed the contamination of black values and behavior to white people and white cultural values and behavior generally. Indigenously black movements such as the civil rights movement and black nationalism (though he was critical elsewhere) were movements in which God was active. They had "God before [them] and over [them]."[108] He suggested that segregation preserved, kept pure, these black ways of being that were different from whites. Once the Jim Crow signs were removed, he maintained, black people believed that they did not need God anymore, and black communities witnessed the genesis of drug abuse and "unnatural sex!"[109] This contagion (i.e., white foreign influence), for Mohammed, seemed to include atheism and same-sex, homosexual relationships: "Trying to show the White man that you can beat him at unnatural sex, and he's been practicing it for many years before you! . . . [Now black people are] all kinds of freaks. . . . In our community, if a boy was a sissy, he was scared, afraid to show it. He would try to walk like a man. He was afraid that he would be jumped on and beat up by another boy. Look what we have done in the face of opportunity."[110] This statement reveals the homophobia that Mohammed believed was a normal and acceptable value in African American culture. He suggested that threats of violence were imminent possibilities for young boys who were gay. Yet he talked about this as though this were a positive attribute of black morality that whites had corrupted through a loosening of the barriers separating the communities. He espoused a particularly low view of "homosexuality," conflating it with bestiality as immorality: "All the things that we read about in the Bible are being done today. Homosexuality and going with animals it's in the Bible."[111] Because of the opportunities that African Americans now had, he contended, they attempted to imitate the ways of whites, immoral behavior in which whites had engaged for years. As part of this pathology, African Americans had even accepted white religious images such as Jesus, God, heaven, and angels as sacred.[112] Mohammed saw white religious iconography as particularly deleterious to the black self-image, maintaining that white religious iconography signified black exclusion from the divine metaphysic and established "white" as transcendental and ultimate. He implied that the issue had deep psychological ramifications and that, as a "student of psychology," he was qualified to make such assertions. Mohammed had started a campaign to encourage Christians, especially African Americans, to remove white images of the Divine from public and private venues.

His terminology is curious, however. Observe that his selection of race nomenclatures (i.e., *White Race, Black*), and even his use of the term *race*, indicated that by the late 1970s and early 1980s (when a radio interview with Carol Hemingway out of Los Angeles called *Religion on the Line* was produced), Mohammed was already revising his positions on race.[113]

Recall that in the mid-1970s, he preferred the terms *Caucasian* and *Bilalian* because he believed that they lifted conversations about race relations out of the historically accumulated weight of racism and that they were more dignified. Yet again, white religious images were another form of foreign objects that pervaded the minds of African Americans and the physical spaces in which they worshiped the Divine.[114] One should not miss the confluence of an Islamic doctrinal issue at this moment, though. Mohammed's appeal to remove white images was also motivated by a desire not to anthropomorphize the Divine (*shirk*).[115] It is for this reason that he most likely objected to suggestion that African Americans have black images of the Divine, rather than white ones.[116]

Where the negative trope of the foreign(er) plays out the most intensely, nonetheless, is in the area of leadership—or, put another way, in who leads black people and who is qualified to be an authentic black leader. Once more, Mohammed used the notion of *foreigner* to establish himself as an organic and authoritative leader who was unique in his standing with the black community. Referring to himself, he proclaimed, "Allah just wants a good model in society."[117] He lamented that African Americans had been following everyone else's model: Arab, Irish, Catholic, African, English, "and for once we have a model that is our own."[118] Never before had a leader existed who was as independent and indigenous as he, for to identify with him was to take on "a new independent mind," a new culture and leadership.[119] He emphasized his belief that his level, style, and independent category of leadership were revolutionary—that they had the power to change black people. He had indicated earlier the incredible deference and authority that he thought black people invested in whiteness. In his perception, he was in such an authoritative position of leadership with black people that it represented an upheaval of historical and extant epistemological authority. He did not answer to anyone who was white; nor was he unduly influenced by whites. He said, "They learned, they understand what I am saying. This is no ordinary leader, you have the boss. I am not bragging, believe me. I do not like bragging. I am not boastful. . . . I am the boss! Allahu Akbar!"[120] Given black people's history with white paternalism, it was critical for him that the leadership of African Americans be independently black. He was also critical of African American leaders who were "backed" or "influenced" by Jews.[121] He explained, "Dear beloved people, we have to have a grip on our life. We have to have leaders that are not made by the outsiders. You have never been successful with a leader that was made by an outsider."[122] He conceded, even as he pleaded, that many African Americans had difficulty seeing authority in someone who came from their own community, who arose out of his relationship with that community: "You cannot break with a foreign image. You cannot break with an image of a man that is not you."[123] Nevertheless, Mohammed offered himself as an opportunity for black people to shun their dependence on and worship of whiteness and white images.

He also established himself as an authority in claiming his right to interpret Islam in the face of immigrant Muslims who wanted to challenge his "orthodoxy" and agency. For Mohammed, it was his right, his duty, to interpret religious truth as a black man for a black religious community. He asserted his authority to do so, since he was neither native-born nor foreign. He considered it a miracle that such a man as he existed, which he expressed anecdotally and, I believe, sarcastically:

> This is a miracle. This is a modern day miracle! **And, I am not White, either!** This is a modern day miracle. It has finally happened! They say, "Oh yes, then, Allah, thank Allah." Father Divine was a Black man. He said, "I am God." They asked, "Upon what basis, what proof are you God, Father Divine?" "On the basis of this son, Jesus Christ." "Oh Father Divine, yes, whatever Father Divine wants is alright with me." Right? Because somewhere in the background, is a white father yes! Here comes the Imam, Warith Deen Muhammad. They say, "who is your power?" "Allah!" "Who is Allah?" "God." "How does he look?" "He doesn't have any looks!" They say, "Well, who is he then, Brother Imam, what is this that you believe in?" "God!"[124]

Mohammed here makes a political, albeit theological, move by locating his authority in a source that can be neither verified nor disproved; nor can it be adequately challenged by religious authorities who make the same epistemological claim to revelation or access to transcendent data. He concedes nothing to those who would challenge his knowledge; he simply dismisses them as foreigners or those who privilege the opinions and veracity of their particular social locations, especially if they are white. He wanted his audience to apprehend the profundity of his claim in the context of their historical experience with whites, and he did so by making the obvious but necessary assertion: "And, I am not White, either!" What a claim—to have the authority and knowledge to espouse religious truths and be neither a foreigner nor white but exactly the opposite: a black organic religious leader. He claimed that his father, and the NOI before him, had worshiped a white man, Master Fard Muhammad.[125]

Mohammed was aware that immigrant Muslims were suspicious of the authenticity of his group of African American Muslims, and that clearly created some tension among groups of Muslims in America. He replied, "I believe the majority of them accept us, but, I do feel that there is still a strain on our relationship. Too many of the immigrant Muslims in the U.S. seem suspicious. They can't believe that we are really as genuine as we appear to be."[126] Yet Mohammed was only modestly interested in accommodating immigrants with respect to his group's Islamic practices, especially their genesis in Fard's and Muhammad's NOI. He seemed unwilling to denounce their NOI origins because he understood the teachings on a deeper level: "So-called orthodox Muslims hate me for continuing to bring up the Honorable Elijah Muhammad and presenting him in a favorable light. Some have told me that I should stop talking about Dr. Fard and my father. They say it just brings up confusion and holds the community back. I know what they know not."[127] Mohammed's language about Islam was that of universality, but he privileged particularity. He saw both the social and the symbolic aspects of the religion as significant, and to that end he was able to dismiss "so-called orthodox" immigrant Muslims as outsiders and foreigners. Mohammed took his right to interpret the religion to its logical conclusion when he suggested that African Americans should develop their own Islamic belief system.

Conclusion

Warith Deen Mohammed was interested in advancing the Nation of Islam's standing among Muslims in the world. He was first and foremost focused on constructing "Islamic" black bodies out-of-place symbolically, since he was concerned with countering racism and with deploying Islam as a religion, history, and culture that would uplift and beautify black bodies. He desired for black bodies to be defined by the practices of Islam and a concomitant worldview.

What Mohammed found as he and the NOI-WCIW embraced Sunni Islam is that being Muslim in a global sense meant that one had to accept a universalism that was unsuitable for all cultural, geographical, and temporal contexts. Therefore, while Mohammed preached this universalism as the ideal, his practice was actively particular. This was a crucial critique of Islam that he never made explicit discursively, but it is glaringly obvious in the entire corpus of his works in the 1970s and 1980s.

One of the most critical aspects of Islam as Mohammed understood it was that, while the body was central, the symbolic and social aspects carried more weight. The social was more significant for Mohammed than for his father, though less than for Malcolm X. That is, the social and political praxis, while important, was not commensurate with the moral teachings and the ideological and theological precepts of Islam. This posture placed Mohammed in tension with both of his predecessors—his father, Elijah Muhammad, and his friend Malcolm X. Yet Mohammed's Islam was consistent with that of his predecessors in that their "Islams" reflected a similar tension between the universal and the particular. To be sure, Mohammed's focus on race, his critique of white supremacy and of America, and his insistence on existential relevance to black life constructed black bodies symbolically out-of-place, in terms of both the American social order and Islamic ideals (i.e., *ummah*) and practice.

As the *mujadid* (reformer) and *mujtihad* (interpreter of law) for his community, race and the experience of being racialized was the primary lens through which he interpreted Islam.[128] At the same time, race and racism in America created some unique problems for this African American religious group—namely, how does one construct a meaningful identity when one's body has been negated and constructed as inferior through violent actual and symbolic practices? Mohammed sought to circumvent the trappings of a racialized identity that rendered black bodies inferior by associating black identity with the figure of Bilal Ibn Rabah, a seventh-century Ethiopian-born Muslim slave and early convert, as well as a close a companion to the Prophet Muhammad. For Mohammed, African Americans were "Bilalians."

This identity was not without serious problems, however. It implied erroneously, for example, that notions of race negated and were mutually exclusive with tenets of culture and history. Like Islamic universal identity and practice, Bilalian identity was reified and totalizing. In addition, it reveals Mohammed's religious chauvinism and pride in that he believed that a Muslim icon that he alone selected could stand as a symbol for an entire "race" of people, on all continents and in all walks of life. And, of course, he ignored the issue of gender in this matter and viewed maleness as normative. Mohammed was able to take such discursive privilege because he viewed himself as the unique and authentic leader of black people.

Mohammed negated things foreign to establish his authority as an African American leader and as a religious leader. Foreign ideas, images, and people functioned as contaminants that inhibited African American communities from realizing their full potential and humanity. This view of the black communities as needing protection from outsiders who sought to invade it and control it corresponded to Mohammed's idealized view of the body as an object to be policed and reflected on because it indicated Allah's creative activity. This necessitated the kind of body-centered morality that Mohammed conveyed in his speeches and writing—codes and discourses that focused on what goes into the body (i.e., food, drugs), what goes on the body (e.g., "pimps' clothes"), what comes out of the body (e.g., foul language), and what people do with their bodies (e.g., "unnatural sex"). The body was regulated by interdictions and by ritual control such as putting a person before the congregation and shaming him or her for deeds that were deemed not in the interest of the collective. It is not surprising, then, that Mohammed did not see Islam as a foreign element invading black communities but, rather, overstated it as the authentic religion of African Americans that was pervasive in the life of the West African slave ancestors.

MOTHERSHIP CONNECTIONS

LOUIS FARRAKHAN AS THE CULMINATION OF MUSLIM IDEALS IN THE NATION OF ISLAM

5

Louis Farrakhan's Islamic thought and praxis is the culmination of that of his predecessors: Elijah Muhammad, Malcolm X, and Warith Deen Mohammed. The title of this chapter, in which I explore these connections, comes from the name of the album *Mothership Connection*, by the 1970s funk music stars Parliament (Funkadelic). The album cover features George Clinton, an African American in funk-inspired space clothes, floating out of the entryway of a spaceship in orbit.[1] The relationship between the Afrofuturistic aesthetics of the album cover and Farrakhan's most significant discourses is apropos, given the correspondence among their ideas both of African American transcendence, space vehicles, and aesthetics, and of black bodies.

Most important, Farrakhan gives his most powerful expression of the nature and meaning of black embodiment in the discourses of his mystical experiences with the Mother Plane/ Mothership, or what he calls the Mother Wheel—literally, a spacecraft.[2] An interpretation of the Mothership is a necessary condition for understanding black bodies out-of-place socially and symbolically in Farrakhan's Nation of Islam (NOI), as attention to the significance of the Mother Wheel for understanding Farrakhan's ministry is all but absent in the literature.[3] Quintessentially out-of-place, Farrakhan embodied an aggressive intellectual and confrontation with America and the US government, and the Wheel is the pinnacle of black bodies out-of-place socially and symbolically. His speeches and activities elevate social and symbolic dynamics to equal status. Meanwhile, his esoteric, mystical, and epistemological experience of the Wheel functions as an organizing metaphor for interpreting black corporeality, and it, indeed, provides the narrative that gives ultimate coherence and purpose to his life and ministry.[4]

Visionary Beginnings: Farrakhan and Mystical Visions

Born Louis Eugene Walcott on May 11, 1933, Minister Louis Farrakhan is the leader of the reconstituted Lost-Found Nation of Islam that "began" in 1977.[5] I use the term *reconstituted* to indicate that the existence of the NOI is disjunctive rather than continuous. Under Warith Deen Mohammed, the NOI existed as such for less than a year before it morphed into the World Community of Islam in the West (WCIW) and, later, into the American Muslim Mission. Both incarnations had Sunni Islamic emphases, though Mohammed maintained his commitment to the particularities of race. The group that Farrakhan "founded" was in many ways a "new" NOI, in that many former members followed Mohammed into Sunni Islam. Believing that Mohammed was corrupting the teachings of Elijah Muhammad, Farrakhan announced to the actor Brock Peters that he was going to reorganize the NOI as the legitimate legacy of Muhammad. Several groups claiming to be legitimate surfaced after Muhammad's death in 1975.

Farrakhan, then Walcott, a former member of the Episcopal Church, a calypso singer, and a nightclub performer, had first encountered Elijah Muhammad in the early 1950s, but it was in 1955, when he was performing at a Chicago nightclub called the Blue Angel, that a friend suggested that he hear Messenger Muhammad deliver his Saviour's Day address.[6] This was a profound moment for Walcott. He was enchanted, even "frightened," by Muhammad's air of mystery and insight.[7] At first, however, Muhammad's broken speech signified to Walcott that the Messenger was uneducated. "I, being a student of English, and verb and subject agreement, heard him speak in a manner that a public speaker who was familiar with English wouldn't do," he says. "So in my head I said, 'O this man can't even talk.'" Immediately and uncannily, Muhammad addressed him directly: "When I said that he looked right at me and said, 'Brother, I didn't get a chance to get that fine education that you got. When I got to school the doors were closed. . . . You pay attention to what I'm saying and then you take it and put it in that fine language that you know. Only try to understand what I'm saying.'"[8]

In the retelling, Farrakhan says, "I was a little frightened that he seemed to know what I was thinking." Nonetheless the event continued, and he stayed. He says, "The rest of the afternoon his teaching was on the birth of a Savior. Now I enjoyed what I heard, but I wasn't overwhelmed to the point where I was going to get up and join. . . . But out of respect for my Uncle I got up and went and got my [membership] form."[9] His wife joined immediately, and his brother would join shortly thereafter.[10]

But Walcott was still not ready to turn in that membership form. He returned to his home in Long Island, New York, after the Saviour's Day convention, and it was several months before he visited an NOI temple (now called "mosque"). He recalls:

> I went back to New York. This was February. I went back [to the meetings] maybe sometime—and March, April, May, June went by and in July I visited the Mosque. I think the first time I went may have been on a Friday night. Brother James 7X was teaching. But on that Sunday, when I went back then I heard Brother Malcolm, I got up and took my form out again. This was July 1955. August, September went by and around the 5th of October I got word that I received my "X." I got my Student Enrollment on that Sunday and five minutes after I had it in my hand, I memorized the ten answers to the ten questions. So that next night I was ready to recite. After I recited, they said well Brother, you're now Brother Louis 2X. Then I went to the class. At the end of the class they called up the new converts.[11]

Here is an illustration of the NOI's focus on issues of the body that we see coming to fruition in the religious life and ministry of Louis Farrakhan. Having received the "X" that would serve as his surname—which, again, denoted that this body was no longer the old black slave body but a new religious one—he underwent an intellectual reorientation, the beginning of which took the form of a short catechism in which new adherents had to learn and formally recite publicly undisclosed information. This learning symbolized that this new black body was an intellectual and religious body that possessed knowledge that was of a private nature.

The catechism allowed Farrakhan to move to the next stage. After reciting the information, which he suggests was elementary for him to learn, he was ready to be affirmed by the religious community. He was then accepted fully as "Louis 2X," the "2" indicating that another "Louis X," existed in the community—he was the second person to have that name. Naming, in this case, was significant because it was an indication to Farrakhan and the community that he was worthy to receive the teachings, rituals, and secrets of the universe, of which the NOI was the sole purveyor.

The new name also signaled that he was ready to be the recipient of ritualized education that took the form of gender-specific regimentation and discipline that it would obtain as a newly embraced member of the Fruit of Islam. Having reached this stage, Walcott, the newly designated Louis 2X, was overtaken by the love and respect that men in the FOI showed him:

> When they called me up to welcome me into the F.O.I. [*sic*] The love that I saw in the eyes and the faces of the Brothers toward me was such a new and beautiful experience. . . .
>
> It was something that you longed to see in Black people. As I started to speak I broke down. But in that short little talk I said "I was going to take this teaching to every nook and cranny, or corner, of the United States of America." Those were the words that I spoke in October 1955.[12]

Farrakhan intimates here that when he was going through the process of membership, he had a "call" experience in which he knew, in the moment, that it was his vocation to become a minister of the NOI and to ensure that its ideals were propagated throughout the United States. In retrospect, Farrakhan thinks, Muhammad gave him the content of this calling in their very first encounter: "But looking back I see that he literally gave me my assignment the first day that he laid eyes on me."[13] Farrakhan understood Muhammad's first comments to him to mean that he was not only to promulgate Muhammad's teachings everywhere, but he was to translate them for a sophisticated and increasingly educated black population. Again, Muhammad's consciousness may indicate his increasing desire to reach more "middle-class" African Americans, as well as his goal for the NOI to reflect more middle-class values and culture.

Farrakhan began worshipping at Temple No. 7 in Harlem, whose minister was none other than Malcolm X. Malcolm was impressed with him, he suggests, and gradually began to see him not as a musician, but as a potential NOI minister.[14] But as Farrakhan moved through the stages that would lead to full membership, he found that his lifestyle conflicted with the philosophy and program of the Nation of Islam. As he did with Muhammad Ali and his boxing career, Muhammad issued an ultimatum to Farrakhan and all new members who were entertainers and athletes that they must abandon their professions to become full members of the NOI; they had thirty days to comply or leave the Nation of Islam.[15] Farrakhan complied with some trepidation, but only after having a vision:

> It was the last day, the 30th day or just about December 26th, or the 27th when I had this engagement in the Nevele Club. Nevele is eleven spelled backwards. It was a Jewish resort. I just said I'm going to get it all out of my system. I sang ballad. I sang some classical. I sang the blues. I played some classical violin. I played jazz violin. . . . [Afterward] I went home to go to sleep. In the night, I saw these two doors. One had *success* written over it and a mound in the floor that came up, maybe as high as this table. It was almost like a pyramid of diamonds and gold. But the other door had *Islam* over it with a black veil over the door. I was told to choose. And I chose Islam.[16]

Farrakhan suggests that this vision, like Malcolm X's prison vision of Master W. D. Fard Muhammad, was authoritative in its effect on his resolve to follow the NOI wholly.[17] His vision sets up the binary decision between "success" and "Islam" as if to suggest that he could have had a prosperous life as an entertainer, but he freely rejected such a life in light of his conviction regarding the precarious circumstances of black people and the role that Islam could play in their liberation and transformation. Also like Malcolm, Farrakhan does not indicate that his "vision" was a dream. Rather, he portrays it as an active and conscious mental image that, for him, was real.

The greater issue here involves the meaning of corporeality in the NOI. Why did Elijah Muhammad discourage participation in sports and popular performance arts such as singing? For Muhammad, black bodies in the NOI were religious bodies; for this reason, he exerted a certain amount of ritual "control" (or, at least, seemed to desire such control) over them. In other words, he wanted to regulate the practices, discourses, and behavior that gave meaning to black bodies. Muhammad also may have been reacting against a history of American entertainment, including sports, that has commodified black bodies for white interests and economic gain but whose representations were ultimately under the control of whites. Consider that professional athletes, while under contract to their leagues, are "owned" like chattel or moveable property. Muhammad wanted to disrupt all forms of white control over black people.

Muhammad rightly perceived that black bodies in-place were depicted as the obsequious, the buffoonish, the criminal, and the amusing—all in service of white desire and domination. He forced Farrakhan either to choose one of those stereotypes or to assent to the total religious ritualization of the NOI, as Edward E. Curtis IV called it, that would give religious importance and control to every aspect of his life.[18] In a sense, the choice at hand was whether or not his body would continue to be the site, like so many others, of American popular representation or of the Nation of Islam's "re-presentation"—that is, an ultimate body that reflects Muslim religious mythology and (black) "middle-class" values and practices.[19]

"Not Them, Just You": The Minister, the Messenger, and the Mothership

Later, Minister Farrakhan linked his 1955 vision to his 1985 experience of the Mothership, or what he calls the "Mother Wheel."[20] He described the details of the 1955 vision retrospectively and suggested that its meaning had become clear only thirty years later, when he experienced another visual revelation. He suggested that the membership form that he completed in 1955 appeared in the 1985 vision: it had a flip side on which something was written in cursive. Moreover, he encountered two voices, one instructing the other to "turn [the form] over, it's not time for him to see this yet."[21] At a subsequent Temple meeting, he saw Malcolm X write the words *Allah* and *Muhammad* on the board in Arabic and realized that this was the language that was written on his form in his vision.[22] Telling the story in 1985, he said: "But the significance of that has been dawning on me, especially now. That was in 1955 and then 1985, or thirty years later comes and I'm up on the Wheel. Then this thing comes down and there's this cursive writing on it. I leaned forward to read it. Then the Honorable Elijah Muhammad speaks and whatever was on that screen disappears. I never consciously knew that I read it."[23] It was this later vision, he suggested, in which the meaning, purpose, and function of the earlier one came to full fruition. He described this subsequent vision in numerous lectures, press conferences, and interviews from the mid-1980s to the 1990s and beyond and assigned it the unreserved religious and political weight that he felt it deserved.

The most provocative version of this vision, akin to UFO abduction narratives, was announced in a press conference at the J. W. Marriott Hotel in Washington, DC, on October 24, 1989. During the conference, Minister Farrakhan related his experience of the Mother Wheel, which he experienced as concrete, on Tepozteco Mountain in Tepoztlán, Mexico, September 17, 1985.[24] I rely on this statement about his Wheel experience, though it was published in 1989 as "The Announcement: A Warning to the U.S. Government," because it continues to this day to be the quintessential statement of his account—so much so, for example, that Farrakhan cited it verbatim during his national Saviour's Day address on Sunday, February 28, 2010.[25] In addition, it continues to inform Farrakhan's knowledge of future events, according to Justine M. Bakker.[26] I cite it here at length:

> In a tiny town in Mexico, called Tepotzlan, there is a mountain on the top of which is the ruins of a temple dedicated to Quetzalcoatl—the Christ-figure of Central and South America—a mountain which I have climbed several times. However, on the night of September 17, 1985, I was carried up on that mountain, in a vision, with a few friends of mine. As we reached the top of the mountain, a Wheel, or what you call an unidentified flying object, appeared at the side of the mountain and called to me to come up into the Wheel. Three metal legs appeared from the Wheel, giving me the impression that it was going to land, but it never came over the mountain.[27]

Farrakhan first lays the foundation by informing listeners that he was on a mountain that was the site of an ancient temple to Quetzalcoatl, a "Christ figure," so that no doubt exists that what he is about to disclose is of a religious and mystical nature. He, I believe, wanted to be viewed in light of Quetzalcoatl and to connect Quetzalcoatl's mystical world to his own.[28] This experience on the mountain in Tepotzlán marks the beginning of a new identity for Farrakhan as mystical sage and chosen apocalyptic spokesman. This numinous turn also signals an enduring change in his candor and confidence: he is now able to speak boldly and openly about the experience. For example, in a *Nightline* interview with the journalist Ted Koppel on October 16, 1996, Farrakhan recounted his experience in Tepotzlán without any hint of trepidation.[29]

Returning to Farrakhan's vision, he proceeds to describe the Wheel as an "unidentified flying object," with three metal legs appearing, which makes him believe that the craft is going to land. The sighting of a circular or disk-like tripod (or three emanating beams of light) is a classic characteristic or feature in UFO reports and depictions in fiction and popular culture.[30] In *The War of the Worlds*, for example, H. G. Wells depicts late nineteenth-century London as being watched and then invaded by a superior intellect—namely, Martians. Written in part as a critique of colonial Europe and England, the novel asks what life might be like if Europe had been dominated by an alien life form in the same way that Europeans had colonized "races" they saw as inferior.[31] Similar to Farrakhan's Wheel, the invasion vehicle or UFO that transported the aliens to conquer this world, which Wells codes as "the Thing," is described as a "tripod," having three metal support and mobility girders extending from the bottom of the craft.[32]

Farrakhan continued with his lengthy press conference, suggesting that the experience frightened him, so he called for members of his party, which included Mother Tynnetta Muhammad; Jabril Muhammad; and Farrakhan's wife, Mother Khadijah Muhammad, who had accompanied him to the mountain. Then a voice from the Wheel replied, "Not them; just you."[33] He reports that the voice told him to relax while he was carried into the vehicle by a beam of light:

> I sat next to the pilot, however, I could not see him. I could only feel his presence. As the Wheel lifted off from the side of the mountain, moving at a terrific speed, I know I was being transported to the Mother Wheel, which is a human-built planet—a half-mile by a half-mile that the Honorable Elijah Muhammad had taught us for nearly 60 years. The pilot, knowing that I was fearful of seeing this great, mechanical object in the sky, maneuvered his craft in such a way that I would not see the Mother Wheel (Plane) and then backed quickly into it and docked in a tunnel. I was escorted by the pilot to a door and admitted into a room.[34]

Farrakhan describes events that for him were literal and physical occurrences. He says that after having been carried "into" the craft by a beam of light, he was transported to the "Mother" Plane, implying that the first "wheel" was not the primary vehicle but merely a transport craft, one of the smaller wheels that took him to the main one—the Mother Wheel. While in the initial craft, he says, he sat next to the pilot, but both the pilot and the Mothership were concealed from his optical gaze, though not from his psychic perception of their presence. After docking the plane in a tunnel, the pilot escorted him into a room.

Here the meaning of the experience would become clear to Farrakhan, and the concrete connection between this experience and his 1955 vision would be revealed (see figure 5.1). Farrakhan intentionally avoids describing this room, insisting that it is extraneous, except to suggest that it was in the center of the room that he heard the voice of his mentor and religious leader, Elijah Muhammad.[35] Muhammad spoke (and Farrakhan heard his voice) as clearly as the press conference audience heard his voice, he contended, as he explained the substance of what he heard:

> He [Elijah Muhammad] spoke in short cryptic sentences and as he spoke a scroll full of cursive writing rolled down in the front of my eyes, but it was a projection of what was being written in my mind. As I attempted to read the cursive writing, which was in English the scroll disappeared and the Honorable Elijah Muhammad began to speak to me. He said, *"President Reagan has met with the Joint Chiefs of Staff to plan a war. I want you to hold a press conference in Washington, D.C., and announce their plan and say to the world that you got the information from me on the Wheel."* He said to me that he would not permit me to see him at that time. However, he said that I had one more thing to do and when that one more thing was done that I could come again to the Wheel and I would be permitted to see him face to face.[36]

Note that Farrakhan uses the phrase "cursive writing" to connect the 1985 events that he is describing to the media to the sacred images that he reported experiencing in 1955. Moreover, the trope is meant, metonymically, to evoke the earlier episode by which he was compelled to commit fully to the NOI after seeing cursive writing on the back of his membership form as part of the vision. To strengthen the linkage further, he uses the report of a voice addressing him in the first person—a voice, as in the 1955 vision, that he experiences as dislocated and not concrete. In other words, these were voices from "somewhere," but he could only "feel" the bodies from which they emanated.

Farrakhan weaves a narrative connected by these two religious experiences against which his ministry must be interpreted, for in these accounts he locates his calling and the ultimate purpose for his involvement in and leadership of the NOI, privileging the latter, which interprets the former. While it is unclear who in his press conference audience would have been aware of the former event, it appears that the Mother Wheel

5.1

Master Fard Muhammad is at the top of this image, with the Mother Wheel above him, Louis Farrakhan is at the bottom left, and Elijah Muhammad is at the right. Farrakhan claims that he experienced the presence of Master Fard and Elijah Muhammad on the Mother Wheel on September 17, 1985. Collage created for the author by David Metcalfe.

episode was meant to validate his leadership and his reconstitution of the NOI, given that the language and the "appearance" of Muhammad function to give coherence and authority to his religious life. Farrakhan is masterful in drawing on earlier NOI mythology and invoking the very language and concepts of Muhammad (at times, he even calls the Mother Wheel the Mother "Plane," as the Messenger did) to connect his revelation, the meaning of which he has yet to be disclosed publicly, to that of his mentor and religious leader. Furthermore, the fact that the Mothership narrative presupposes knowledge of his call experiences and 1955 vision may suggest that his message here was intended for multiple audiences.

Perhaps Farrakhan's "Announcement"—which, he contended, he was making because Muhammad directed him to do so—was meant for the white media and the US government and, simultaneously, for followers of Warith Deen Mohammed and rival NOI groups, such as those founded by Silis Muhammad, John Muhammad, and Royall Jenkins after Elijah Muhammad's death. All of these groups claimed to be legitimate and authentic successors to Muhammad's NOI; they also claimed that Farrakhan, in reality, was corrupting Muhammad's teachings.[37] The most powerful "evidence" that Farrakhan is the genuine heir to Muhammad's religion is his experience of Muhammad as physically alive and dwelling in the Mothership.

Moreover, Farrakhan's vision implies that Elijah Muhammad exists bodily in some realm or dimension that is only epistemologically and experientially accessible to the mystically adept. Hence, his identification with Quetzalcoatl constructs his identity as an avatar or "Christ figure" who has privileged, if not exclusive, spiritual gnosis, foresight, and experience that has given him at least a glimpse of the ultimate wisdom and truth of the universe—in other words, the ultimacy of black bodies. Black bodies, the Mothership reveals, render death irrelevant; they are enduring, and their animation and function do not end with ostensible death, as seen in the persistence of Muhammad. Jabril Muhammad, a close colleague of Farrakhan (who was with him on Tepozteco Mountain) and the author of *Is It Possible That the Honorable Elijah Muhammad Is Still Physically Alive???*, confirms this reading of the Mothership and what it uncovers about the persistence of such bodies:

> The importance of that issue has been publicly heightened by means of the vision from the Honorable Elijah Muhammad to Minister Louis Farrakhan, on September 17, 1985, and the Minister's report of it to America and

the world. . . . It is, of course, beyond the purpose of this introduction to this little book to go into those details necessary for the best understanding of the "vision" of Minister Farrakhan, and how it relates to the fact that the Honorable Elijah Muhammad is alive; is well; is in power; and is doing that which was written that he would do even as you read these words. . . . Furthermore, Minister Farrakhan's experience in Mexico, was next to actually [*sic*] seeing him in his physical body. . . . Certainly, many of us heard the Honorable Elijah Muhammad state that he would one day be with the God who raised him up and that he would return.[38]

Jabril Muhammad acknowledges that it is appropriate to read Farrakhan's description of his UFO "encounter" with Elijah Muhammad as an interaction with Muhammad's physical body—that is, actual contact with the Messenger and not an apparition or hallucination—though he was unable to gaze on Muhammad directly. According to Farrakhan, a full and tactile experience in which he would be allowed to see Muhammad would come later: "He said that I had one more thing to do and when that one more thing was done that I could come again to the Wheel and I would be permitted to see him face to face."[39] Jabril Muhammad offers additional evidence that Farrakhan's vision suggests Muhammad is alive—namely, that Farrakhan states explicitly that Muhammad survives.

Mother Tynnetta Muhammad confirms Farrakhan's experience as authentic and affirms its implication that black bodies—in this case, Elijah Muhammad's body—endure after ostensible death.[40] As one of the most important theological thinkers in the NOI, Mother Tynnetta, a former secretary and now a leader of the NOI, is so significant that, Bakker concludes, she "should be seen as Farrakhan's 'right hand' in guiding the world to the Hereafter."[41] With all of her own creativity, authority, and esoteric system of thought, Mother Tynnetta's dreams verify, for her, the truth of Farrakhan's vision of Muhammad as "alive and well"; that "he is not dead."[42]

Farrakhan himself says that Muhammad was "alive" bodily. He observes that Master Fard Muhammad (God for Elijah Muhammad's NOI) is also living. Furthermore, the two—Fard and Muhammad—are together, meaning that the Mahdi and His Messenger are aboard the divine vehicle known as the Mothership or the Wheel. Finally, Farrakhan's phrase "in power" suggests that Elijah Muhammad (rather than Fard Muhammad) is sovereign. The phrase also implies conscious activity on the part of Muhammad, that things are still under his control and moving toward the apocalyptic denouement that he prophesied in the Yakub narrative: that the Mother Plane will end the age of white domination.[43]

Farrakhan signals that his vision has a double meaning. The original message that he received from Muhammad may have involved President Ronald Reagan and a war directed at Muammar Qaddafi and Libya: not only does Farrakhan constantly refer to Reagan, he does so in relation to the Mother Wheel in speeches after his experience of September 17, 1985. He maintains that Reagan (and President Jimmy Carter) and the US government were aware of the existence of the Wheel, which they called a UFO.[44] Ironically, President Reagan apparently did believe in the existence of UFOs and extraterrestrial beings. He referred to them in speeches that he delivered during his presidency. In a speech titled "Remarks to Students and Faculty at Fallston High School," delivered on December 4, 1985, for instance, he claimed in reference to his conversations with Soviet leader Mikhail Gorbachev regarding US-USSR relations and defense (including his Strategic Defense Initiative, or "Star Wars" defense system) that the two countries should not have to be attacked by an "alien race" to realize all people are humans.[45] In another, "Address to the 42d Session of the United Nations General Assembly in New York," on September 21, 1987, President Reagan remarked, "I occasionally think how quickly our differences worldwide would vanish if we were facing an alien threat from outside this world."[46] Both of these public addresses might have served to confirm Farrakhan's suspicion that the US government was aware of an extraterrestrial presence—which is to say, the Mother Wheel—especially since the implication is that white nations might unite if faced with an "alien" threat.

Notwithstanding Reagan's discourses on extraterrestrials, the revelation from Muhammad was ambiguous, Farrakhan reports, because it also was to serve as a symbol for the deeper meaning of the communication—a warning of a covert war on black people, especially on African American youth, to be carried out several years later by President George Bush.[47] Farrakhan described this in his press conference:

> The reason that the Honorable Elijah Muhammad did not tell me who the President and the Joint chiefs [sic] of Staff had planned a war against was because Moammar Qaddafi, the Muslim Revolutionary leader, and the small nation of Libya, was only to serve as a sign of an even more significant and consequential war which would come several years later. I am here to announce today that President Bush has met with his Joint Chiefs of Staff, under the direction of General Colin Powell, to plan a war

against the Black people of America, the Nation of Islam, and Louis Farrakhan, with particular emphasis on our Black youth, under the guise of a war against drug sellers, drug users, gangs and violence—all under the heading of extremely urgent national security.[48]

Farrakhan proposes that Elijah Muhammad was deliberate about making his communications cryptic and ambiguous to give Farrakhan the time he needed to apprehend the dual and futuristic messages in Muhammad's words. Observe that Minister Farrakhan reports having been taken into the Wheel in 1985, but he did not hold the press conference until 1989, allowing for the necessary duration of time to acquire the full intent of the disclosure. And when he declared to the world the ultimate meaning of his religious leader's words, it was devastating: the true meaning and objective of Bush's "War on Drugs" was not "national security" but, rather, a genocidal conspiracy by the US government to destroy black people.

Farrakhan does not emphasize that Colin Powell, whom he cites as complicit in the pernicious plan, was also "black." He simply points to the president and the government, especially the Federal Bureau of Investigation, as the culprits in the demonic plan.[49] Later, however, he does make an effort to mention Powell's racial heritage and how Powell's cultural identity was important in the conspiracy to destroy black people.[50] Generally, Farrakhan contends, when whites elevate an African American, they do so because they intend to use him or her against other black people, as a means to deflect the charge of racism and conceal racial motivations in particular actions and policies. It is integral to the conspiracy, Farrakhan implies: "Why would President Bush assign a Black man to be chairman of the Joint Chiefs of Staff, jumping over 30 white men, who are reportedly more qualified, to be chairman? Ofttimes [sic], when a Black man is elevated to a high position, it is generally because of a desire to use him against the legitimate aspirations of his own people, or to use him as window-dressing to make the masses of Black people believe that an unjust system is working on their behalf."[51]

Farrakhan makes the point that it is not he who is saying that many other white men were more qualified to be the chairman of the Joint Chiefs of Staff; he has heard rumblings to that effect, indicated by his use of the phrase "*reportedly* more qualified."[52] In such an instance, it was illogical for a black person to hold such a position unless that person's elevation to the post or rank was purposefully to be used surreptitiously in service of maintaining white supremacy and domination. Powell could also be used to justify sending African American, Hispanic, Native American, and poor white people to foreign lands such as Panama and Colombia and then on to Cuba and Africa to fight against liberation movements there, he intimates.[53]

While Farrakhan's words are ambiguous about how all black bodies could inherit the experiences that he has had, he is intentional about connecting the Mother Wheel to all black bodies. It defines them all as esoteric and as the sites of divine ultimate concern in the cosmic contest between the forces of good and evil, which Farrakhan represents as "black" and white, respectively. Farrakhan suggests that the representation of black bodies by the media works in concert with those government forces that want to destroy them. By portraying black youth in Southern California, New York, and Washington, DC, as "Crips and Bloods," drug dealers, and violent and well-armed criminals, federal and local law enforcement may be seen by the public as justified in their violent treatment and incarceration of, and focus on, African American young people under the pretext that such youth are a threat to national security. It is interesting to compare Farrakhan's words from this press conference in 1989, expressing his "abduction" narrative of 1985, to the present-day prison-industrial complex in which black bodies are commodified as products in the billion-dollar corporatizing of incarceration, often for low-level marijuana and other nonviolent offenses that are unevenly distributed among, and devastating to, black and Latino families, while whites, who are just as likely, if not even more likely, to commit such offenses are not the public face or the victims of the War on Drugs of the Reagan, Bush, Clinton, and Obama eras. This is exactly the point of Michelle Alexander's monumental legal analysis of race and the criminal "justice" system, *The New Jim Crow: Mass Incarceration in the Age of Colorblindness*.[54] Uttered more than thirty years before Alexander's study, Farrakhan's words—that he represented as coming from Elijah Muhammad—were perhaps prophetic, indeed.

Farrakhan ends by warning the president and the government against such a cabal, for African Americans are the "People of God," and Allah will fight for their liberation: *"And so in the present case, I say to you, stay away from these men and leave them alone, for if this plan or action should be of men, it will be overthrown; But if it is of God, you will not be able to overthrow them; or else you may even be fighting against God."*[55] Farrakhan emphasizes, again, that this "announcement" pertains to all black bodies, that they are significant to God and are the recipients of God's divine attention, even though all black people are not literally members of the NOI. The warning was meant to reach the highest halls of government and into the shadows of the covert, where violent machinations are devised by those whose insidious goals entail the destruction of the (entire) black race.

But in making this declaration, Farrakhan makes a faulty question-begging assertion, a cardinal error that puts him in line with other African American religious traditions that have argued that God is on the side of black people and against oppression. William Jones, author of *Is God a White Racist?: A Preamble to Black Theology*, points out that such declarations assume the existence of "God" and God's goodness, and they fail to prove that God is on the side of black people or that God has "chosen" them. Jones argues that such faulty theological methodologies can actually imply the opposite: that God is a white racist who can just as easily be the cause of black suffering, since God has not prevented it or brought it to an end. The tradition that Farrakhan invokes is a prominent theme that has its roots in nascent nineteenth-century black theological development:[56] fighting against African Americans will, in reality, be a futile fight against God. Hence, black people are all God's people, and for Farrakhan the Mothership proves it. Lest anyone seek to mock him for his UFO-inspired warning to America, he reminds them that they will see "UFOs in abundance over the major cities in America."[57] Farrakhan interprets the entire history of UFOs in light of the Mother Wheel. Although sightings of it were misrecognized and misrepresented as UFOs throughout history, they were all the Mother Wheel, which he also sees as Ezekiel's Wheel or the smaller wheels that come from within it. He concludes by cautioning the government that the calamities that America was experiencing at the time would increase to the end that they might humble themselves to heed the "Warning contained in this Announcement."[58]

The Meaning of the Mothership

Farrakhan's UFO encounters can be given some coherence through selected readings in the psychology of religion, particularly psychoanalysis.[59] I offer a detailed psychoanalytic interpretation of Farrakhan's relationship to the Mother Wheel and its male occupants in an article that was published in the *Journal of the American Academy of Religion* in 2012, so I will not repeat that in this space. I will say only that Farrakhan's Mother Wheel moments can be understood as a *real* experience that was in response to exigent racialized circumstances, a threat against black people both now and in the 1980s that tied all black bodies together in purpose and meaning. That is, instead of relegating Farrakhan's visionary experience (or Muhammad's, for that matter) to the realm of science fiction or pathology, we can understand it as ontological in the sense that it had real and numinous effects on him. Moreover, we can read Farrakhan's longing to see Muhammad (and Fard) as a homoerotic experience or aim-inhibited "male bonding" that perhaps is deflected by the "Mother" (i.e., the feminine) of the Mother Wheel. In fact, Jabril Muhammad, one of Farrakhan's closest companions, has described his adoration for Muhammad in very erotic terms:

> He is the example of the perfect love of a student for his teacher. It's similar to when a woman loves a man, she submits herself totally to him. She desires to be "*wit*" him at all times; so much that she devotes her life to his life. She wishes she could be apart [*sic*] of his very genetic makeup. . . . The pain of being without the loved one is so unbearable, that she begins to take on the characteristics of the object of her love and affection. She becomes one with him.[60]

One could argue that the asymmetrical analogy is sexist, in that the longing is not reciprocal and is expressed only in terms of a woman strongly desiring a man. The analogy also requires that one of the partners of the *relationship* (a term that Jabril uses over and over) be imagined as a woman and be put in the symbolic position of the feminine. Jabril changes the terms of the relationship between Farrakhan and Muhammad to an apparently more acceptable heterosexual conceptualization to ease the obvious tension of describing their male-to-male relationship as a "love affair." The analogy functions to recast the otherwise same-sex framing of the relationship, just as "mother" functions as the symbolic language that veils desire to unite with the male occupants of the Mother Wheel.

Farrakhan's longing for "mother" is not a Freudian Oedipal conflict (since there is no apparent contest with a "father" over the "mother"), but Freud and, to an extent, Jung might see the wheel-like Mothership as a symbolic vagina or womb into which Farrakhan was carried and from which he could emerge, born anew with a new identity, new purpose, and new significance. In addition, the Mother Wheel may represent a exoticized symbolic space in which Farrakhan experiences love, affirmation, and peace. At the same time, the Wheel, as a symbol of technology and intellect, may serve to counter white supremacist discourses of black inferiority and empower black quests for freedom from oppression.

In the narrative of Yakub, the Mothership functions as a metaphor for black bodies, revealing them, in turn, as symbols of the NOI collective culture and cosmology; it brings them to full idealized fruition and uncovers their connection to the mythological and cosmic origins that render them transcendent. That is, the Yakub epoch, which ends with the return of the Mothership, connects black bodies to ultimate meaning that is not located in earthly sources and sociopolitical and historical spaces. This by no means indicates that black bodies have no material or political relevancy, only that these are less important. But in Farrakhan's vision, the opposite is true: these were religious bodies whose very existence signifies the importance of sociopolitical conditions for the religious life and meaning for the Nation of Islam. Nowhere in NOI philosophy and theology is this more factual than in the ministry of Louis Farrakhan.

The Mother Plane establishes and discloses the reality of the meaning of black bodies. That is, Farrakhan had heard Elijah Muhammad teach about the Wheel for twenty years.[61] With his personal contact with the Mother Wheel Muhammad's teachings became "real" and manifested in the world. Farrakhan knew then, if he had had any doubts before, that all African Americans were God's special people and that God was a "man" just like he was and human just like black people. After all, he "saw" Muhammad and Master Fard in the Wheel.[62] Consequently, we learn two important things from Farrakhan's reflections on his vision. Grounded in Master W. D. Fard Muhammad as the originary and ideal black body, Farrakhan is now privy to the material veracity of Elijah Muhammad's claims about black bodies being the preeminent bodies in the universe and their connectedness, as the ultimate and standard for humanity. In communicating this vision, he suggests to all black people that this, too, could be their destiny, though one might infer that such a destiny may only be accessible through Farrakhan as the Christ figure. This actuality of persistent black bodies reveals the truthfulness of all of the history and teachings of Muhammad. The other thing that can be gleaned from this notion, as Farrakhan suggests in his lecture *The Wheel and the Last Days*, is that black people do not require weapons to fight against the government and the forces of oppression: they have the "power to make things happen if you come in tune with the Almighty," just as he has.[63] In other words, black bodies generally have power that is based on and driven by "spiritual" alignment with God and with Farrakhan. This power comes to fruition through the highest religious ideals of Farrakhan and the Nation of Islam.

The power of black embodiment, then, is not simply to be understood as rooted in pure physicality. It is also to be understood in symbolic—which is to say, religious—realities. Aligned with and connected to divine ideals and bodies, African Americans have epistemological and creative mental and psychic power to create substantive realities in their own lives. In fact, the Mother Wheel itself is a sign that African Americans, related to the creators and navigators of the Wheel, are a superior intelligence. Farrakhan notes that the "plane is a sign of that greater wisdom."[64] Simultaneously, the Wheel signals a revolutionary shift in Farrakhan's theology in that he seems to eschew Elijah Muhammad's traditional view that Master Fard was God in exchange for a more mystical New Age perspective. Instead, Fard was god-*like* and represents the same consciousness, power, and creativity that all African Americans can possess. Master Fard, he says, is "a great god . . . the Great Mahdi" but not the originator of all creation.[65] Fard has only grown to God-type knowledge and power.

Farrakhan suggests that he has access to God directly, so he does not worship the Prophet Muhammad or Jesus. Rather, Black people are "joint heirs" (I assume he means co-creators) with God. Once they come to the godlike self-consciousness, the same consciousness that Farrakhan himself is realizing, they will see that they have creative psychic abilities. Farrakhan contends, for instance, that "black people don't need God to make things happen if they come back to God" because God wants to give them the power to "control the destiny of things on earth."[66] In some ways, we might read such discourses as a critique of all his predecessors, in that the role of human beings in creation of their own divine realities is much greater. Thus, humans have greater agency, consciousness, and power than seen in the theologies of Elijah Muhammad, Malcolm X, and Warith Deen Mohammed, and the level of human dependence on God is diminished.

Farrakhan says that after his initial encounter with the Mother Wheel, the Wheel continued to be present in his everyday life. He was able to feel and see it from his airplane as he traveled after his vision; in his words: "The Wheel performed for me, letting me know that it was there."[67] It is clear that this numinous experience was authoritative for him. And he says that it was not simply a phantom or a result of psychiatric pathology: there were witnesses and evidence. A Japanese military pilot saw the wheel—or, in fact, "strange light, small circular planes following his plane" for at least four hundred miles of travel or for "approximately fifty minutes."[68] According to Farrakhan, the smaller wheels that have been seen are what Muhammad suggested were the 1,500 hundred "little wheel-like planes" within the Mother Wheel.[69] The pilot also "noticed the silhouette of a very huge object . . . [that] appeared to be the size of two aircraft carriers . . . a half mile by a half mile."[70] The pilot drew a picture of it; Farrakhan shared the sketch at the 2010 Saviour's Day meeting.[71] Farrakhan appeals to Elijah Muhammad's teachings and suggests that the Japanese pilot's observations of the size of the Wheel correspond to Muhammad's declaration of the Wheel's size. Farrakhan also claims that the wheel left physical traces on US military radar.[72] It interfered with a US aircraft carrier's communications, he says, concluding: "Before you can call me a nut or call me crazy, these wheels will be seen all over America."[73] He also asserts that all US presidents since 1930 (when Master Fard "arrived" in North America), including Reagan, Ford, and Carter, have known that the Mothership exists, but they do not want to admit "that there is a power and technology in the world" that renders Western technology inferior.[74] Farrakhan contends that the Wheel is poised and ready to exact retribution on the government or anyone who harms him, even if the harm is accidental. "If I just get scratched accidentally by you, you will be destroyed completely," he says.[75]

Indeed, Farrakhan sees himself as unique among black bodies.[76] As suggested earlier, his role, derived from his mountaintop experience in Mexico, is Christ-like—soteriological and protective with respect to black people and apocalyptic with respect to America. His presence in the world is protective: without it, cataclysmic upheaval, via the Wheel, will ensue.[77] Farrakhan tells America, "I am here as a mercy to you or to end your civilization."[78] Even more, knowledge of the Wheel's constant watchful protection should empower all black bodies to be boldly confrontational with the world physically and psychologically—that is, socially and symbolically out-of-place.

The tone and candor of Farrakhan's own attitude and oratorical castigations of America changed dramatically after his encounter with the Wheel and are examples of what all black bodies can, and perhaps should, be. This shift in the intensity of symbolic acts can be seen not only in his announcement and warning to the US government but in many of his subsequent public addresses. The Mothership signals perpetual symbolic out-of-placeness for black bodies in America, which Farrakhan promotes with force. Michael Lieb, for instance, quotes Farrakhan's *The Shock of the Hour* (1992) address in which Farrakhan proclaims: "We are a strange people in your midst. . . . You look at us, but you do not know us. . . . We are people of the Wheel. It protects us, it guides us, it stands as a constant reminder of our difference, our otherness."[79] Farrakhan proclaims that black bodies are distinct and mysterious and that they have an intimate relationship with the Wheel—a symbolic and esoteric relationship that no other people share.

Farrakhan makes it clear that he views black people as being defined by something other than the racist social system. His cosmic consciousness that resulted from the UFO encounter implies a black bodily transcendence that, because he was in a sense so otherworldly, meant he could engage the material world without fearing the racist backlash via sociopolitical public discourses or losing his life. His life and destiny were in the "hands" of Master Fard, the Great Mahdi, and his Messenger, Muhammad, who himself had taken on characteristics of divinity, having survived death and being primary occupants of the Mother Wheel.

Farrakhan's bold pronouncements illustrate newly acquired aggression that for him was a matter of ultimate religious and, ironically, patriotic import. He proclaims:

> Sexism is sinking the country. Classism is sinking the country. Racism is sinking the country. White supremacy is sinking the country. Black inferiority is sinking the country. . . . God has chosen from among the former slaves, the blacks. He has put in the head of the Honorable Elijah Muhammad and in the heads of those of us who follow him, a light; a torchlight that shows the way out of America's worsening conditions, for blacks and for all America. But America's treatment of us and America's treatment of the Honorable Elijah Muhammad is like the treatment of Daniel by the proud kings of Babylon. It's terrible that some of those with power and influence label me a Hitler, a racist or a hater, so that they can justify their own people, or agents among our people, in attempts to defame and otherwise harm me. This is hiding the light. This is scapegoating.[80]

Farrakhan speaks as one who is uniquely called to cure the ills of America, arguing that being a member of the most oppressed class of people has had the reverse effect. He intimates that God chose to raise from among the oppressed class someone with a prophetic voice and insight that could save the sin-sick soul of the country; however, in his rendering, the entire class of people is chosen. In a way, having been a member of a historically oppressed people afforded him a privileged religious position, though he did not seem to intend to valorize the suffering and violence (not here, at least) that is part and parcel of oppression. Moreover, he connects the relationship of black people in America to the biblical figure Daniel and the officials of Babylon. But he also reveals a patriotic commitment to America and a concern that it be a just country.

Farrakhan offers his truth as a "torchlight" that can lead the United States out of its present darkness into the light of day that is free from classism, racism, sexism, and white supremacy. Farrakhan says that America intentionally defames him (i.e., a response to his perceived symbolic out-of-placeness) to conceal the enlightenment he offers and as a means to do continued violence to black people and to him. This policing of black bodies is, in part, a response to the ignorance of Americans and white supremacy; they do not recognize him for who he is. Farrakhan signals that his *new* identity is cosmic and beyond human understanding: "I am more than what you I think I am and I am more than what I thought I was."[81] He is audacious in calling out Presidents Reagan and Bush for their alleged plots to destroy black people, and his attitude reflects an intellectual and religious self-importance that is beyond that of any human intellect, governmental or otherwise.[82] Like the argument here, Lieb connects Farrakhan's apocalyptic sermons about the government, whites, and Jews to the Wheel.

This symbolic out-of-placeness is connected to social out-of-placeness. The Mothership brings forth activities in which the body as a symbol exchanges meanings with the physical body, emboldening it, that are cast as social out-of-placeness in radical new ways Given that social out-of-placeness entails the physical body crossing established boundaries of acceptable and racially structured social activity for black people, it is fueled and motivated by beliefs and attitudes of symbolic out-of-placeness, as described earlier, and vice versa. In this case, Farrakhan opted to defy government orders in terms of his own political excursions in the 1980s, 1990s, and beyond and to confront the government bodily are a direct result of his being defined not by the system, but by the Mothership and by NOI mythology and cosmology.

Dennis Walker, author of *Islam and the Search for African-American Nationhood: Elijah Muhammad, Louis Farrakhan and the Nation of Islam*, notes numerous examples of Farrakhan's activism, claiming that they have an influence among Middle Eastern Arabs and American electoral politics. Walker also claims that NOI leaders generally have had greater access to American seats of power; for instance, Minister Robert Muhammad, Farrakhan's southwestern regional representative, was invited to meet with former Texas Governor Anne Richards in 1992 to contribute to the Governor's Citizen Action Task Force. Farrakhan also suggests that many African American groups have responded to NOI activism with increased political vigor, including "black political classes," "black leftist and unionists," "black Christian churches," and "women and feminists," and as well as Latinos in America and Latin America and Arabs—too many instances to enumerate here.[83]

Soon after he experienced his vision of the Mother Wheel, Farrakhan embarked on an international journey that included nations on the US list of terrorist nations to which American citizens were forbidden to travel. He commenced his "World Friendship Tour" in January 1986 and traveled to Iraq, meeting with Saddam Hussein; to Libya, meeting Muammar Qaddafi and to Iran, Sudan, and Syria.[84] Most upsetting to the US government was Qaddafi's offer to give the NOI $1 billion to found a bank, which would serve the cause of African American freedom.[85] The US State Department insisted that Farrakhan register henceforth as a foreign agent. As a form of insolence, Farrakhan and the NOI sought a license from the US Treasury to receive the donation. Allowing the NOI to receive the money, Farrakhan argued, would be "an act of expiation," a goodwill gesture to African Americans that America could make as recompense for its history of brutality and oppression.[86] Needless to say, no evidence indicates that the NOI received the money.[87] But Farrakhan's very travel to these nations was an excellent illustration of black bodies that were socially out-of-place, and the government's reaction showed that it considered Farrakhan a *danger* to its interests. Farrakhan even notes that it was Allah and the Mother Wheel that made it possible for him to slip in and out of the United States without being detected by government surveillance.[88]

Another direct result of Farrakhan's encounter with the Mothership, and his subsequent conviction that that black bodies are socially out-of-place, was his and the NOI's involvement with the "Navaho and Hopi Indians" in the year after his vision.[89] On July 6, 1986, he made a commitment to these Native American communities when the government and the military sought to move them from their land. They needed him, he said, because "the U.S. government is a very murderous government."[90] As a result, Farrakhan; his wife, Mother Khadijah; Mother Tynnetta Muhammad; and Jabril Muhammad traveled to Arizona to challenge officials at odds with the Native American communities.[91] Farrakhan reports that the four of them prayed in Arabic, and after the prayer, he maintains, "It came to me. Your prayer is answered."[92] Apparently, God was with them in their quest and was protecting and guiding them; so was the Wheel, Farrakhan says.[93]

His comments about his presence in the government–Native American relocation controversy are revealing: "We were not to go in the fringe, we are to go right to the frontlines where death is . . . We are to go wherever death is to challenge death . . . because death has no power today over the force of life that is with us."[94] In the context of his July 13, 1986 lecture, *The Wheel and the Last Days*, it seems reasonable that this "force of life" to which Farrakhan refers is the Mother Wheel, which sustains his life and empowers him to risk bodily harm, even "death," to confront what he sees as injustice. Part of the larger goal in these events was to fulfill Muhammad's contention that Native Americans are part of the original "black" nation, and Farrakhan informs us that he was "born to bring about union between the black people and the red people."[95] In the end, he saw his goal as uniting two communities of people who were perhaps the most maligned in the history and development of America, a defiant act of symbolic and social out-of-placeness that might remind the country of its violent and white supremacist origins.

Conclusion

Farrakhan intimates that the vision of Elijah Muhammad and Master Fard Muhammad in the Mother Wheel ultimately gave his life and destiny coherence and comprehensibility, to the extent that previous events and visions, such as the 1955 experience that led him to commit fully to the Nation of Islam, came to fruition and found their meaning in that "technology of epistemology" known to the world as a UFO.[96] He ties the shining moment of his ministry, the Million Man March—when countless African American men assembled on the mall in Washington, DC, on October 16, 1995—to inspiration from his experience on the Mothership, especially in his speech *The Vision for the Million Man March*.[97] Farrakhan also suggests the connection in his *Nightline* interview with Ted Koppel in 1996. In fact, Lieb argues that the Million Man March was one of several acts of "bearing witness" to the visionary encounter on the Mother Wheel.[98] The Million Man March address, titled "Toward a More Perfect Union," is an enactment of his role as an oracle, the purveyor of esoteric truths in the form of numerology and symbolic parallels, such as the Washington Monument as a Masonic symbol (i.e., Masonry as the origin of the NOI) and an African-Egyptian (i.e., the ancient classical African civilization) creation that is tied directly to the Wheel in theme and esoteric content.[99] In other words, the hundreds of thousands of black (male) bodies gathered on the Mall that day were cosmically and mythologically connected to the origins and truthfulness of the NOI that received concrete expression on September 17, 1985, when Elijah Muhammad reportedly engaged Farrakhan on the UFO.

Black bodies out-of-place symbolically and socially, as represented by Farrakhan, were enactments connected to the Wheel. It was no coincidence, then, that what may have been the two most poignant acts of perceived out-of-placeness—the Million Man March and "The Announcement," in which the social and the symbolic could be seen concurrently and intertwined—took place in Washington, DC, the seat of power in the United States. Those two performances brought together the bodily sensibilities of Farrakhan's predecessors and mentors—Elijah Muhammad, Warith Deen Mohammed, and Malcolm X. In Farrakhan, we see both the profound religious and symbolic commitments that characterized his leader and Messenger, Muhammad, and the bodily (social) crossing of boundaries in a confrontational manner that his former friend Malcolm desired so deeply to perform in his own life. These acts and others were empowered and compelled by Farrakhan's visionary encounter, without which his reconstitution of the Nation of Islam in 1977–78 might have faded into relative obscurity.

Farrakhan reinstituted all of the discourses and practices of Elijah Muhammad, including the eminence of the Fruit of Islam, which Imam Warith Deen Mohammed had disbanded.[100] But like Mohammed, Farrakhan desired a much closer connection to the global community of Muslims—a longing that, strangely enough, was also tied to his vision of the Wheel via the Million Man March and many other acts and events. Farrakhan notes, for instance, that one of the two main reasons for holding the Million Man March was to link the NOI to Muslims of the world; the second was to connect African Americans to Africans on the continent.[101] Farrakhan, like Mohammed, jettisoned the term *temple* for the place where the NOI holds worship and meetings for "mosque." After his vision, Farrakhan embarked on a goodwill international tour in which he visited almost exclusively Muslim nations, such as Iran, Libya, Syria, Sudan, and Iraq. Even other countries on the tour that were not "Muslim" per se, such as Ghana, had large Muslim populations.

Farrakhan's commitment to social and symbolic out-of-placeness may help to elucidate why he and the NOI (i.e., black bodies in the NOI) have been perceived so harshly as subversive and *dangerous*. Consequently, certain segments of the public have responded violently. For example, in response to a Farrakhan speech delivered at New York City's Madison Square

Garden in 1985, Mayor Ed Koch and Governor Mario Cuomo denounced him, and the Jewish Defense League held a "Death to Farrakhan" rally in the city. Perhaps their own institutional and cosmological commitments impeded them from perceiving any "truths" in Farrakhan's social critique of white supremacist values and practices in America and made it difficult for them to ascribe epistemological authority to black bodies.

As Mary Douglas informs us in her book *How Institutions Think*, such oppositional commitments exert a tremendous influence on cognition, rendering it difficult, at best, for those in dominant institutions to hear the other as legitimate.[102] Judith Bradford and Crispin Sartwell argue similarly that "the voices of those who would protest their consignment to a social identity can be de-legitimated in advance by the expectation on the part of authoritative listeners that those bodies do not count."[103] That is, the policing of bodies is a means to render them mute and illegitimate socially and symbolically. Nevertheless, it is interesting to note that Farrakhan tied a UFO sighting in Tucson, Arizona, on the morning of his New York City address, delivered just days after his UFO episode, to persecution by whites and white Jewish groups.[104] In other words, the Mother Wheel was protecting him and revealing itself as a sign of Farrakhan's religious authority.

On *Nightline*, Koppel summed up prevailing perspectives of Farrakhan's vision as "gibberish."[105] To Farrakhan, however, the vision was not gibberish but a religious, and ultimately significant, event that defined, empowered, and guided his ministry from that day forward and that rendered meaningful events that happened thirty years earlier. Farrakhan connects the eternal truths of the Nation of Islam, Elijah Muhammad, and Master Fard Muhammad to his vision and suggests that the evidence is global and ancient. Which is to say, his collected responses to the issue of the Mothership imply that the history of ufology and UFO encounters is, indeed, the history of the Mothership, but only he and the NOI hold the key to understanding its meaning and what it means in terms of the identity of all black bodies on the planet.

The Mothership defines all black bodies for Farrakhan and delineates the breadth of his activity, for which and to which the Mothership gives significance. Because the Wheel is transcendent in its meaning and immanent in its direct implications, it reflects a cosmology that regards the transcendent and immanent aspects of the world as ultimate and as the objects of religious concern—bringing the religious, the everyday, and the political together. The Mother Wheel, as a (indeed *the*) carrier of the meaning of black bodies, denotes that these bodies are divine in their physicality (social) and their cosmic transcendence (symbolic). This may help to explain why, despite ideological pressure from Sunnis and other Muslims, as well as media scrutiny of UFOs and Farrakhan, the institutional ideals and doctrines of the NOI remained durable.

(RE)FORMING BLACK EMBODIMENT, WHITE SUPREMACY, AND THE NATION OF ISLAM'S CLASS(IST) RESPONSE

This book offers a new way to understand the Nation of Islam (NOI) not as a black nationalist group but as an organization shaped by multiple religious, cultural, and social traditions. Thus, the NOI can best be understood within the framework of religious nationalism. In fact, Ernest Allen, the author of "Religious Heterodoxy and Nationalist Tradition," argues that the NOI provides one of the best examples of a religiously oriented nationalist movement, both embracing and challenging Islamic traditions. He identifies the ideological sources, constraints, and compulsions that made the NOI part of a religiously oriented nationalist movement, specifically citing the tension between black people in America wanting to fight for their human and civil rights and, at the same time, to express a willingness to be left alone to determine their own destinies. For Allen, this contributed to a militant part of the NOI made up of black people with relatively few economic resources and an economically secure part of the group. He concludes, "African American Muslims as a whole will remain a conservative political force wedded to the vision of economic empire."[1]

Garrett Felber, the author of *Those Who Know Don't Say*, misses the point that I, along with Allen and others, make about the NOI as a religious nationalist group. Instead, Felber contends that the NOI's concerns with black suffering—namely, the killing of black people by the police and other forms of violence directed toward them—are indicative of "Black nationalism as an ideological current of Black politics."[2]

To be sure, the NOI was and is first and foremost a religious community. This should not seem like a controversial proposition, but, unfortunately, it is common for scholars to regard the NOI as a black nationalist group, which obscures the religious nature and meaning of its symbols and practices. For example, how would one make sense of unidentified flying objects (UFOs), black life on other planets, and the fact that "black" for the NOI refers to the majority of the people of the Earth (see chapters 2–3), all of which figure so prominently in Nation of Islam theology? Much of the matter surrounding the understanding of the NOI as a black nationalist stems from early studies of the NOI, such as sociologist C. Eric Lincoln's *The Black Muslims in America* (1961); black nationalism was the primary lens through which Lincoln interpreted the doctrines and practices of the NOI. The political scientist E. U. Essien-Udom followed Lincoln in his study of the NOI, *Black Nationalism: A Search for Identity in America* (1962). These classic texts exerted a major influence on subsequent scholarship, and the NOI has been branded *black nationalist* ever since.

But the meaning and function of the rituals, discourses, and symbols of the NOI become clear when one gives theoretical attention to the religious meaning of UFOs, for instance, through which engagement of its practices should be mediated. Ideas and narratives that seem bizarre otherwise inform the NOI's practices, which then become coherent. My concern for the academic location of such a project in religious studies may be read as both a conciliatory overture and a critique of intellectual arenas that have almost wholly ignored the importance of black religion.

I follow Tracey E. Hucks in calling the NOI *religious nationalists*; as she argues, black nationalism is too rigid to account for black religion, for it often requires an untenable notion of racial homogeneity, emigration, and the establishment of a nation-state. The Nation of Islam's religious nationalism recasts epistemology and ontology in service of new ways of knowing the world and identifies itself in the sacred cosmos. Mars, Venus, and "East

Asia" (see chapter 1) reauthenticate black identity for the NOI in ways that allow African Americans to reformulate what it means to be human beyond racist notions of blackness as evil and inferior. A state, then, is unnecessary for religious nationalists, for their beliefs and practices function to "create a space of transcendence. . . . Most often, this transcendence involved the search for a trans-American identity that equipped African Americans to navigate their very real social location within North America."[3] The NOI used "transcendental symbols" as a means of authentication or reauthentication, in Hucks's terms.

The NOI was an important religious institution; like African American religion more generally, it forged spaces as resources for liberation and subjectivity, where African Americans could experience authentic humanity or create new "humanities." Indeed, the historian of religions Charles H. Long has argued that the experience of Africans in America is grounded in the "absurd meaning of their bodies" as material commodities and as the loci of Enlightenment ideologies that justified their enslavement and oppression.[4] Thus, the experience of blackness, making meaningful sense of the world that is lived in and experienced through black bodies, is central to the activity of African American religion. Anthony Pinn extends Long's line of reasoning to offer a theory of religion that regards the body as the primary site of religious meaning. He sees African American religion as a push against and beyond the bodily and psychic constraints and controls that African Americans have experienced historically in America. Subsequently, the rituals of the slave auction and practices of lynching, whose function, along with discursive, oppressive, and discriminatory practices, was to maintain the social order, had a particular effect on the construction of black bodies as objects.

Moreover, religion is a deep and fluid reservoir in that it allows for what Long calls a "new and rich counter-creative signification"—that is, a critique of racist and sexist depictions of black as inferior and the re-envisioning of the meaning of black bodies through cultural sources that are not circumscribed by white supremacy.[5] The NOI constructed a metaphysical notion of race that I call *transcendent blackness*, which emerged from a quilt-like *bricolage* of sources that include science, extraterrestrial and UFO narratives, transcendental symbols, black history, sacred religious texts, other religions, and more.

Indeed, embodiment is at the heart of the Nation of Islam's brand of religious nationalism—specifically, the function and symbols of the body that simultaneously advance and undermine the NOI's goal of retrieving black bodies from white subordination. Thus, the black body is best understood, through the lens of the NOI, as a theological category. This study connects the body to the NOI, but the linkages between the black body and black political and theoretical traditions are also evident.

Reclaiming and reforming black bodies has been at the heart of racial uplift ideologies, associated, most notably, with Booker T. Washington and E. Franklin Frazier and with the politics of respectability of the early twentieth-century Women's Convention movement of the National Baptist Convention, which, together, constitute a *perichoretic politics of racial uplift* that is evident in the NOI. Moreover, the body and embodiment are central to preserving, promoting, and maintaining a male-dominated ideology, which I name *metaphysical masculinity* in an effort to reify the role and position of black women's bodies according to the whims and will of the NOI's male-centered religion.

The NOI has sought to (re)form bodies that for it were disfigured in every conceivable way by a white supremacist culture that affected and structured all major aspects of black social life, including its religion. Christianity, for the NOI, has participated in this grotesque construction of black corporeality as socially and symbolically in-place, attaching negative meanings to black embodiment and constricting the activities of African Americans so they cannot attain their own liberation. Elijah Muhammad, Malcolm X, Warith Deen Mohammed, and Louis Farrakhan viewed "Islam," in its various forms and in general terms, as the appropriate vehicle to raise the status of African Americans—enculture them, beautify them, ennoble them—and give them the motivational, ideological, and metaphysical grounding to push toward fullness with regard to their material existence. This is not to suggest, however, that these leaders agreed on the nature of "Islam" or on the means—social or symbolic—by which to accomplish this. Their perspectives and practices have been diverse, and they have been critical—sometimes implicitly and other times explicitly—of one another.

Without question, the NOI has been only partially successful in its grand project to reimagine and (re)form African Americans. What Elijah Muhammad, Malcolm X, Warith Deen Mohammed, and Louis Farrakhan share is, in a sense, a poststructuralist praxis that regards the dominant structures of white supremacy as fluid and socially constituted, not as natural and given. Black bodies are *recalcitrant*, as all bodies are, and they resist being fully totalized or wholly determined by any social system. And black bodies in the NOI have been particularly obstreperous, always out-of-place socially and symbolically and thus especially dangerous to the maintenance, perpetuity, and reproduction of white supremacy. The absence of reflexivity—or strategic denial and obfuscation—among those who benefit from whiteness does not, and perhaps cannot, admit that their responses are tied to a cosmology of the naturalness of white domination. They blame the victims of oppression rather than systems of oppression that structure the world hierarchically and that axiologically privilege white over the larger world of color as *given*. Thus, they misrecognize the NOI as the problem—or worse, they name it *black supremacist*, as if such a system exists.

The dominant discourse of whiteness that functions as "truth" to keep the "lower classes" in-place and that posits the social order as natural and desirable may best be understood as a form of *symbolic violence*.[6] Moreover, a long history of antiblack violence; slavery; lynching; inferiority discourse; and laws, machinations, and practices have made the current order appear inherently normal and insurmountable. The NOI has apprehended the discourses and practices of white supremacy not as fixed, natural, or given but as structures that can be disrupted and overcome by finding new meaning for African Americans via transcendental symbols such as UFOs, extraterrestrials, and heroic figures, or via practices that give them a new sense of being and physical vitality. It has also given the Nation of Islam a sense of transcendence against an American history that casts black bodies as pure immanence.

Nonetheless, the ways in which the NOI has reconstituted bodies in the face of seemingly overwhelming obstacles—the bodies that it has constructed as ideal and how that these bodies have functioned in relation to other African Americans—are enormously problematic. The NOI, like many social institutions, limits and restricts some forms of individual thought—that is, ideas that do not support its values and maintenance. These institutions, with their self-policing conventions and thought worlds, legitimate themselves through naturalizing principles that ultimately are located in the body as an analogy. (Recall Warith Deen Mohammed's idea of the body as a model for society and government in chapter 4.) Such embodied principles serve as a form of social control where the majority rules.[7]

In response to the perceived need to (re)form black bodies in the face of whiteness, the NOI ontologized blackness and constructed black bodies through resignified symbols of white supremacy and a creative conglomeration of practices and discourses that, in effect, produce an ambiguous and indeterminate class dynamic. The significance of this dynamic cannot be overstated. The NOI's class system was nascent and underdeveloped, yet its discourses and practices were efficacious when it came to deciding, for instance, who would be most prominent in its leadership class. Importantly,

I do not argue that class is a category that can parade as universal against a background of slavery and labor in which black people *were* the economic medium of exchange; they were traded as capital, rather than classed by it. Rather, I am deploying the work of Pierre Bourdieu. Bourdieu's monumental social theory in *Distinction: A Social Critique of the Judgement of Taste* and *Outline of a Theory of Practice* offers conceptual language about this classed body and how it functions to structure discourses directed not at white bodies, but at black bodies within and outside the NOI.[8] That is, the NOI has very creatively navigated the pitfalls and problems of race, but not those of class: it has reproduced systems that rank and order relationships of authority. The NOI, then, has deployed a classist gaze outward toward poor black people and African American Christians, in particular, and an inward gaze that has functioned to establish the bodies that would be the most prominent among the leadership within the group. In short, rather than resolve problems of race to which it was reacting, the NOI transmuted issues of race into issues of class. Hence, black bodies in the NOI have been classed and structured by each of the four NOI leaders highlighted in this book.

Elijah Muhammad's *ideal black embodied economy*, introduced in chapter 2, was his way to counter white supremacy and its relationship to his belief that it disfigured black people and made them ugly. The problem is that this body and these conversations did violence to other black people: they collapsed African American complexity and diversity, ontologized an ideal black body as if it corresponded to something *real* in the world, and legitimized class distinctions based on the approximation of bodies to this ideal. As a result, they rendered particular black embodiments problematic and left unmarked and stable intersecting—white supremacist, classist, sexist, homophobic, ableist—systems of oppression. In short, they made a qualitative *distinction* between NOI bodies and other black bodies. This can generally be seen in the thought not only of Elijah Muhammad, but also of Malcolm X, Warith Deen Mohammed, and Louis Farrakhan.

Elijah Muhammad's Ideal Black Embodied Economy: Bourdieu's *Habitus* and Classed Bodies in the Nation of Islam

Muhammad's black embodied economy was in operation in all of the four moments of the NOI. As a symbol of institutional values, it functioned to influence the nature of who was prominent within the organization, particularly with respect to its leaders. The conversation within the chapters indicates when and where elements of Muhammad's bodily matrix appeared. The characteristics that make up this ideal economy can be understood as Muslim, male, masculine, physically healthy, adult, "middle class," heterosexual, mystical-esoteric, light-complexioned, and intelligent/"gifted." Clearly, President Barack Obama embodied many of these features, though not "Muslim." One could suggest that this economy functioned in African American communities to garner such strong support and intense loyalty that it served to shield Muhammad from activists' and scholars' critiques of his policies and practices. Many features of this economy, when aggregated and embodied, signify authentic blackness for some, which may help to explain the racial piety evoked by Obama regardless of the effects his policies have had on African Americans and marginalized groups. Most assuredly, this bodily matrix has been important in the NOI.

What is effectively eschewed and marginalized is a body constituted by any combination of features from the default, or "lower-class," black embodied economy, which can be viewed, conversely, as Christian, female, effeminate male, dark-complexioned, accommodationist/"integrationist," working class/poor, disabled, and so on. This contrast serves as the basis for an exploration of the demarcation between valued embodiments within the NOI and bodies that were castigated and disparaged, which existed primarily outside of the NOI. To this end, Bourdieu's notion of *habitus* theorizes how such features become embodied and why they are always classed.

The grand vision that concerns Bourdieu is to ascertain how social systems replicate—that is, how societies reproduce themselves. He concludes that replication occurs at the level of the body. His notion of habitus theorizes that, through nondiscursive bodily techniques of social reproduction, individuals acquire a set of dispositions, including habits, tastes, and cultural practices, that become second nature and seemingly unconscious, and in this way a society's values and norms are transmitted and transposed to successive iterations of the culture.[9] For Bourdieu, these *embodied* dispositions are always classed in the sense that habitus will benefit those in the society who hold power and authority, given that they function to duplicate the established social order, particularly rising in its effectiveness in concert with the degree of cultural homogeneity.[10] That is to say, the more cultural systems share characteristics, the easier they are to reproduce.

In the context of the United States broadly, Bourdieu, I would argue, would concede that habitus—embodied dispositions—is not only classed but also gendered and raced, given that gender and race are co-constitutive of, or are both essential elements that occur jointly in, how human beings are generally recognized and categorized. According to Judith Bradford and Crispin Sartwell, "Race and gender cannot be compared because they are in fact inextricable."[11] They understand both race and gender as political processes that consign bodies to social categories that structure them into political, economic, and other positionalities, and they note that race and "gender" intersect in all bodies in which the human taxonomy is assigned.

That is, the hierarchical order of society, which privileges some men, is socially replicated on and in the bodies of the members of a given society through various techniques that constitute habitus. Social homogeneity ensures concealment or misrecognition of power relations that are involved in the processes theoretically, given that the hierarchical order of society then appears "everyday" and naturally occurring.[12] This is why oppressive social environments are resistant to diversity of bodies and ideas: presumed sameness and assent are necessary conditions for perfectly reproducing social norms and social arrangements along the lines of race, gender, class, and so on.

In social circumstances that are much more complex and diverse, it would seem, the power relations that serve to establish classed, gendered, and racialized habitus might then be in jeopardy of apprehension because their complexity might allow difference to be *seen*. That is to say, when difference is introduced within a particular set of social arrangements, it allows for the possibility that one might recognize the power relations that were at work and that constituted the arrangements in the first place. Diversity, complexity, and difference are significant, therefore, because they heighten the potential for the recognition of power relations that can potentially be disrupted. Disruption of the bodies that were constituted by way of white supremacy is what the NOI was attempting to accomplish. With respect to Muhammad's ideal black embodied economy, conversely, the NOI reproduced hierarchy and nascent classes, with those whose bodies more closely approximated the bodily economy being the guarantors or leadership class.

Habitus, then, is physical and symbolic, since it reflects a particular social system or collective such as the NOI. Simultaneously, it is inhabited as the material locus of the self. That said, a habitus becomes embodied (or "in-bodied") through what Bourdieu calls *bodily hexis*, a complex of modalities of bodily comportment, motor functions, postures, behaviors, facial expressions, tones of voice, and styles of speech, along "with a host of social meanings."[13] That is, habitus is *in-corporated* through experience and imitation. The experiential nature of bodily hexis accounts for its durability.[14] This also explains why NOI rituals such as dietary codes, physical activities, dress codes, and so on, were so important: reproducing bodies occurs, in part, through inculcation and mimicry. Bourdieu suggests that bodily hexis begins with childhood imitations of adults within a given culture. This implies that it could also apply to neophytes or new converts of any age to a religious, cultural, or social system. It also suggests that successful social replication, or the strength of the durability of such replication, may depend on inculcating the values and norms of a society in a person at a young age so that the order of the society and its practices are more easily normalized and naturalized. While I could conceive of such a process working with new converts to a religion, ensuring their misrecognition of power relations—and, hence, the construction of a religious body that reflects the religious collectivity and cosmology—would seem to be more difficult and potentially less durable.

Nevertheless, the body for Bourdieu is a political body in the sense that it is produced by unspoken, undisputed, and "taken-for-granted" values that are imposed on dominated classes by those who rule. Bourdieu calls these tacitly posited suppositions and taxonomic systems of classification that appear as self-evident *doxa*.[15] Doxa become epistemologically legitimated by the *lower classes* through *symbolic violence*, which obscures the power relations that allow it to operate indiscernibly.[16] That is to say, the masses accept *as given* the values, perceptions, and categories of thought imposed on them by the guarantors of the culture or leadership class and acquiesce to the desired hierarchical social order (partly because it is seen as "natural"), which allows for the perpetuation of the structures of action via the habitus. I would add that religious authority plays a part in symbolic violence in that sanction from gods or other divine beings functions to legitimize discourses, practices, and social arrangements that privilege some bodies and not others.

Subversive speech and practices that reconstructed black corporeality may have been well intentioned and partially successful reformative ventures, but they were also susceptible to the power dynamics of social reproduction, centered on and in bodies, that produced racialized and classed hierarchical modes of being in the larger culture. Indeed, it is strategies such as these, whose primary intent may be subversive to the dominant order, that invariably reproduce and re-create the very inequality they seek to destabilize and eliminate.[17] This is not to suggest the NOI produced a system of marginalization commensurate with the intense level of enduring violence and oppression or anything close to the well-developed, centuries-old global dynamics of white supremacy; rather, in response to white supremacy, the NOI reproduced its basis for distinguishing and valuing certain bodies as structured along lines that Bourdieu would understand as social *classes*. Such classes are conceived in terms of social relations, generally, rather than relations of production and economics. These groups may share the same habitus that represents a set of dispositions that result from similar material conditions of existence and conditioning.[18] Thus, the NOI has done what we have seen many colonized groups do: institutionalize, toward one another, many of the practices of their experience of having been dominated. Colorism, in which people of color whose complexions are viewed as closest to whiteness hold greater social positions or status, is just one example.

The inevitability of such reproduction of inequity is due to several factors. First, habitus are always classed. Further, in the absence of sufficient sociocultural complexity that would enable the recognition of habitus by the rank and file, relative homogeneity like that found in the NOI, which seeks to constrain and control aspects of its members' activities, limits the cognition of its members and hence the potential to disrupt of social replication.[19] Moreover, misrecognition by the membership of the arbitrariness of the principles that serve to legitimate leadership domination—and, hence, the concealment of social stratification and reproduction—is attained through *symbolic violence*, so that members come to see the order as given and natural, and even desirable.[20] The principles that are used to "naturalize" the social order are generally located by analogy in the body to conceal them from recognition. In *How Institutions Think*, Douglas explains the logic of analogies directly:

> The incipient institution needs some stabilizing principle to stop its premature demise. That stabilizing principle is the naturalization of social classifications. There needs to be an analogy by which the formal structure of a crucial set of social relations is found in the physical world, or in the supernatural world, or in eternity, anywhere as long as it is not seen as

a socially contrived arrangement. When the analogy is applied back and forth from one set [*sic*] social relations to another form and from these back to nature, its recurring formal structure becomes easily recognized and endowed with self-validating truth. . . . The institutions lock into the structure of an analogy from the body.[21]

Elijah Muhammad, of course, appealed to the Divine as the spokesperson or Messenger for God and the natural.

Muhammad appealed to agriculture metaphors and the physical body to stabilize and legitimate social relations between men and women in the NOI and to validate male dominance when he asserted that women are a "man's field to produce his nation." That is to say, biology and "nature" indicate that men are active and aggressive and women are the passive recipients of male activity and desire; as "fields," women are men's to traverse and manage, albeit by enthusiastic consent of and participation by women.[22] Finally, such social replication and reproduction via the experience of the violence and discourses of oppression is deeply sedimented in the bodies and psyches of African Americans and other oppressed communities, making it challenging, though not impossible, to curtail them.

These strategies as found in the NOI ultimately hierarchize and order bodies as what Judith Butler calls "bodies that matter."[23] They structure, normalize, and police the bodily habitus of the marginal—in this case, those who do *not* closely approximate the ideal bodily economy within the NOI and those who *cannot* attain the ideal because they are outside the NOI. Such strategies, as exemplified in the religious dimensions of the NOI, are often practices such as rituals, diets, and clothing styles, which ultimately seek to structure the body according to a rigid, inflexible, and normalizing economy.

As daunting as it may be, inequality does not need to be reproduced by historically oppressed groups that are struggling for self-determination. Disruption of inequality is possible by recognizing that social systems are fluid and constructed and that they therefore can be overcome. Disrupting inequality is also possible by changing the field of relations and practice. A *field* is a system of social positions and valued cultural knowledge arranged in power relationships in specific social spaces. Changing the field creates new forms of capital and modalities of practice, meaning, and value. In this case, being religious—or the social position of "Messenger" or "Muslim," for example—offers a new social economy that is potentially capable of subverting racist and hierarchical modalities in (other) social arenas. The

NOI changed the field from a more general social one to a religious life-style. Class expresses itself in lifestyle, which the NOI frames as "Islamic" or "Muslim," that is coded aesthetically across preferences or tastes (e.g., food, music, fashion).[24] Again, such class distinctions are not dependent on quantifiable factors such as income or wealth: that is the difference between what I am arguing (that class is a function of embodiment in the NOI) and the notions of C. Eric Lincoln, E. U. Essien-Udom, Lawrence Mamiya, Edward Curtis, and others (who theorize the NOI as a vehicle for class mobility and as imitating white middle-class practices).[25] Such discussions of class are helpful but ultimately limited because they view class in, well, classical terms of income, education, and prestige. Various forms of capital (especially cultural and symbolic capital) that construct classes are given meaning and weight within the particular field or arena in which they operate. Changing the field to one of lifestyle within the religious organization, according to Bourdieu, would cause the value of the forms of capital to be determined within that particular arena.[26] Thus, class is always embodied and, in its sense for Bourdieu, not necessarily associated with the traditional markers. Where conflicts existed due to the co-optation of practices and values traditionally associated with middle-class white America, the NOI ritualized those practices and values within the field of religion to obscure their origins and claim them as Muslim and hence as "black."

In addition, disruption requires self-awareness and acute attention how an experience of hegemonic white supremacy might have affected the manner in which oppressed people see themselves (i.e., the extent to which they have internalized white supremacy). This also means paying attention to how power has been and is used in forms of domination.[27] Reverend Albert B. Cleage is critical of the NOI in this sense and says in *Black Christian Nationalism: New Directions for the Black Church*: "Under the same circumstances the Black man [*sic*] *will* act the same way. Some day the circumstances will be the same unless we create a community in which Black people can establish a different value system. The Black Nation is important because we do not want to become the 'beast' that the white man has become. We want to secure power within a communal framework that will enable us to preserve our humanity."[28] Cleage demonstrates this type of awareness in his quest to build a black Christian nation when he speaks about power in the context of how white people have used it and how black people, being no different from whites ontologically, must use it. Finally, disruption of marginalization necessitates the deployment of counter-discourses, values, and practices that not only resist the social reproduction of white supremacy as a form of oppression but also defend against responses to racism that conceal themselves in other, coconstitutive forms of oppression such as sexism, heterosexism, and indeed, classism. This is the major point that Cleage was making. Hence, while the NOI successfully recognized categories as fluid and changed the field of relations and practices, it failed to recognize the possibility that it had internalized white supremacist frameworks or to deploy counter-practices against them and against related discourses and practices of oppression.

God's ("White") Body: Class Discourse and the Aesthetics of Mythology

The bodies that most approximated Muhammad's ideal black religious body and how these bodies appeared and functioned in the social world were grounded in the Nation of Islam's mythology of Yakub and God's own phenotypically "white" body, which was also mythicized in the Yakub saga. In addition, such aesthetic judgment or taste (e.g., preferences in food, attire, etc.) functioned to mark the class distinction between the NOI and other black bodies, even as it determined significance within the Nation of Islam. Operating out of a Bourdieuian notion of class rather than a Marxist one ameliorates the need for quantitative analysis, which is of limited use and not of interest for my purposes. For Bourdieu, class is a sum of cultural capital, which can take the form of general knowledge and cultured tastes and material possessions that are valued in a field of practice.[29] Likewise, the naturalizing, normalizing, and ordering of the body, both physical and symbolic, as Muhammad did through speeches, mythology, theology, and rituals make up what it meant to be a sublime black religious body in the NOI.[30] The categories of Muhammad's economy can be aggregated and represented generally as religion, color/complexion, class, and gender/sexuality; thus, these factors were expressed in the life of the NOI as forms of intraracial and intrareligious consciousness and, further, they distinguished the NOI hierarchically and qualitatively from other black bodies, such as poor people and Christians. These social markers can be seen in the lives and thought of all four moments of the NOI that are outlined throughout this book.

Through its mythology, theology, and rituals, the NOI reproduced a system that resembles the classifications and restrictions of white supremacy as it was attempting to reform the lower-class habitus tied to violent practices of racialization and discourses of black inferiority.[31] Paulette Pierce and Brackette F. Williams's "And Your Prayers Shall Be Answered through the Womb of a Woman: Insurgent Masculine Redemption and the Nation of Islam" concludes something similar when the authors argue that the myths and gender norms of the NOI "bear stunning resemblance to the most cherished notions of race, manifest destiny, gender precepts, and bourgeois ideals of (White) American nationalism, particularly during the Victorian period."[32] Bodies were constructed according to the NOI's own cosmology as found in the mythology of Yakub, and this mythology ordered bodies and social relations within the Nation of Islam, with respect to religion, gender, sexuality, class, color, and so on. This reproduction of inequality is analogous to other strategies that have been employed by "middle-class" black people by means of a primary function of religious ideology. For example, Evelyn Brooks Higginbotham claims in *Righteous Discontent: The Women's Movement in the Black Baptist Church, 1880–1920* that many black women in Baptist churches employed what she calls a "politics of respectability," interpreted as a strategy to counter the white supremacist normative depictions of black people in general as inferior, immoral, and uncouth.[33] This notion of a politics of respectability is related to the theory or cult of domesticity—developed by white men, in this case—given that such strategies functioned not only as tools to police women's bodies but also to mark particular bodies as having middle-class status (i.e., "Victorian"). Furthermore, "domestic" space functioned as a marker that allowed for the policing of bodies through excessive ordering or tidying.[34] As a result, African Americans invariably altered and monitored their own bodies and behavior so that they conformed to what they believed whites would deem respectable. At the same time, they policed and sanitized the bodies and practices of lower-class African Americans through morality discourses.[35]

Final Thoughts

The overarching problem, however, is that the NOI failed to take seriously its own practices and therefore appeared aesthetically as black composites of bodies constructed through white discourses. Some of the more problematic aspects were the ideas of "gender" and sexuality that the NOI attempted to police and control in its practices and discourses. Farrakhan comes the closest to reconciling the matter. Moreover, the NOI's critique of African American Christianity, while sometimes valid with respect to its social analysis, obscures a significant part of the Nation of Islam's origins, which it borrowed from black churches. In short, because of the absence of reflexivity and institutional structures that would allow it to avoid becoming the oppressor that it despised, the NOI came to be an organization that policed bodies within the group and in African American communities in unhealthful ways.

Having recoded terrifying experiences of racism in terms of class-consciousness, the NOI, in its attempt to (re)form black bodies and reimagine black origins (e.g., through transcendental symbols of extraterrestrials and UFOs), produced hierarchies in its discourses and practices. These "classes" were stabilized by the ritualizing and performance of the aesthetics of mythology found in the cosmic narrative of Yakub and grounded in the body of Master Fard Muhammad, whose physiognomy was "white." Therefore, leadership and prominence in the NOI was, and continues to be, determined partially by proximity to the ideal. This ideal can be seen functioning throughout the life of the NOI. The durability of Muhammad's ideal was due to the fact that it was mythologically located in God's body. The body was sacralized but not sufficiently criticized and deconstructed as virulent by the leadership of the NOI.

Evidence indicates that implicit in such an economy is its own taxonomy and its own notion of "dirt," which is embedded in its own mythology; further, this "lower-class" economy may represent what is *dangerous* and potentially polluting to its own cosmologies. In the end, the NOI, via Master Fard Muhammad, created its own classificatory system that lacked the sophistication and fluidity to account for the enormous complexity and diversity among African Americans. Many of the people it claimed to represent and "save" were marginalized by discourses. Ensconced in its own institutional commitments, the Nation of Islam was perhaps unable to see some of its own practices as oppressive. It was unable to apprehend within it the influences and practices of white supremacy.

What was revolutionary was the profound sense of pessimism that Anglo values and their benefits were unattainable as "white," which the NOI quite obviously could never be. What was exceedingly creative was the manner in which the NOI disconnected Anglo values from their original signification, which was attached to white bodies, and redeployed and ritualized them to obscure their origins and, hence, any ideological conflicts. With the co-optation, nonetheless, came the problematic issue of class discrimination, regardless of how indiscreetly class functioned and how ambiguously it was developed. What is also quite radical was that the NOI co-opted white Anglo ideals of civilizationism as resistance to the negative meanings that were attached to black bodies and gave them a new name: "Muslim."

WHEELS, WOMBS, AND WOMEN
AN EPILOGUE

Research about and by women scholars at the intersection of race, gender, and religion has expanded over the past few years. It ranges from works that question "the promise of patriarchy" to those that explore the experiences of Muslims of color and hip-hop in America.[1] In addition, scholarship over the past two decades on women in the Nation of Islam (NOI) has been helpful in that it has created a space in which to establish the primary sources that women in the NOI were writing and publishing, what their contributions to the NOI and African American communities were, and how they engaged with the culture and practices of the NOI. For example, in *American Muslim Women: Negotiating Race, Class, and Gender within the Ummah,* Jamillah Karim "portrays Muslim women with a richness and detail that reveal what it means to negotiate a religious sisterhood against America's race and class hierarchies."[2] Furthermore, published works have been considerate regarding the perspectives of the subjects and the language that they assign to their own reality. What the preceding chapters of this book and my previous work point to are critical areas for future research—areas that heretofore have garnered scant and inadequate attention. This epilogue signals directions for future research that I hope others will pursue.

My push is for a fuller engagement of women in the NOI and embodiment, which simply cannot be accomplished without understanding the significance of Louis Farrakhan's UFO experience and UFOs in the NOI generally, especially since the Nation of Islam regards UFOs as being of the utmost importance, as NOI member Ilia Rashad Muhammad's *UFOs and the Nation of Islam: The Source, Proof, and Reality of the Wheels* indicates.[3] Moreover, much of the work that engages the subject of women in the Nation of Islam fails to give significant attention to the religious meaning of women in the NOI, embodiment, and the study of religion more generally. Perhaps because it wants to present viewpoints fairly, it lacks interpretive and critical vigor. To this end, psychoanalysis—especially object relations theory—and womanist and black feminist scholarship can be helpful.

While I find value in most books, articles, dissertations, and essays about the NOI, the most suggestive material, for my purposes, has been Sonsyrea Tate's *Little X: Growing Up in the Nation of Islam* (2005); multiple works by Ula Yvette Taylor, including "As-Salaam Alaikum, My Sister: The Honorable Elijah Muhammad and the Women Who Followed Him" (1998), "Elijah Muhammad's Nation of Islam: Separatism, Regendering, and a Secular Approach to Black Power after Malcolm X" (2012), and *The Promise of Patriarchy: Women and the Nation of Islam* (2017); and Carolyn Moxley Rouse's *Engaged Surrender: African American Women and Islam* (2004).[4] Tate gives a courageous first-person account of being a little girl who grew up in the NOI that helps to give nuance to the many apologetic accounts of women who defend the NOI, Muhammad, and Farrakhan. Rouse's book is limited on this subject, however, since she is most interested in Sunni women, many of whom held prior membership in the NOI. Most important, although both Taylor and Rouse make the crucial move of acknowledging the importance of embodiment, which is significant for scholarly understandings of women in the NOI, they do not offer sustained and theoretical engagement with it.[5] No other work makes the connection among wheels, wombs, and women as essential to apprehending the religious meaning of NOI women and the context for their agency.

The appeal of some of these works is that they attempt to highlight women's own voices from limited and repetitive sources such as *Muhammad Speaks*—for instance, the chapter titled "Raising Her Voice" in Bayyinah S. Jeffries's *A Nation Can Rise No Higher Than Its Women: African American Muslim Women in the Movement for Black Self-Determination, 1950–1975* (2014) and her very closely related essay, "Raising Her Voice: Writings by, for, and about Women in *Muhammad Speaks* Newspaper, 1961–1975 (2012)."[6] In addition, one finds engagements with the *Final Call* newspaper and other NOI newspapers and publications—for instance, Dawn-Marie Gibson's "Ebony Muhammad's *Hurt2Healing* Magazine and Contemporary Nation Women" (2017), which attempts to look at one magazine producer and draw conclusions about greater potential trends among women in the NOI.[7] None of these sources engages the topic of women's embodiment substantially; nor, oddly enough, do many significantly engage the matter of religion.

That is, much of this work makes sweeping claims that are beyond the strength of the interview data that many of these publications and subsequent dissertations employ. For example, in the early 1990s, Cynthia S'thembile West, after interviewing only sixteen local women who had been members of the NOI in Newark, New Jersey, in the 1960s, concluded: "Through the promotion and teaching of African history, and that blackness is something to be proud of, Black Muslim women laid a foundation for the Afrocentric movement today."[8] This conclusion is unsubstantiated, and this is one such claim of many. Kathy Makeda Bennett Muhammad similarly asserts, without evidentiary support, that "during chattel slavery, millions of Muslim slaves were imported to the U.S. [*sic*] to work on the plantations of the South."[9]

More specifically, previous scholarship has been incomplete by either failing to give attention to the fuller body of work on women in the NOI or by truncating the matter and stopping at the descriptive—which, again, is mostly monotonous. That is to say, this scholarship has failed to give theoretical consideration to the meaning of women's embodiment in the NOI. The descriptive nature of the work is the primary reason for this restriction. However, what I read as disciplinary hegemonies that regard religious studies and theory of religion as negligible is evident as well. Rarely do the authors of these works cite scholars whose primary training and work are in the study of religion. This dynamic is curious since the NOI is first and foremost a religious group.

While this book is about embodiment in the NOI and what that means to the religion and its discourses and practices, it offers an interpretation of gender—of both men and women (and implied nonbinary identities)—in the thought of various thinkers in the movement. Despite the increasingly productive scholarship that engages the subject of women in the Nation of Islam, much of it is, as noted earlier, is descriptive, repetitive, and defensive of the NOI. West's unpublished dissertation, "Nation Builders: Female Activism in Nation of Islam, 1960–1970" (1994), exerts a great deal of force by functioning as a model that almost all subsequent works follow.[10] Those works include her article "Revisiting Female Activism in the 1960s: The Newark Branch of the Nation of Islam" (1996), a condensed version of her "Nation Builders" project, and the follow-up essay, "Take Two: Nation of Islam Women Fifty Years After Civil Rights" (2012).[11]

The available literature describes NOI women in areas such as education, domestic life, business, and security, as well as their sartorial and aesthetic interests, from a variety of sources to illustrate their agency, reiterating to a certain extent West's project, including her method of ethnography. For example, in *Women of the Nation: Between Black Protest and Sunny Islam* (2014), Dawn-Marie Gibson and Jamillah Karim purport to represent women in their own voices and context.[12] But, as I argue later, there is a larger context in which "women's voices" and activities must be interpreted, and ignoring that context is what skews research toward caretaking approaches that point to a genealogy of repetition that structures and constrains subsequent projects.

A few more recent doctoral projects may be seen in relation to West's dissertation and the larger critique being made here. The projects are understandably self-protective in nature, given their relationships to the NOI and to West's endeavor as a model. The first is "An Analysis of Womanhood: The Portrayal of Women in the Nation of Islam Newspaper: *The Final Call* 1982–1995" (2002), by Toni Y. Sims (Muhammad).[13] It is unclear exactly what its thesis is, but the dissertation seems to suggest that the lack of attention to women in the NOI has to do with scholarly and media foci on "orthodox Islam," "Judeo-Christian" perspectives in analyses, and the NOI's "radical" ideology. Sims thinks the *Final Call* presents a more accurate view of women in the NOI, since it discusses issues such as their education, family life, career advancement, and leadership.[14] She contends that the thrust of the newspaper is that the success of the Nation of Islam depends on women and highlights their "nontraditional roles," such as having voice. Therefore, neither *Final Call* nor Farrakhan is sexist, the work contends. Of course, suggesting that women are necessary for a nation to "rise" does not, in and of itself, deflect sexism. I offer a different perspective in the next section.

Likewise, Bennett Muhammad's doctoral project, "Humble Warrioress: Women in the Nation of Islam: A Comparative Study 1930–1975 and 1978–2000" (2008), reports building on the "theoretical contributions" of West, Molefi Asante, and others.[15] While the dissertation's thesis is ambiguous, Bennett Muhammad contends, against the weight of recent scholarship, that "previous research is miniscule and extremely androcentric" without engaging or even naming the work. She also implies that scholars who study the NOI should be Muslim.[16]

Jeffries likewise claims originality in *A Nation Can Rise No Higher Than Its Women* when she reports that "this book reveals an unacknowledged agency of previously invisible and nameless Muslim women, as demonstrated in both their private roles as mothers and wives and their public roles as leaders, instructors, business owners."[17] Jeffries's book focuses on selective sources, remarking, without justification, that she chose to engage only "major" works on the NOI.[18] It remains unclear what this means but does lead to the exclusion of many published works cited here. Jeffries focuses her argument, instead, against Taylor, a black feminist scholar, claiming that she follows "her male counterparts in positioning the NOI women as easily duped and less important than their male counterparts."[19] It is a dubious claim, which may explain why these "male counterparts" are never mentioned. Scholarly studies by men on women in the NOI were absent when Taylor published her article in 1998, and very few have written on women in the NOI since then.[20] It is imperative, henceforth, that scholars take up the challenge of addressing this deficiency in the literature.

Part of what makes the literature apologetic is the idea of *reform* in the NOI that seems so positive on the surface. We see this valorization in the works of West, Sims, and Jeffries, and we see it reflected in the positive testimonies of women in Gibson's and Karim's studies, and those of so many others, which they leave largely critically unmarked. This is not true of Paulette Pierce and Brackette F. Williams's "And Their Prayers Shall Be Answered through the Womb of a Woman: Insurgent Masculine Redemption and the Nation of Islam" (1996). Pierce and Williams tracked the notion of reform genealogically to interpretations of ideas that appear in the work of the sociologist E. Franklin Frazier. This notion of reforming a people is inevitably sexist and classist, they contend, since "for Frazerians, the reform of the

Black woman and the improvement of Black family through the creation of proper bourgeois domesticity was the *sine qua non* of racial redemption in U.S. society."[21] What they also show is that such reform narratives are not necessarily creative but are part of larger narratives that circulated in African American communities as part of class(ed) discourses. What also remains unmarked critically in the literature is the idea that for Elijah Muhammad and Louis Farrakhan, who follows him, the logic of reform is significantly, but not exclusively located in women's bodies. As Farrakhan says, it requires "re-building and reforming the woman of that people."[22]

Farrakhan, UFOs, and Black Women's Bodies as Metaphysical Spaces

Let me be explicit: what this book and my work on women and embodiment in the NOI show is an undeniable connection—missed by most scholars—among UFOs; what Farrakhan, following Muhammad, calls the Mother Wheel and the Mother Plane; and black women's bodies. Specifically, wheels, wombs, and women are inextricably linked, and one must give theoretical attention to the religious meaning of women's embodiment and UFOs to make sense of the numerous discourses and symbols in the present-day NOI and its iterations. In fact, Farrakhan's most significant religious narrative, expressed most clearly in chapter 5 of this book and in my article "The Meaning of 'Mother' in Louis Farrakhan's 'Mother Wheel': Race, Gender, and Sexuality in the Cosmology of the Nation of Islam's UFO" (2012), signals the connections among gender, women's bodies, and the ultimate meaning of religion and black embodiment in the NOI.[23] Yet the article has been all but ignored in scholarship on NOI women and embodiment and their meaning for Farrakhan's NOI religion. Two essays by the Jewish studies scholar David Halperin, a professor emeritus at the University of North Carolina, posted on his *Diary of a UFO Investigator* blog are thoughtful exceptions.[24]

Edward E. Curtis IV offers another essay that cites the article in which I make the connection between UFOs and "gender" in the NOI. I agree with his contention that most works on the NOI erroneously deal with it as a form of political organization rather than a religion. Curtis makes reference to my article in his "Science and Technology in Elijah Muhammad's Nation of Islam: Astrophysical Desire, Genetic Engineering, UFOs, White Apocalypse, and Black Resurrection" (2015).[25] Yet I have given much more substantial scholarly attention to the intersection of race, UFOs, embodiment, and metaphysics than his article suggests. What I argue here and elsewhere is that UFOs are essential to an interpretation of what motivates the work of the NOI, including gender. In fact, "The Meaning of 'Mother' in Louis Farrakhan's 'Mother Wheel'" concludes that "the Mother Wheel as a form of UFO not only offers hermeneutical possibilities, it is a *hermeneutical necessity*. Inattention to this point in scholarly work . . . calls into question all supposed interpretations of [Farrakhan's] religious experience and threaten[s] to render the Mother Wheel mundane—or worse, 'gibberish.'"[26] It also calls into question interpretations of NOI cosmology, including implications for race, gender, class, women, and beyond. What I mean by this is that scholarly works on the NOI that do not explore the ways that UFOs connect to Elijah Muhammad, Farrakhan, women, race, and so many matters that seem mundane are truncated. Subsequently, I give significant attention to UFOs in "From Mistress to Mother: The Religious Life and Transformation of Tynnetta Muhammad in the Nation of Islam" (2013), the first published essay-length treatment of Mother Tynnetta; "Hidden Away: Esotericism and Gnosticism in Elijah Muhammad's Nation of Islam" (2013); and "Mathematical Theology: Numerology in the Religious Thought of Tynnetta Muhammad and Louis Farrakhan" (2015).[27]

Once more, my argument about future research on NOI women's embodiment as the obvious direction to which this book points is that the meaning of black women's bodies emerges from a close reading of the works by Farrakhan, the leader of the NOI and the purveyor of truth for his community (and ostensibly the world), on the subject and many of his speeches about African American women. It is in the religious thought that appears in these speeches and writings (often transcribed speeches) that Farrakhan enacts a metaphysical reduction of the meaning of African American NOI women's embodiment to wombs.[28] This is, in part, why I have argued for a nuanced perspective on men in the NOI that I call *metaphysical masculinity*. Indeed, women's bodies are structured as metaphysical spaces for the reproduction of the black nation and the possibility for the creation and reproduction of metaphorical "Farrakhans." Farrakhan illustrates this in the speech "Why Do They Blame Farrakhan for the Assassination of Malcolm X?" In it, he claims that the reason to respect women is precisely because they have wombs that can reproduce men: "But your wife, though not your mother, has a womb that you should revere and honor, because that sacred chamber is going to reproduce you, to keep you alive on earth when you are gone."[29]

In what perhaps gives greater support to my contention, he mentions "wombs" no fewer than *twenty* times in a speech given on June 25, 1994, in the lead-up to the Million Man March.[30] In it, he claims: "When you respect God, you must respect woman because the womb of a woman is a place of sacredness, and it should be reverenced, held in awe, and even a thought—not of worshipping women, but women should be held in awe, because of the majesty of her womb. When God and woman cooperate, Jesus comes forth, Moses comes forth, Abraham comes forth, greatness comes forth, when God and woman cooperate."[31] And Farrakhan comes forth. He positions himself intimately with respect to women's embodiment. His body holds the key to what women mean. Women's bodies are read through his. As Pierce and Williams note, "In these terms, NOI also 'borrowed' from the Western cultural tradition the mythologic for the concealment of female generativity/power, transforming it into a property of the male body."[32] Therefore, men's bodies become "father and mother" as the wombs of the black nation become "absorbed" by father figures such as Farrakhan and those father figures become the "real women/womb whence life comes."[33]

That is to say, Farrakhan erases much of the material meaning of women's embodied pursuits, activities that are the overwhelming focus of research on women in the NOI, which almost without exception lacks explicit attention to the body.[34] In short, he imbues their discursive and metaphorical bodies with religious meaning that negates and objectifies their material bodies, and he subjects their material activities to the religious meaning that is dependent on both him and UFOs (i.e., wheels). In short, Farrakhan and the NOI androcize and mythicize wombs; the earlier quotations can be read as valorization of wombs as the raison d'être to "respect" women incidentally. Pierce and Williams may not apprehend the relationship of these matters to UFOs, but they are acutely aware of the contestation over black women's wombs.[35] Such statements are exorbitant and superfluous and can be found in many of Farrakhan's discourses on women.[36]

In other words, the significance of the activities of NOI women to which scholars point—as educational leaders and regarding their cleanliness and health, diets, and attire—serve only to constitute, support, and stabilize their bodies as sites of religious meaning and vessels of containment for their wombs. I pointed this out in previous work when I said that "Farrakhan argues that the womb (a recurring theme for him) is the sacred location that is the genesis of good or bad that happens in black communities."[37] Farrakhan is fixated on black women's wombs and, hence, the control of African American women's bodies. This is an extension of

Elijah Muhammad's discourses of which the controlling metaphor was an agrarian representation of women's bodies as "fields" of production for African American men. In her article "Nation Women's Engagement and Resistance in the *Muhammad Speaks* Newspaper" (2015), Gibson claims that "Nation women remain an invisible cohort in scholarly treatments of Elijah Muhammad's Nation of Islam."[38] The article cites exceptions to this in the first footnote, which does not include, among others, the essay in which Margarita Simon Guillory and I engaged the idea of black women's bodies being regarded as passive and their responses to it, highlighting their voices and agency: "'That Girl Is Poison': White Supremacy, Anxiety, and the Conflation of Women and Food in the Nation of Islam" (2012)—Elijah Muhammad's Nation of Islam.[39]

While we did theorize embodiment, we drew from the work of many African American women scholars and some of the first-person experiences of women in the NOI that were available at that time. We make some important assertions, such as, "In *Message to the Blackman in America*, Elijah Muhammad utilizes agricultural metaphors to establish cosmological, divinely ordered, gendered, and sexual identities within the NOI." We continue, "Since the male examines, oversees, and protects the crops from pestilence, he is equated with activity, but the field, which Muhammad metaphorically designates as the woman, serves as a vessel of reception. Therefore, she symbolizes immobility, passivity, and utility."[40] As a matter of fact, the policing of black women's bodies; the subjugation of those bodies to men's desire and direction; the circumscription of women's activities, against which they sometimes resist are, in the strongest and most intentional terms, a technology meant to produce a particular form of black humanity, a religious body that is akin to "a god." "Black man, god, that's who you are," Farrakhan asserts.[41] In *Women, Race and Class*, the black feminist scholar Angela Davis traces the notion of women as domestic workers and sites of production; she concludes that those roles are not naturally occurring but owe their historical appearance in the nineteenth century and their bourgeois logic to the very white capitalist order that the NOI decries, in which "women began to be ideologically redefined as the guardians of a devalued domestic life."[42] Davis concludes: "Black women have needed relief from this oppressive predicament for a long, long time."[43] In practical terms, as I argued in the conclusion, these bodies are classed and classist, given that they are held superficially in high regard over and against other black bodies, especially Christian ones, and women's bodies are seen as the route to a hierarchized black upper status.

Notwithstanding the discomfort brought about by his attentiveness to wombs, understanding the connection of wheels, wombs, and women requires acknowledging Farrakhan's own biography and his UFO encounter of 1985, about which I have written significantly in the book and elsewhere. It should come as no surprise that I disagree with at least the second part of the contention by Toni Sims (Muhammad): "As for the Nation, most mass media attention focuses directly on Minister Louis Farrakhan and that produces limited data for gender notion analysis."[44] I demonstrate why it is imperative to talk about Farrakhan and gender and how he has everything to do with the meaning of women's embodiment in NOI religion. The first matter, however, is to note that Farrakhan is particularly sensitive about his mother's admission of her three attempts to abort him in utero. "My mother tried to abort me in the womb three times," he says, which scarred and marked him for life.[45] As I have surmised, "In his own words, his mother's wish for an abortion wounded his subconscious mind in a way that affected him . . . throughout his lifespan and accounts for his many mistakes."[46] Farrakhan laments his mother's decision and the trouble that it has caused him by saying, "She begs the pardon of God for trying to kill this which was in her womb, but she marked me with her own thinking."[47] This is significant in that Farrakhan sees himself at a psychological deficit because of his mother's actions. He was damaged. Saidiya Hartman's *Lose Your Mother: A Journey along the Atlantic Slave Route* (2007) talks about this sense of mourning and loss of a "mother." Reminiscent of my interpretation of Farrakhan, and using Sigmund Freud's "family romance" notion to reenvision Farrakhan's sense of yearning for a mother that the Mother Wheel plays for him, Hartman says, "It is only when you are stranded in a hostile country that you need a romance of origins; it is only when you lose your mother that she becomes a myth."[48] The language is so strikingly similar that Hartman had to have Freud in mind. Therefore, Farrakhan's driving quest is for a new "mother" and, subsequently, a new beginning, a rebirth.

Farrakhan finds fulfillment of this longing desire in the UFO, the Mother Wheel. Since I rehearse this in chapter 5 and in multiple articles and essays, I will not repeat, in great detail, here the fascinating aspects of his description of events in his account of the Mother Wheel into which he reports being taken on September 17, 1985. But I do want to summarize some of what I have argued elsewhere, because it is most relevant to the meaning of wheels, wombs, and women in the NOI. To this end, it is consequential that the UFO is called "mother." Recall that Farrakhan and Muhammad referred to the 1,500 planes/wheels within the Mother Wheel as "baby planes" and "baby wheels." I both agree and disagree with Michael Lieb (as, by inference, do Pierce and Williams), who contends in *Children of Ezekiel: Aliens, UFOs, the Crisis of Race, and the Advent of the End Time* that the Mother Wheel is a metaphor for black bodies.[49] It is, but it is clear that it is a particular signifier for black women's embodiment.

Using classical psychoanalysis and object relations theory, I have argued that the experience of being inside the Mother Wheel was analogous to being in a *womb*, from which Farrakhan was reborn as someone new—a sage, a prophet, a Christlike figure. I demonstrate that he also intimates his experience as such, as he "envisions himself returning to her [the Mother Wheel's] womb and being (re)born as someone profoundly significant. Indeed, the Mother Wheel *is* his *real* 'mother' and indicates who he really is. He expresses it this way explicitly in relation to the Mother Wheel: 'I don't mean to boast. I am more than what you think I am, and I am more than what I thought I was.'"[50] He made this proclamation to the world in the speech *The Wheel and the Last Days*, in which he also warned President Ronald Reagan and Vice President George Bush about the power that was now his.[51] Subsequent to his emergence, Farrakhan expressed in revelatory and enlightened terms that he was more than he thought he was and that the Mother Wheel followed and protected him. His newfound self-awareness gave him the boldness and candor to warn the US government that, were he only "scratched" by its agents, the Wheel would destroy them. Farrakhan, then, became the contemporary prototype for what wombs can produce, symbolizing the vast potential of what that sacred space (i.e., black women's wombs) can generate under the right conditions. His transformation, which takes place in/on the UFO, thus becomes the quintessential object lesson of the possibility for the creation of African Americans who are akin to the Divine.

Wheels, wombs, and women cannot be dissociated in the theology of the NOI. This is why black women's bodies become imperative: *they* have the *power* to reproduce "Farrakhan" and the great sages. Wombs and UFOs—at least, the Mother Wheel—thus exchange meanings. They represent each other. Yet while the Mother Wheel is perfection, African American women have to be curated; their activities, cleanliness, eating, attire, and contact with men outside the Nation of Islam have to be monitored so as not to garner the negative meanings attached to their bodies, negative signifiers that point to African American women who are not members of the NOI. The activities that scholars point to in their descriptive work should be understood in this context and against these existential conditions.

This is precisely what Margarita Simon Guillory and I did. In reference to Sister Clara Muhammad, who was basically the executive director of the NOI while her husband, Elijah Muhammad, was in prison for draft evasion (1942–46), and other women in the NOI, we said: "It is essential to illustrate the means in which some women transformed a seemingly restrictive space into one of productivity. However, it is equally important to present women who did not agree with the marginalized localities that they were placed in by the NOI. . . . While these women practiced verbal protest, others demonstrated their objections via personal action."[52] Notwithstanding my trepidations over the gratuitous use of "patriarchy" as a transcendental analytic, Taylor is likely correct, despite the objections of some of the scholars on women and the NOI. She argues that gendered language in Elijah Muhammad's NOI that assigns obedience to women in exchange for men being taught to love them, "helped to camouflage gender inequities and entice Black women into the Nation despite its patriarchal core."[53] The same is true for Farrakhan's NOI. Despite the recurring tropes of "respect" and "protection," women's bodies are surveilled to ensure their physical and spiritual purity in service of religiobiological reproduction and the reproduction of "gender" in the NOI—that is, to stabilize and replicate gendered relations between men and women and to create gods.

Justice or Else (10.10.15): A Brief Reflection

Moreover, Farrakhan illustrates the significance of wheels, wombs, and women, which is most evident in the high-profile speech he delivered on October 10, 2015, the twentieth anniversary of the historic Million Man March (October 16, 1995), also convened in Washington, DC. The theme of the 2015 march was "Justice or Else"; the event is also referred to as "10.10.15." Farrakhan's keynote address was more than two hours long. In the early part of the speech, he picked up where he often does: talking about women and wombs:

> Every woman is from the creator. Her womb is the workshop of God. . . . For she is in labor, enduring the pain of death to bring forth new life. And there is always a show of blood before the birth, so the man is trying to equal himself to the woman. That means that the Native man, who disrespects your female, you have lost your way. And any Black man under the sound of our voice, any red man, any yellow man that will traffic women and girls, you are worthy of death itself. [Applause]. Now, through a womb of a woman, every great one was born.[54]

Farrakhan continued to address the subject of women for quite some time. He raised the matter of abortion, again, which he opposes: "My mother tried three times to abort my life because the circumstances under which she was pregnant were uncomfortable for her." He talked about the nature of the *womb*, using the word numerous times. Farrakhan returned to the subject of women and sexuality toward the end of the address. Yet I find Farrakhan's and the NOI's concern with "justice" ironic, since the perspectives described in this epilogue raise all kinds of issues for what Loretta Ross calls "reproductive justice" and what Treva B. Lindsey and Jessica Marie Johnson call "sexual subjectivity" of women, since their bodies are co-opted by men and they are seen as the recipients of men's desire, whose bodies are the location of the mythologic, originating in slavery, of the reproduction both of "Farrakhan" and of the black nation.[55] Women's bodies are never regarded as having sexual agency and desire for pleasure that might also play a part in liberation.

As I watched Farrakhan's speech on *C-Span* and streamed live on the NOI's site, one scene caught my attention more than others: Minister Farrakhan asked some Nation of Islam women to come before him (see figure E.1). They were to be seen as an example to women and men alike of what a woman *should* be. Ten women joined him onstage. Red, blue, brown, yellow, fuchsia, turquoise, peach, orange—their garments were brightly colored and beautiful. As the ten women in the many-colored garments were on display, I was reminded that even instrumental objectification could be veiled in the language of respectability. Farrakhan said:

> These are warriors. These are scholars. They know how to cook. They know how to sew. They know how to rear children, and, uh oh—[This is the point at which they took the stage.] Look at them, brothers and sisters. If a sister came up and stood behind them with a miniskirt and a low-cut dress that is beckoning nursing babies, which of these sisters would somebody say, "Hey baby"? They don't talk like that to our women. If they do, it is a terrible mistake. When our women are clothed, they **earn** respect. The beauty of your form is for your husband. If you don't have a husband, keep it covered. . . . Them beautiful hips. Those succulent lips. Lord have mercy. My sisters, all of them, they are very highly intelligent.[56]

He dismissed the women with a "thank you." As they processed off the stage, I was astounded by how much work is yet to be done on women and

E.1

Farrakhan invites women of the Nation of Islam to join him onstage
on October 10, 2015, during his address for the twentieth anniversary
of the Million Man March in Washington, DC. He lauds them as
examples of the ideals of womanhood in the Nation of Islam. Collage
created for the author by David Metcalfe.

embodiment in the Nation of Islam. These African American women were beautiful, but everything that was said about them diminished them and reduced them to womb-bearing organisms who could cook. Their highest purpose was domestic and reproductive. This book points to new directions in this conversation.

THE "LOUIS FARRAKHAN" THAT THE PUBLIC DOES NOT KNOW, OR DOESN'T WANT TO KNOW?
AN AFTERWORD

Much has happened since I initially researched, then composed, this book, necessitating a final glance at the Nation of Islam (NOI), as in the epilogue, with an eye toward future research and to clarify misnomers and misunderstandings about the group. And they are many, both in public and in published scholarship. I offer this afterword as an effort to clear up, and tie up, what I have argued here and elsewhere and as a refutation of glaring errors regarding Farrakhan and the NOI.

"The Criterion: A Message to the World"

It was 12:30 p.m. central time. The day was July 4, 2020. It was a beautiful sunlit day. The weather was warm. The sky was clear and blue. The setting was a colorful lush garden—the NOI's Michigan Farm, to be precise. Birds were singing loudly in the background. Minister Louis Farrakhan approached the podium, which was adorned with a large image of a single white dove. The dove is often used to signify peace, which was a major thrust of his speech, "The

Criterion," on the ninetieth anniversary of the founding of the Nation of Islam on July 4, 1930.[1] The audience was masked and socially distanced. The women wore all white, typical of formal gatherings of the NOI, while men wore black and dark-colored suits. The frail-looking eighty-seven-year-old leader of the NOI was escorted by two gentlemen, one of whom was his son, Mustafa. His many years as leader of the NOI showed in his admission that he stumbled twice getting to the podium. He indicated that this address might very well be his last speech.

And it might very well be his most important speech.

I watched, like tens of thousands of others, by live stream as it happened.

In one of the most expansive, universal public speeches he has ever delivered, Farrakhan weighed in on some of the most important issues of our time, including the global COVID-19 pandemic and the police killing of unarmed black people, including George Floyd. In doing so, he dispelled many of the commonly held myths about him and the NOI. But the thrust of his argument was that peace among people of the Earth requires justice.

Draped in crisp, white, ornamented Muslim garb, Farrakhan clarified, during the three-hour speech, which ideas were most momentous to the NOI—namely, the significance of his experience with UFOs, the story of Yakub, and the importance of the Mother Wheel. He drew on all of them, explicitly and implicitly, to develop his narrative. He also disrupted many popularly held negative tropes about himself, about his attitudes and beliefs toward women, American Jews, and LGBTQ+ communities, notions about him that require no explicit examples. They are superfluous and ubiquitous. It was an amazing speech that I recommend everyone who wants to understand Farrakhan listen to and, as my colleague and friend Biko Mandela Gray always says, "sit with it."

But on this day, the public would not recognize Farrakhan, whose media representation has been populated by all kinds of notions of him as hateful, antiwhite, and anti-Jew. I have refuted all of those notions in the corpus of my work, even as I have been critical of Farrakhan in this book; and I have indicated how the Southern Poverty Law Center's (SPLC) declaration of the NOI and other African American religious organizations as "hate and extremist groups" is inaccurate, inappropriate, inflammatory.[2] And antiblack. The SPLC's listing lacks nuance, scholarly rigor, and depth; adding depth and scholarly rigor to the narratives about the NOI's story of Yakub and how it has to be read and interpreted against a history of white racial terror and violence to make sense of its absurdity in the world, largely motivated me to write "'The Secret . . . of Who the Devil Is': Elijah Muhammad, the Nation of Islam, and Theological Phenomenology" (2017). This does not mean that Farrakhan has not been critical of Jews and other white people. He has been. But he has also been critical of Muslims and Christians—Protestant and Catholic—and the violence that they have enacted and enabled in the world. Yet in "The Criterion," he spoke lovingly of a white Catholic priest, Father Michael Pfleger, who was sitting, masked, in the front row, as "my brother in Christ" whom he loved, and of the Jewish comedian Chelsea Handler as "truthful, so sweet, and wonderful" after she spoke affirmingly of him after seeing him on *The Phil Donahue Show* in the 1990s.

In "The Criterion"—again, probably his final major public address—Farrakhan devoted a substantial amount of his attention to the COVID-19 pandemic and the Trump administration's mishandling of it, as well as to President Donald Trump's call for white nationalists, white supremacists, and white extremists—real extremists, not the African American religious groups who are falsely equated with them—to support his presidency and his bid for reelection. This call, of course, culminated in the US Capitol insurrection of January 6, 2021, activities about which my colleagues Biko Mandela Gray, Lori Latrice Martin, and I theorize in *The Religion of White Rage: White Workers, Religious Fervor, and the Myth of Black Racial Progress*.[3] Farrakhan could not have seen the events of January 6, 2021, coming. Or maybe he did. We did, too.

Farrakhan seemed to have a sense of his approaching death as he spoke, but he was neither worried nor melancholy. He was going to the Mother Wheel, he claimed longingly, to join Master Fard Muhammad and his teacher, Elijah Muhammad:

> I asked them to show you the Wheels because I have also asked Allah to send them over just to confirm what I have said today. That the men that I represent today. . . . You know those two men? They are masters of the Wheel, and that's where I got what I got to tell you over the last twenty, nearly thirty, years; the planning of the Presidents of the United States, I got it on the Wheel. You all laughed at me and thought I was crazy. I'm about to go back to the Wheel. I have to go under extraneous circumstances. I don't care what the circumstances is [*sic*], but I wanna get back because my teacher says, 'If you're faithful and don't change the teaching while I'm gone, I can say I've been faithful. . . . I have been given insight into his teaching.'"

The "extraneous circumstances" that will enable him to return to the Wheel involve his "death," or what appears as death to the rest of us; he intends to inhabit the Wheel bodily. Here Farrakhan confirms what I have said in this book and in many earlier essays and articles: that to understand what Farrakhan and the NOI are doing and saying, one must take their notion of UFOs, the Mother Wheel, seriously, since the Wheel signals that Black embodiment, NOI bodies, and Farrakhan's body, in particular, are special. His body is unique among them, however; it is the quintessential black body out-of-place, socially and symbolically, in which American culture sees little intrinsic value. Farrakhan is different. "I'm no ordinary Negro. No. Hell no," he proclaimed. While Farrakhan's body gains its meaning through relationship to the Wheel, his true "mother," Farrakhan is connected to the meaning of black women's bodies and to all "black" people's bodies—black in all the colors and "races" of blackness—historically, Native Americans, Asians, Latinxes, and the people of African descent, among whom African Americans are most significant.[4]

Indeed, the speech was framed by a concern for the pandemic and the people who lost their lives in it, and it is here that Farrakhan spoke most forcefully and universally. The NOI has always been one of the most universal religious groups in deed, rather than in mere rhetoric. It has cultivated relationships historically with the Hopi and the Navajo; with Japanese and Koreans, such as with Sung Myung Moon's Unification Church; with the Latino Nation of Islam and with Arab, African, and South Asian Muslims; and now, officially, with Scientology. So much for being "anti-white"; it is hard to be whiter than Scientology. And let's not forget Father Pfleger. Farrakhan has also made multiple conciliatory gestures toward Jews that defy register in mainstream media, as the Jewish scholar Michael Lieb, the author of *Children of Ezekiel: Aliens, UFOs, the Crisis of Race, and the Advent of the End Time*, has documented. His words are worth reading at length. Regarding the Million Man March in 1995, whose theme was "atonement," Lieb notes:

> In its own way, the act of reaching out made a point of addressing the ongoing conflicts that the Nation has had with the Jewish community. What might well be viewed as an attempt to reconcile difference is the professed allegiance of those who formulated the march to underlying concepts of Judaism, an allegiance that made no distinction between those deemed "true Jews" and those branded "so-called Jews." . . . It was accordingly no accident that the march was designated the Day of Atonement. Both in his speeches and in his writings, Farrakhan made clear his indebtedness to Yom Kippur in the formulation of his conception of the march.[5]

Lieb explores many such efforts at reconciliation but concludes, "In conjunction with the emphasis on atonement in his march speech, Farrakhan makes a point of appealing to the Jewish community for reconciliation. . . . [I]t would be an error to dismiss Farrakhan as an 'opportunist,' a 'demagogue,' a 'fanatic,' and 'hate monger' who deserves nothing more than contempt, denunciation, and castigation."[6] Farrakhan has done so much to foster unity with the requirement of justice that the universal tone of reconciliation does not surprise me. It might only shock those whose sole information about Farrakhan and the NOI comes from the mainstream media, the internet, or an SPLC list rather than from primary data and published scholarship.

Farrakhan began his message by lamenting the loss of Minister Abdul Hafeez Muhammad, the NOI's East Coast representative, to COVID-19: "His passing affected me like no other. It affected me like that because God wanted me to stop and think because there was a message that He wanted to give me, that He wanted me to give to you." What was that message? In my estimation, it was a message of peace and justice in the midst of a pandemic, a peace for which justice was the criterion. "The Message" wasn't without controversy, given that Farrakhan viewed the novel coronavirus as purposeful and intentional for "population control"; that immediately made me wonder what he might have thought about President Joe Biden's commitment to buy a half-billion doses of the COVID-19 vaccine for distribution throughout the poor world.[7] Farrakhan must have been mortified and probably interpreted Biden's gesture not as goodwill but as potentially fulfilling his prophetic utterances regarding nefarious development and uses of the vaccine.

However, Farrakhan also struck a chord that would be unrecognizable to most. He cast all lives lost to the pandemic, including women, as martyrs according to Islam. He lamented sexism. He championed human rights for LGBTQ+ communities more than once, going as far as to mention explicitly "queer" and "trans" people who also died as martyrs. He expressed love for righteous people of goodwill, including Jews, Christians, and Muslims. He tacitly valorized interracial marriage and procreation—at least some of them—since Master Fard had a black father and a white mother. About Fard's white mother, he asked his audience: "Do you have a problem with that?"

Likewise, Farrakhan maintained that, as a large African American man who under fair circumstances could have beaten all four police officers (including Derek Chauvin) who participated in his murder, George Floyd was a symbol of peace. He submitted to authority. This black body—Floyd's black body—came to represent peace and African Americans who have died by white racial violence and state-sanctioned police violence.[8]

Similarly, Farrakhan invoked Freddie Gray, saying his impassioned wailing in the throes of death at the hands of Baltimore police in 2015 reminded him of Floyd's desperate pleas for mercy and for his mother. Thus, Farrakhan tacitly enshrined Ahmaud Arbery, Daunte Wright, Breonna Taylor, Lejuana Phillips, Sandra Bland, Michael Brown, Philando Castile, Tamir Rice, Eric Garner, Michelle Cusseaux, Crystal Danielle Ragland, Latasha Nicole Walton, April Webster, Trayvon Martin, and so many others, as transcendent—too many names to mention, of course.

Farrakhan returned frequently to the pandemic. It evidenced injustice, as well, since it has affected black and brown people disproportionately. The method of his address was a hermeneutics of suspicion, so common in African American religious thought about America. He cited the Tuskegee experiment in which black men were intentionally left infected with syphilis and who then infected black women; government experiments on Native Americans and smallpox; and many others. He concluded: "How can you trust them with a vaccine after what they have done? . . . We can't trust you no more, white folks, not with our lives." Notwithstanding his suspicions of the government and the health-care industry, he was not opposed to vaccines. He called for African American scientists to develop a vaccine that black people could trust, including those that use alpha interferon, a naturally occurring cytokine that the body produces to elicit immune responses. Moreover, Farrakhan advocated safety, the wearing of masks, and social distancing.

Finally, and perhaps most astounding to some, after praying in Arabic and then in English for peace in the world, especially in India, Pakistan, Asia—all around the globe—Farrakhan ended with an excursus that could be understood only as American exceptionalism: "I would never tell you to disrespect the flag even though we have suffered under it and been blessed despite it. I thank Allah for living in America. We are the most educated black people in the world." Soon the world would be "set free," he concluded. This is not the Farrakhan that the world knows, or perhaps wants to know. He is illegible against the defaming discourses that assail him.

About two-and-a-half hours into his presentation, an airplane then flew overhead. Farrakhan looked up. Then he looked at his watch, and looked up again. It was a plane that commemorated the ninetieth anniversary of the Nation of Islam, pulling a banner that had pictures of Elijah Muhammad and Master Fard Muhammad displayed on it, along with "Happy 90th birth anniversary of the Nation of Islam." Among Farrakhan's last words that followed was the proclamation, "When I close down in the garden, the God, will do some work," implying that the presence of his living body is holding the apocalypse against injustice at bay. Furthermore, perhaps it was an allusion to Jesus in the Garden of Gethsemane before his crucifixion. Maybe that is why the Michigan Garden was chosen to symbolize moments before Farrakhan's approaching death. "The government will be interested in ending my life," he said of the Central Intelligence Agency (CIA) and Federal Bureau of Investigation (FBI).

After three hours, the video version of the speech ends with a fifteen-minute YouTube video of UFO sightings, beginning with one that took place in New York on July 4, then one in South Side Chicago, the location of the NOI's headquarters, Mosque Maryam, and the minister's home, also on July 4, the very night after his speech. The video progresses with sighting after sighting: Colorado, July 4; Tacoma, Washington, July 4; Minneapolis, July 4; two others in Chicago; several others elsewhere in the "USA," July 4; Fresno, California, July 4; Daytona Beach, July 4; Beijing, July 4; Dubai, July 5; Tennessee, July 7; San Jose, Costa Rica, July 8; Slovakia, July 8; Puerto Ordaz, Venezuela, July 9; Mexico City, July 9; Utica, New York, July 9; USA, July 10th; and China generally, July 14. Images of UFOs were intermingled with periodic cameos of Farrakhan talking about the Mother Wheel. These were the baby wheels about which Elijah Muhammad and he had spoken.

The video was also an allusion that was meant to evoke a speech on October 24, 1989, in which Farrakhan declared to the public that he had a vision of being taken into the Mother Wheel on September 17, 1985. In that press conference, held at the J. W. Marriott Hotel in Washington, DC, Farrakhan proclaimed to the world that UFOs would appear all over American cities to testify to the truth of his experience and that he was, indeed, a sage prophet whose time on earth was drawing to a close.[9] At that time, UFOs appeared all over the world; UFOs and science testified on Farrakhan's behalf. This is what he and the NOI contend.

Perhaps the most interesting recent phenomenon—at least for me—is the debate in elite scientific journals about 'Oumuamua, an interstellar object that was detected in our solar system on October 19, 2017. The astrophysicists Shmuel Bialy and Abraham "Avi" Loeb, who chairs Harvard's Astronomy Department, published an article in 2018 in *Astrophysical Journal Letters* that argued for the possibility that 'Oumuamua's origins were artificial and alien. They wrote: "Considering an artificial origin, one possibility is that 'Oumuamua is a lightsail, floating in interstellar space as debris from advanced technological equipment. . . . Alternatively, a more exotic scenario is that 'Oumuamua may be a fully operational probe sent intentionally to Earth vicinity by an alien civilization."[10] Not all astronomers agreed, of course, but this is a fascinating debate about alien life and UFOs that, for Farrakhan, would serve as validation, despite the fact that he would say scientists are wrong or duplicitous about the identity of such objects. The NOI contends that the objects that are misidentified as UFOS are the Mother Wheel or one of the 1,500 military vehicles, called "baby wheels," that are housed within it. Incidentally, or *co-incidentally*— that is, occurring in meaningful relationship to the NOI's ideas of UFOs— Farrakhan's speech took place just over a month after the government disclosure that UFOS (using the updated nomenclature *unexplained aerial phenomena* [UAP]) are "real."[11] What is more, the CIA released thousands of pages of its declassified and digitized UFO files in January 2021. They were obtained through a Freedom of Information request and are hosted on the Black Vault website, owned by John Greenewald Jr.[12]

Indeed, likely of most immediate interest to Farrakhan and the NOI is the recent report by the Office of Defense National Intelligence's Department of Defense Unidentified Aerial Phenomena Task Force (UAPTF) that was announced by Pentagon Press Secretary John Kirby on June 25, 2021.[13] In his statement, Kirby said that the government considers UAPs (UFOS) a "threat" to national security and that Deputy Secretary of Defense Kathleen Hicks had directed the Office of the Undersecretary of Defense for Intelligence and Security to develop a plan to formalize the continuing work of the UAPTF, which has a $50 billion annual budget. The plan is to include the collection of UAP data and, perhaps most pressing, "provide recommendations for securing military test and training ranges."[14] The military and security concerns would make the most sense, given Elijah Muhammad's and Farrakhan's contention that the Mother Wheel is a military vehicle about which the government is aware.

Prepared with input from multiple government agencies, including the FBI and the National Security Agency—agencies within all military branches and intelligence services, as a matter of fact—the nine-page Defense National Intelligence report, "Preliminary Assessment: Unidentified Aerial Phenomena (Intelligence Assessment)," claims at least 144 cases of UAP for which the military has no explanation since 2004, the year the UAPTF was authorized and initiated.[15] Eighty of these cases were observed "with multiple sensors." Astoundingly, most of the UAP reported probably do represent physical objects, given that a majority of UAP were registered across multiple sensors, including radar, infrared, electro-optical, weapon seekers, and visual observation." Perhaps *unidentified flying object*, then, is a more appropriate term than *unidentified aerial phenomena*. Consistent with the government report, the NOI recognizes UFOs as *objects*, as crafts with propulsion, as its video at the end of "The Criterion" indicates. The Mother Wheel, at least, is a physical object with propulsion. The report also notices patterns in military UFO sightings, two of which are significant. First, the reports cluster around US military installations; and second, UFOs/UAP exhibit unusual movement, including advanced speed, without discernible means of propulsion, unusual flight patterns, stationary status in winds, and so on, all of which may represent "breakthrough technologies."[16]

To this end, the video includes screen after screen displaying words about the Mother Wheel as a mechanical craft that indicates the genius of the black people; the genius of the God, Master Fard Muhammad, who created it; and the transcendence of black bodies. A screen appears that says, "These sightings (and many others) can be viewed on YouTube.com. Search 'July 2020 UFO.'" The credits then roll.

Like the NOI, Louis Farrakhan has been a hero to some and a villain to others and is misunderstood by many, especially, as noted earlier, by those whose information about him comes only from the so-called mainstream media. His most recent major speech may not have been intended to debunk long-standing and gross myths about him and the religion. But it did. Regardless of what people think about Farrakhan, his effect on how we understand the diversity of black people and their place in the world is undeniable. He challenged the way that scholars, the general public, and black people understand their place in and out of this world. He contended that black lives matter long before social media and the movements they help to empower. Lieb is right when he says: "As repugnant as his [ostensible] message might be to those content with the delineation of him in the headlines, he is an individual who invites, perhaps even demands, analysis. This is no ordinary mortal: whether demonized or idolized, whether shunned as a pariah or worshipped as a messiah, he cannot simply be dismissed as an ephemeral, if disturbing, aberration."[17]

FARRAKHAN'S SWAN SONG?
A POSTSCRIPT

Louis Farrakhan is the "Messiah." This is not my claim; it is his and the NOI's. Did I mention that the apocalypse is nigh? Farrakhan proclaimed that the age of white domination is coming to an end. This age cannot culminate while *his body* is still on earth, however. He's leaving soon; he's returning to the Mother Wheel to join Master Fard Muhammad and Elijah Muhammad, whom he encountered there in 1985. Once he does, the world as we know it is over. And Farrakhan has multiple wives! But I am getting ahead of myself.

Let me paint the picture.

It is Sunday, February 27, 2022, only three days after Russia invaded Ukraine. The location is Mosque Maryam, the headquarters of the NOI in Chicago. After roughly an hour of preliminary matters, Farrakhan approaches the podium. His assistants ask him to use the high chair that they have provided rather than to stand. Farrakhan remarks on it, smiles, and remains standing. He is eighty-nine years of age. He speaks for almost five hours, a personal record for the leader known for delivering lengthy addresses.

His Muslim attire is a beautiful, bedazzled, emerald green robe and matching hat. His message on this day? "The Swan Song." His earlier address, "The Criterion," wasn't Farrakhan's last speech, though it still may be his greatest, but he has more to say in "The Swan Song." Presumably swans sing their most beautiful songs as they approach death, and the term *swan song* is meant to convey a final message, a retirement, a note that one is moving on from a particular station in life, or a testimony before death. Was this Farrakhan's swan song?

The occasion is Saviors' Day. Farrakhan addresses a wide range of issues but devotes a substantial amount to time to COVID and vaccinations. Farrakhan spends no less than forty-five minutes of his speech addressing vaccines. It is, for Farrakhan, a matter of urgency. Farrakhan and the NOI reference Nixon's and Kissinger's National Security Study Memorandum 200 of April 24, 1974, which suggests the possibility of reducing the global population by two to three billion people. Perhaps he perceives this global pandemic and push for a new vaccine as yet another attempt to end his life prematurely—and that of many black and brown people across the globe. Farrakhan goes so far as to describe vaccines as "a death plot." He reports that his entire family, household staff, and he had COVID. They received an alternate treatment of monoclonal antibodies, ivermectin, and other therapies, rather than CDC-approved vaccines, Farrakhan says. It cured them all, quickly. The NOI still does not trust the government or coronavirus vaccines because vaccines are a government depopulation plot to reduce earth's most undesirable populations. Black bodies remain in jeopardy in this world, for Farrakhan and the NOI.

Neither COVID nor the vaccine could kill the Messiah and alter the course of events. Farrakhan says that he is the messiah, in part, because Elijah Muhammad was the messiah, and Farrakhan claims to be his "first and only national representative." Malcolm X was only his "spokesperson," he says, not his representative. Farrakhan distinguishes himself from Malcolm X and Warith Deen Mohammed, who were great teachers, but he is the authentic representative of Muhammad. Maybe this is why Farrakhan chose multiple wives—because Muhammad did also? This is his first public disclosure of polyamorous relationships. The matter of taking wives was the first thing he asked Elijah Muhammad about on the Wheel. Muhammad rebuffed him, he says; it wasn't time for that. He praises Mother Khadijah, his first wife. He tries to make all his children one family and claims they defend him. To my knowledge, he has never admitted publicly to having multiple wives. This may provide some evidence that this could be Farrakhan's swan song.

Farrakhan has done his work here on earth; he has been faithful to Muhammad's message for sixty-seven years. According to him, he's leaving soon, only to return later. It will appear that he died—Elijah Muhammad never died, either, claimed Farrakhan during the address—but Farrakhan will be with him and Master Fard on the Wheel, learning. There are ten thousand years left in this twenty-five-thousand-year cycle, which you may recall I described in chapter 1. Farrakhan doesn't know if he will be permitted to learn ten thousand years' worth of knowledge before he comes back to this world as the Christ; he hopes so.

Cataclysms will ensue after he leaves, but they cannot happen until he does, Farrakhan contends. He predicts that the United States will enter the war against Russia in defense of Ukraine at which point the US government will "come for" him; he expects that the government will carry out their "death plot" using black people. Recall that he referred to COVID and vaccines as a "death plot." This time the plot would be carried out. Sounding like an Afropessimist, Farrakhan says this white-dominated world must end so that a new world might be established. He claims that God will make America pay for many wrongs against black people, Native Americans, Mexicans, and others around the world. This war will bring an end to the age of white domination, since the majority of that war will be fought in Europe and will cause the end of the United States as it is known—*the end of America*. Hence, this speech is not Farrakhan's swan song; it was America's; it is white supremacy's. This is the thesis of his presentation.

It is not clear when Farrakhan expects to return to this world. Toward the end of his speech, he mentions the NOI Executive Council, the leadership board made of thirteen women and men, which may correspond to the thirteen tribes of the Original People, which I discuss in chapter 1. He charges them and his followers not to change his teaching.

At the end of his remarks, the camera pans out as he exits, but like a messiah, he returns. Back at the podium, he calls for his "Omega brothers," a reference to the Omega Psi Phi Fraternity, Incorporated, a fraternity of which I am also a member. Omega, the final letter of the Greek alphabet, may symbolize the end, and perhaps the beginning, of a new era.

Introduction

1. See Allen, "Identity and Destiny"; Allen, "Religious Heterodoxy and Nationalist Tradition"; Allen, "When Japan Was the 'Champion of the Darker Races.'"

2. Rouse, *Engaged Surrender*, 8–9.

3. Spillers, "Mama's Baby, Papa's Maybe"; Hartman, *Scenes of Subjection*, 8.

4. Douglas, *Purity and Danger*, 50.

5. Douglas, *Purity and Danger*, 43.

6. Douglas, *Purity and Danger*, 49, 119–20.

7. Douglas, *Purity and Danger*, 44.

8. Douglas, *Purity and Danger*, xi. Julia Kristeva extends Douglas in a helpful way here in *Powers of Horror*. Using psychoanalysis as a primary tool of interpretation, Kristeva examines the stuff (i.e., the abject) that in Douglas's schema would be considered "out-of-place," again, those things that were seen as *dangerous* to the system because they were considered potentially contradictory or defiling and therefore subversive to the purity of the social order and worldview.

9. See Outlaw, *On Race and Philosophy*, xii–xiii; Yancy, "Whiteness and the Return of the Black Body," 114–65.

10. See, e.g., Leder, *The Absent Body*, 91–92.

11. Douglas, *Purity and Danger*, 44, 49, 119–20.

12. hooks, *Black Looks*, 61–73, 87–107.

13. Muhammad, *How to Eat to Live, Book 1*, 102–3.

14. Douglas, *Natural Symbols*, 72.

15. Alexander, *The New Jim Crow*. It should be noted, however, that Anthony Pinn, using a Foucauldian analysis, had already theorized about the role of the prison system as a means of controlling and shaping black bodies and how this extended the system of control of slavery and lynching that affected the development of black religion: see Pinn, *Terror and Triumph*, 68–70, 75; cf. Foucault, *Discipline and Punish*.

16. Finley, "The Meaning of 'Mother' in Louis Farrakhan's 'Mother Wheel.'"

17. Lee, *The Nation of Islam*, 92. See also *Chicago Tribune*, March 7, 1976, 38.

18. McCloud, *African American Islam*, 37–38.

19. See Farrakhan, *The Announcement*, 6.

20. Finley, "The Meaning of 'Mother' in Louis Farrakhan's 'Mother Wheel.'"

21. See, e.g., Muhammad. *The Supreme Wisdom*, 1:33–34; Muhammad, *The Supreme Wisdom*, 2:16. These practices and counter-discourses were only moderately successful, in that some of the negative ideas about black bodies that the NOI deplored were reproduced and deployed in their own narratives. For example, the story of Yakub explained African physical features, including "kinky hair," as resulting from the corruption of original black phenotype when an early dissatisfied God-Scientist in East Asia (i.e., the Nile Valley and Mecca) suggested that members of the Tribe of Shabazz, or the original black people, go into the "jungle" to live there and prove that they could conquer wild beasts. Accordingly, this experience would harden black people and make them able to endure the vicissitudes of life. The resulting aesthetic effect was the appearance of modern black features such as full lips, wide noses, and tightly curled hair.

22. See Finley, "Mathematical Theology, 123–37; Finley, "The Meaning of 'Mother' in Louis Farrakhan's 'Mother Wheel'"; Finley, "From Mistress to Mother"; Finley and Guillory, "'That Girl Is Poison.'"

Chapter One: Elijah Muhammad, the Myth of Yakub, and the Critique of "Whitenized" Black Bodies

1. Tsoukalas, *The Nation of Islam*; Finley, "'The Secret . . . of Who the Devil Is.'"

2. Jackson, *Islam and the Problem of Black Suffering*, 6–8.

3. See Muhammad, *Message to the Blackman in America*, 34–35.

4. Evanzz, *The Messenger*, 350.

5. Muhammad, *The Science of Time*, 27, emphasis added.

6. See Muhammad, *Message to the Blackman in America*, 31.

7. Muhammad, *The Supreme Wisdom*, 1:17.

8. Cf. Wilson, *Black-on-Black Violence*.

9. Young, "Five Faces of Oppression," 57.

10. Young, "Five Faces of Oppression," 57.

11. See Pinn, *Terror and Triumph*, 77. Pinn calls this consciousness and ever-present fear "terror."

12. Muhammad, *History of the Nation of Islam*, 26–27. According to Muhammad in this 1964 interview, his maternal great-grandfather was a slave master.

13. Evanzz, *The Messenger*, 19.

14. Evanzz, *The Messenger*, 20. See also Berg, *Elijah Muhammad and Islam*, 32.

15. Evanzz, *The Messenger*, 20.

16. Clegg, *An Original Man*, 10.

17. Evanzz, *The Messenger*, 23–24; Clegg, *An Original Man*, 10.

18. Clegg, *An Original Man*, 10.

19. Pinn, *Terror and Triumph*, 74–75.

20. Clegg, *An Original Man*, 10. Clegg suggests that Elijah was traumatized by the inactivity of black people in response to lynchings: "Though a most savage object lesson, Elijah could not understand how this could have happened to a young man 'in the midst of his own people' while 'all our grown men right there in the section' watched and dare not intervene."

21. Evanzz, *The Messenger*, 39.

22. Evanzz, *The Messenger*, 39–40; cf. Pinn, *Terror and Triumph*, 75.

23. Elijah Muhammad, quoted in Evanzz, *The Messenger*, 40.

24. Clegg, *An Original Man*, 10.

25. Evanzz, *The Messenger*, 41–43.

26. Evanzz, *The Messenger*, 46.

27. Evanzz, *The Messenger*, 47.

28. Evanzz, *The Messenger*, 39.

29. Evanzz, *The Messenger*, 47.

30. Evanzz, *The Messenger*, 47.

31. Evanzz, *The Messenger*, 51.

32. Evanzz, *The Messenger*, 54–5.

33. Muhammad, *The Science of Time*, 26–27.

34. Finley, "'The Secret . . . of Who the Devil Is.'"

35. Cone, *A Black Theology of Liberation*, 83–85. See also Pinn, *Terror and Triumph*, 77.

36. Gossett, *Race*, 178–85; Muhammad, *Message to the Blackman in America*, 42, 54, 78, 101–22.

37. See esp. X, *The End of White World Supremacy*, 42–60; Muhammad, *The Fall of America*; Muhammad, *Message to the Blackman in America*, 100–34. See also, e.g., Muhammad, *Birth of a Savior*; Muhammad, *The Flag of Islam*; Muhammad, *The History of Jesus' Birth, Death and What It Means*; Muhammad, *History of the Nation of Islam*; Muhammad, *I Am the Last Messenger of Allah*; Muhammad, *Our Savior Has Arrived*; Muhammad, *The Science of Time*; Muhammad, *The Secrets of Freemasonry*; Muhammad, *The Supreme Wisdom*, vol. 1; Muhammad, *The Tricknology of the Enemy*; Muhammad, *The True History of Master Fard Muhammad*; Muhammad, *Yakub*. See also Clegg, *An Original Man*, 41–67; Pinn, *Terror and Triumph*, 120–27. The fact that

the story of Yakub has no singular source suggests that acolytes had to be disciples for an indeterminate period of time before they would have gained a full sense of NOI mythology.

38. Muhammad, *Message to the Blackman in America*, 16–17.

39. Muhammad, *Message to the Blackman in America*, 17.

40. Muhammad, *Message to the Blackman in America*, 17.

41. Muhammad, *Message to the Blackman in America*, 17.

42. Finley, "Hidden Away," 279.

43. Muhammad, *The Supreme Wisdom*, 2:2.

44. Muhammad, *Yakub*, 48; Clegg, *An Original Man*, 41.

45. See Hoyle, *The Nature of the Universe*.

46. Muhammad, *Birth of a Saviour*, 51, 56; Muhammad, *Theology of Time*, 121; Muhammad, *Yakub*, 48. Time equals motion. See also Clegg, *An Original Man*, 42.

47. See, e.g., Muhammad, *Message to the Blackman in America*, 42.

48. Clegg, *An Original Man*, 42.

49. Muhammad, *The True History of Master Fard Muhammad*, 167–68; cf. Muhammad, *History of the Nation of Islam*, 8; Muhammad, *Yakub*, 59.

50. For a discussion of the intersection and relevance of race and cosmology, see Denzler, *The Lure of the Edge*.

51. Muhammad, *Message to the Blackman in America*, 111.

52. Clegg, *An Original Man*, 45. Such language describing the gods as mortal may be intended to counteract the notion that God is eternal and to reinforce the notion that God is embodied.

53. Clegg, *An Original Man*, 44–45.

54. Muhammad, *Message to the Blackman in America*, 108.

55. Muhammad, *The Flag of Islam*, 10.

56. Muhammad, *The Flag of Islam*, 14; cf. Muhammad, *Yakub*, 26; Clegg, *An Original Man*, 44–45.

57. Clegg, *An Original Man*, 44–45.

58. Du Bois, *The Souls of Black Folk*, 2–3.

59. Muhammad, *The Supreme Wisdom*, 1:33; Muhammad, *Message to the Blackman in America*, 31. The saga also makes an unexplained temporal leap from trillions of years ago to tens of thousands of years ago.

60. Muhammad, *Message to the Blackman in America*, 31; Muhammad, *The Supreme Wisdom*, 1:33–34; cf. Clegg, *An Original Man*, 48–49.

61. Muhammad, *Message to the Blackman in America*, 31–32.

62. The term *nappy hair* has negative connotations. The reference to "rough climate" is from X, *The End of White World Supremacy*, 48.

63. Clegg, *An Original Man*, 48.

64. Muhammad, *The Supreme Wisdom*, 2:15; Diop, *The African Origin of Civilization*.

65. Clegg, *An Original Man*, 49; Muhammad, *Message to the Blackman in America*, 110; Muhammad, *Yakub*, 61. Recall that the world functions in twenty-five thousand-year cycles in which new gods reign and new scriptural histories are written.

66. Muhammad, *Message to the Blackman in America*, 110.

67. Muhammad, *Message to the Blackman in America*, 110.

68. Muhammad, *Message to the Blackman in America*, 110–11; Muhammad, *The Flag of Islam*, 30–31; Muhammad, *The Supreme Wisdom*, 2:15.

69. Muhammad, *Message to the Blackman in America*, 111–12.

70. Muhammad, *Message to the Blackman in America*, 112.

71. Muhammad, *History of the Nation*, 6–9; Muhammad, *The Supreme Wisdom*, 1:38; cf. Evanzz, *The Messenger*, 75.

72. Muhammad, *Message to the Blackman in America*, 112.

73. Muhammad, *Message to the Blackman in America*, 113.

74. This could also be read as a critique of Christianity, which exploits black people economically by promising them wealth in return for obedience.

75. Muhammad, *Message to the Blackman in America*, 113.

76. Muhammad, *Message to the Blackman in America*, 161–52, 226. "Naturally we would need help for the next 20 or 25 years. After that, we would be self-supporting!"

77. Muhammad, *Message to the Blackman in America*, 113.

78. Muhammad, *Message to the Blackman in America*, 171.

79. Muhammad, *Message to the Blackman in America*, 115–26; cf. Muhammad, *History of the Nation*, 35–36. Note that the physical characteristics of whites—that is, pale skin and blue eyes—that have come to represent purity and the ideal image in the West are reversed here and seen as the apex of physical and moral corruption.

80. Pinn, *Terror and Triumph*, 123; West, *Prophesy Deliverance!*, 47–65.

81. Muhammad, *The Flag of Islam*, 17–19; Muhammad, *The Science of Time*, 20–21; Muhammad, *The Tricknology of the Enemy*, 10; Clegg, *An Original Man*, 51.

82. Muhammad, *Message to the Blackman in America*, 117.

83. Dogs are taboo in Islam and can be kept only for guarding herds and property: see Hopfe and Woodward, *Religions of the World*, 334; Muhammad, *Message to the Blackman in America*, 120. The dog as "man's best friend" to white men can be traced

historically to these caves, in which they lived with whites. Muhammad, *Message to the Blackman in America*, 119; Clegg, *An Original Man*, 52–53.

84. Muhammad, *Message to the Blackman in America*, 119. This grafting process accounts for the existence of the entire monkey family.

85. Muhammad, *Yakub*, 31–32.

86. Muhammad, *The History of Jesus' Birth, Death and What It Means*, 20–21.

87. Clegg, *An Original Man*, 55; cf. Muhammad, *The Supreme Wisdom*, 1:13, 16; Muhammad, *The History of Jesus' Birth, Death and What It Means*, 22.

88. Muhammad, *Message to the Blackman in America*, 55; Muhammad, *Birth of a Savoir*, 30.

89. Muhammad, *Message to the Blackman in America*, 212–23; Muhammad, *The Flag of Islam*, 17–18.

90. Muhammad, *The Science of Time*, 20; Muhammad, *The History of Jesus' Birth, Death and What It Means*, 53.

91. Clegg, *An Original Man*, 59.

92. One will note frequent terminological and conceptual slippage by Muhammad's uses of "mankind" to refer to the original people. Elsewhere, "mankind" can refer only to the devil, who is a kind, a genus. The original man is just that—original, not a kind. Consider Muhammad's explanation: "Mankind, who is mankind? mankind is the caucasian [*sic*] race, often called the white race. They are a made people so God has taught me and so the scripture verifies, that not created from the original man, but came after him and a grafted man from the original man." See Muhammad, *The Science of Time*, 21.

93. Muhammad, *The Supreme Wisdom*, 1:13–24.

94. Muhammad, *Message to the Blackman in America*, 3, 230; Muhammad, *The Tricknology of the Enemy*, 1. Clegg, *An Original Man*, 58.

95. See, e.g., Muhammad, *The Supreme Wisdom*, 1:16–27.

96. Muhammad, *Birth of a Savior*, 32–33; Muhammad, *The History of Jesus' Birth, Death and What It Means*, 17; Muhammad, *History of the Nation of Islam*, 32–33; Muhammad, *The Science of Time*, 50.

97. Muhammad, *Birth of a Savior*, 28. See also Lincoln, *The Black Muslims in America*, 72; Muhammad, *Message to the Blackman in America*, 70, 78.

98. Muhammad, *The Science of Time*, 57; cf. Walker, *Islam and the Search for African-American Nationhood*, 313–16.

99. Muhammad, *The Science of Time*, 57.

100. Muhammad, *Message to the Blackman in America*, 241.

101. Muhammad, *Message to the Blackman in America*, 173.

102. Muhammad, *Message to the Blackman in America*, 47; Muhammad, *The Science of Time*, 55–57.

103. Muhammad, *The Science of Time*, 54.

104. Muhammad, *Message to the Blackman in America*, 241.

105. See "Martin Luther King Jr.—Biography," NobelPrize.org, 1964, accessed January 5, 2020, http://nobelprize.org/nobel_prizes/peace/laureates/1964/king-bio.html.

106. Muhammad, *Message to the Blackman in America*, 240.

107. Muhammad, *Message to the Blackman in America*, 242; cf. Walker, *Islam and the Search for African-American Nationhood*, 316.

108. Muhammad, *The Science of Time*, 54.

109. Washington, *Up from Slavery*, 47–48.

110. Clegg, *An Original Man*, 27.

111. Muhammad, *The Supreme Wisdom*, 1:14.

112. Walker, *Islam and the Search for African-American Nationhood*, 316.

113. Muhammad, *The Tricknology of the Enemy*, 5–6. The notion that "Islam" is associated with or means "black" may antedate the transmission of the Yakub narrative from Master Fard Muhammad to Elijah Muhammad, and at the same time, it may be part of the theoretical genealogy of the mythology. However, the details lie beyond the purview of this chapter. See Turner, "Edward Wilmot Blyden and Pan-Africanism."

114. Muhammad, *Message to the Blackman in America*, 47, cf. 83.

115. Muhammad, *Message to the Blackman in America*, 83.

116. Muhammad, *The Supreme Wisdom*, 1:6.

117. Muhammad, *The Supreme Wisdom*, 1:6. See also Muhammad, *The Science of Time*, 41.

118. Muhammad, *Message to the Blackman in America*, 236.

119. On Scripture as a "poison book," see Lincoln, *The Black Muslims in America*, 74; Muhammad, *The Supreme Wisdom*, 1:12–13, 25–26, 30; Muhammad, *Message to the Blackman in America*, 90. Muhammad, *Birth of a Savior*, 8, 14, 24, 38; Muhammad, *The History of Jesus' Birth, Death and What It Means*, 10–12, 14, 20, 22–24, 29, 44; Muhammad, *The Science of Time*, 25, 47, 83–84; Muhammad, *The True History of Master Fard Muhammad*, 101; Muhammad, *Yakub*, 98.

120. Muhammad, *The Tricknology of the Enemy*, 16. "We must forget that old slavery talk and thinking that one day God is going to rise us up out of the grave and we're going to heaven—get that out of your mind. This is heaven now if you want to go in it. The coming of God and His words, teaching here among us is heaven."

121. See, Muhammad, *The History of Jesus' Birth, Death and What It Means*; Muhammad, *History of the Nation of Islam*.

122. Muhammad, *Message to the Blackman in America*, 3, 5, 7, 10; Muhammad, *The Science of Time*, 47.

123. Muhammad, *Message to the Blackman in America*, 15.

124. Muhammad, *Message to the Blackman in America*, 1.

125. Muhammad, *Message to the Blackman in America*, 2.

126. Muhammad, *Message to the Blackman in America*, 15.

127. Elijah Muhammad claimed that Martin Luther King Jr. called whites the devil in a private meeting: see Walker, *Islam and the Search for African-American Nationhood*, 316.

128. Muhammad, *Message to the Blackman*, 226, 226–27; cf. Muhammad, *The Tricknology of the Enemy*, 11–12, 17.

129. Muhammad, *Message to the Blackman in America*, 318.

130. Curtis, *Black Muslim Religion in the Nation of Islam*, 12.

131. Muhammad, *Message to the Blackman in America*, 317; cf. Muhammad, *The Supreme Wisdom*, 2:18, 24.

132. Muhammad, *Message to the Blackman in America*, 312.

133. Muhammad, *Message to the Blackman in America*, 217.

134. Muhammad, *Message to the Blackman in America*, 218.

135. On slave food, see Muhammad, *The Supreme Wisdom*, 1:22–23; Muhammad, *The Tricknology of the Enemy*, 18. On slave masters' names, see Muhammad, *The Supreme Wisdom*, 1:14; Muhammad, *The Tricknology of the Enemy*, 9.

136. Walker, *Islam and the Search for African-American Nationhood*, 313–14.

Chapter Two: Elijah Muhammad, Transcendent Blackness, and the Construction of Ideal Black Embodiment

1. Berg, *Elijah Muhammad and Islam*, 2–6.

2. Higginbotham, *Righteous Discontent*, 185–229.

3. Washington, *Up from Slavery*, 127–39.

4. Washington, *Up from Slavery*, 127–39.

5. Frazier, *The Negro Family in the United States*.

6. Pierce and Williams, "And Their Prayers Shall Be Answered through the Womb of a Woman," 197.

7. Gardell, *In the Name of Elijah Muhammad*, 333.

8. Baker-Fletcher, *Dancing with God*, 56. Baker-Fletcher uses the term *perichoresis* to describe the relationship of the members of the Christian Trinity to one another. It

implies that they are inextricable from one another and that they are in a "dance" or are "enveloped" together.

9. Finley, "The Meaning of 'Mother' in Louis Farrakhan's 'Mother Wheel,'" 458.

10. Cf. Hanegraaf, *New Age Religion and Western Culture*, 1–20.

11. See Cooey, *Religious Imagination and the Body*, 5; Curtis, "Islamizing the Black Body"; Muhammad, *History of the Nation of Islam*, 43.

12. Essien-Udom, *Black Nationalism*, 8–9.

13. Essien-Udom, *Black Nationalism*, 8.

14. E.g., Muhammad, *How to Eat to Live, Book 1*, 102–3.

15. Muhammad, *How to Eat to Live, Book 1*, 1.

16. Muhammad, *How to Eat to Live, Book 1*, 2–3.

17. Muhammad, *How to Eat to Live, Book 1*, 8.

18. Curtis, *Black Muslim Religion in the Nation of Islam*, 169–70.

19. See Muhammad, *Message to the Blackman in America*, 17. See also Essien-Udom, *Black Nationalism*, 205–6; Curtis, *Black Muslim Religion in the Nation of Islam*, 98–109.

20. Muhammad, *How to Eat to Live, Book 1*, 13.

21. Muhammad, *How to Eat to Live, Book 1*, 14, 72.

22. Muhammad, *How to Eat to Live, Book 1*, 103.

23. "Chickens are not fit to eat. You have to nurse them so carefully to keep them away from filth": Muhammad, *How to Eat to Live, Book 1*, 11. See also Muhammad, *How to Eat to Live, Book 1*, 4–6, 63, 90–92, 109; cf. Curtis, *Black Muslim Religion in the Nation of Islam*, 98.

24. Muhammad, *How to Eat to Live, Book 1*, 41; Muhammad, *How to Eat to Live, Book 2*, 4–6, 85.

25. Witt, *Black Hunger*, 107.

26. Witt, *Black Hunger*, 107.

27. Muhammad, *How to Eat to Live, Book 1*, 13.

28. See, e.g., Muhammad, *How to Eat to Live, Book 1*, 2, 19–21.

29. Muhammad, *How to Eat to Live, Book 1*, 19, 52–53, 80–81.

30. Essien-Udom, *Black Nationalism*, 203.

31. Turner, *Islam in the African American Experience*, 3.

32. Muhammad, *Message to the Blackman in America*, 26.

33. Muhammad, *Message to the Blackman in America*, 43.

34. Turner, *Islam in the African American Experience*, 1.

35. Muhammad, *Message to the Blackman in America*, 19.

36. Muhammad, *Message to the Blackman in America*, 43.

37. Muhammad, *Message to the Blackman in America*, 34.

38. Muhammad, *The History of Jesus' Birth, Death and What It Means*, 54.

39. Essien-Udom, *Black Nationalism*, 207.

40. Curtis, *Black Muslim Religion in the Nation of Islam*, 109.

41. Essien-Udom, *Black Nationalism*, 207.

42. Muhammad, *The Supreme Wisdom*, 2:56–57.

43. Curtis, *Black Muslim Religion in the Nation of Islam*, 109.

44. Essien-Udom, *Black Nationalism*, 191.

45. Muhammad, *Message to the Blackman in America*, 321.

46. Muhammad, *Message to the Blackman in America*, 277.

47. Muhammad, *Message to the Blackman in America*, 277–78.

48. Muhammad, *Message to the Blackman in America*, 277.

49. Curtis, *Black Muslim Religion in the Nation of Islam*, 136–37.

50. Evanzz, *The Messenger*, 233. Muhammad's Supreme Captain was his son-in-law Raymond Sherrieff.

51. Curtis, *Black Muslim Religion in the Nation of Islam*, 138.

52. Muhammad, *History of the Nation of Islam*, 21.

53. Essien-Udom, *Black Nationalism*, 150, 157.

54. Essien-Udom, *Black Nationalism*, 157. Here again, Essien-Udom erroneously refers to the MGT-GCC as the "Moslem" (rather than "Muslim") Girls Training and General Course in Civilization.

55. Muhammad, *The Supreme Wisdom*, 2:58.

56. Essien-Udom, *Black Nationalism*, 157–58. Curtis, *Black Muslim Religion in the Nation of Islam*, 146–53.

57. Essien-Udom recognized prayer as an important ritual but erred in his contention that the prayer service was the only religious ritual in NOI praxis, concluding, "There is virtually no religious ceremony or ritual at Temple meetings except the prayers said at the opening and closing of meetings and perhaps a verse or two read by the minister from the Koran or from the Bible during the course of his lecture": Essien-Udom, *Black Nationalism*, 232. His failure to recognize the ritual and religious nature of NOI praxis and principles is due in part to a matter of methodology, since he interprets the organization not by the theories and methods that constitute the field of religious studies, which are themselves multidisciplinary and transdisciplinary, but rather opts for a theory of black nationalism, which obfuscates the religious nature of the movement. In fact, such an approach seems only to allow him to interpret the group as a

sociopolitical movement. This approach, indeed, continues to mark studies of the NOI that fail to recognize that NOI "politics" result first and foremost from their religious orientation. Conversely, Curtis makes similar observations as mine, noting that there are numerous examples of behavior and circumstances that Essien-Udom mentions in his detailed oeuvre that "many contemporary students of religious studies would view as religious ceremony and ritual": Curtis, *Black Muslim Religion in the Nation of Islam*, 161.

58. Muhammad, *Message to the Blackman in America*, 138.

59. Muhammad, *Message to the Blackman in America*, 138.

60. Muhammad, *Message to the Blackman in America*, 144.

61. Muhammad, *Message to the Blackman in America*, 135, 148–52.

62. Curtis, *Black Muslim Religion in the Nation of Islam*, 27.

63. Muhammad, *Message to the Blackman in America*, 137.

64. Muhammad, *Message to the Blackman in America*, 143.

65. Muhammad, *How to Eat to Live, Book 1*, 67, 81–86; Muhammad, *How to Eat to Live, Book 2*, 89–90, 118, 179.

66. See Finley and Guillory, "'That Girl Is Poison.'"

67. Eilberg-Schwartz, *God's Phallus and Other Problems for Men and Monotheism*.

68. Muhammad, *How to Eat to Live, Book 1*, 85.

69. Muhammad, *Message to the Blackman in America*, 64–65.

70. Muhammad, *Message to the Blackman in America*, 60.

71. Muhammad, *Message to the Blackman in America*, 127.

72. Muhammad, *Message to the Blackman in America*, 127.

73. Douglas, *Purity and Danger*, 4.

74. Muhammad, *Message to the Blackman in America*, 44.

75. Brown, *Religious Aesthetics*, 128. See Muhammad, *The Supreme Wisdom*, 2:16, where he calls Negroes "Sacred Vessels," and Muhammad, *The Flag of Islam*, 22, where he refers to black people as "Gods of the Universe."

76. Evanzz, *The Messenger*, 367.

77. I have argued in at least two essays for the consideration of esotericism as an important interpretive lens for the NOI: Finley, "Hidden Away"; cf. Finley, "From Mistress to Mother." See also Bakker, *On Knowledge of God, Self and Enemy*.

78. Hanegraaff, *New Age Religion and Western Culture*, 388.

79. Finley et al., "Africana Esoteric Studies and Western Intellectual Hegemony."

80. Finley et al., "Africana Esoteric Studies and Western Intellectual Hegemony," 165.

81. Finley et al., "Africana Esoteric Studies and Western Intellectual Hegemony," 165.

82. Hanegraaff, *New Age Religion and Western Culture*, 388, 397; cf. Essien-Udom, *Black Nationalism*, 8.

83. Curtis, *Black Muslim Religion in the Nation of Islam*, 158.

84. Evanzz, *The Messenger*, 402; cf. Clegg, *An Original Man*, 73, where Clegg refers to "the theosophy of Fard Muhammad."

85. Hanegraaff, *New Age Religion and Western Culture*, 397.

86. See, e.g., Beynon, "The Voodoo Cult among Negro Migrants in Detroit"; Walker, *Islam and the Search for African-American Nationhood*, 318, 405–6, 568.

87. Essien-Udom, *Black Nationalism*, 35–36.

88. Walker, *Islam and the Search for African-American Nationhood*, 319. Clegg, *An Original Man*, 36, draws the same conclusion.

89. See Lévi-Strauss, *The Savage Mind*, 1–34.

90. Curtis, *Black Muslim Religion in the Nation of Islam*, 18; cf. Lee, *The Nation of Islam*, 138, for whom gnosis is a characteristic of millenarianism.

91. Muhammad, *Message to the Blackman in America*, 52; cf. Muhammad, *The Supreme Wisdom*, 2:14, for a similar discourse that is verbatim in places to the one cited here.

92. Muhammad, *Message to the Blackman in America*, 14.

93. Muhammad, *The True History of Master Fard Muhammad*, 9.

94. Muhammad, *The Secrets of Freemasonry*, 15, 24.

95. Muhammad, *The Secrets of Freemasonry*, 24, 31.

96. Muhammad, *The Secrets of Freemasonry*, 24.

97. Muhammad, *The Secrets of Freemasonry*, 45.

98. Essien-Udom, *Black Nationalism*, 74.

99. In what are arguably the three most important texts on the theology of the NOI—Muhammad's *Message to the Blackman in America* and *The Supreme Wisdom*, vols. 1–2—the discourses privilege this order of information: the identity and nature of Allah and the divine origin of the black race.

100. Muhammad, *The Supreme Wisdom*, 2:14. An identical text appears in Muhammad, *Message to the Blackman in America*, 53.

101. Muhammad, *How to Eat to Live*, Book 2, 7, cf. 54.

102. The people on Mars and other planets ended up there after Yakub exploded the earth. The thirteenth tribe, the one called Shabazz, ended up on what is now known as the earth: see, Muhammad, *The Supreme Wisdom*, 2:15.

103. Muhammad, *The True History of Master Fard Muhammad*, 167–68; cf. Muhammad, *History of the Nation*, 8; Muhammad, *Yakub*, 59.

104. Muhammad, *The Science of Time*, 63.

105. Muhammad, *Our Savior Has Arrived*, 39.

106. Evanzz, *The Messenger*, 87.

107. Essien-Udom, *Black Nationalism*, 43.

108. Cited in Essien-Udom, *Black Nationalism*, 315; Evanzz, *The Messenger*, 395, 414. Only a few pictures were known other than the prison pictures of Wallace Dodd Ford; the Federal Bureau of Investigation (FBI) claims it exposed Fard's true identity. Elijah Muhammad owned one that the FBI confiscated. Evanzz says that the NOI had another picture that the Detroit Police Department took on May 26, 1933.

109. Essien-Udom, *Black Nationalism*, 315.

110. Clegg, *An Original Man*, 21–22.

111. Muhammad, *Message to the Blackman in America*, 19–20. See also Muhammad, *History of the Nation of Islam*, 31–34; Muhammad, *The History of Jesus' Birth, Death and What It Means*, 51.

112. Muhammad, *Message to the Blackman in America*, 24.

113. Lincoln, *The Black Muslims in America*, 25–26. Lincoln suggests that the majority of NOI members were "ex-Christians" or came from Christian homes in which their parents or grandparents were Christians.

114. Muhammad, *History of the Nation of Islam*, 4.

115. Muhammad, *Birth of a Savior*, 31.

116. Muhammad, *The Secrets of Freemasonry*, 9.

117. Muhammad, *The Supreme Wisdom*, 2:30.

118. Muhammad, *The Supreme Wisdom*, 2:32.

119. Muhammad, *Message to the Blackman in America*, 290.

120. Muhammad, *The Mother Plane*, 28.

121. Muhammad, *Message to the Blackman in America*, 291; Muhammad, *The Mother Plane*, 55.

122. Muhammad, *The Mother Plane*, 13–14.

123. Muhammad, *Message to the Blackman in America*, 291.

124. Muhammad, *Message to the Blackman in America*, 291; Muhammad, *The Mother Plane*, 28.

125. Muhammad, *The Mother Plane*, 25, 27.

126. Muhammad, *The Supreme Wisdom*, 1:25–26.

127. Muhammad, *The Supreme Wisdom*, 1:25.

128. Lieb, *Children of Ezekiel*, 3.

129. Lieb, *Children of Ezekiel*, 3, 42. See also Denzler, *The Lure of the Edge*.

130. Lieb, *Children of Ezekiel*, 13.

131. Lieb, *Children of Ezekiel*, 14.

132. Rojcewicz, *The Gods and Technology*, 47.

133. Lieb, *Children of Ezekiel*, 17.

134. Lieb, *Children of Ezekiel*, 34, 164; cf. Kickelmans, *Heidegger on Art and Art Works*, 163.

135. Lee, *The Nation of Islam*, 63. By the mid-1960s, Muhammad was reporting sightings of UFOs as a definite sign of impeding judgment and the "Battle in the Sky."

136. Lieb, *Children of Ezekiel*, 164.

137. Long, *Significations*, 136–38.

138. Lieb, *Children of Ezekiel*, 131. Lynchings were a "commonplace occurrence" for Elijah Muhammad.

139. Muhammad, *The Mother Plane*, 16–17.

140. Muhammad, *The Mother Plane*, 29.

141. Lieb, *Children of Ezekiel*, 176.

142. Lieb, *Children of Ezekiel*, 176.

143. Lee, *The Nation of Islam*, 130.

Chapter Three: Malcolm X and the Politics of Resistance

1. Cleage, "Myths about Malcolm X," 14.

2. Cleage, "Myths about Malcolm X," 15–16.

3. Dyson, *Making Malcolm*; Marable, *Living Black History*.

4. Dyson, *Making Malcolm*, 23.

5. X and Haley, *The Autobiography of Malcolm X*.

6. Marable, *Malcolm X*.

7. Baraka, *Eulogies*.

8. Baraka, *Eulogies*, 1.

9. See Finley, "Homoeroticism and the African American Heterosexual Male Quest for Meaning in the Black Church"; cf. Finley and Guillory, "'That Girl Is Poison.'"

10. Anderson, *Beyond Ontological Blackness*, 11–19.

11. Taylor, "Premillennium Tension," 52.

12. DeCaro, *On the Side of My People*.

13. DeCaro, *On the Side of My People*, 6.

14. Taylor, "Premillennium Tension."

15. Taylor, "Premillennium Tension," 53.

16. Muhammad, *Birth of a Savior*, 38.

17. Muhammad, *Birth of a Savior*, 45.

18. X and Haley, *The Autobiography of Malcolm X*, 161–63.

19. X and Haley, *The Autobiography of Malcolm X*, 161–62.

20. X and Haley, *The Autobiography of Malcolm X*, 162–63.

21. Taylor, "Premillennium Tension," 53. Taylor seems to suggest that it was Malcolm's perspective that he adopted from Muhammad.

22. Cone, *Martin and Malcolm and America*.

23. Taylor, "Premillennium Tension," 59. For detailed discussions, see also Muhammad, *Message to the Blackman in America*, and chapter 1 in this volume.

24. X, *The End of White World Supremacy*, 23–66.

25. X, *The End of White World Supremacy*, 44.

26. X and Haley, *The Autobiography of Malcolm X*, 161–62.

27. X and Haley, *The Autobiography of Malcolm X*, 162–63.

28. X and Haley, *The Autobiography of Malcolm X*, 2. On Marcus Garvey and Black Nationalism, see Carew, *Ghosts in Our Blood*, x.

29. X and Haley, *The Autobiography of Malcolm X*, 3, 19.

30. Cleage, "Myths about Malcolm X," 19.

31. Cleage, "Myths about Malcolm X," 21.

32. Malcolm X, "Message to the Grass Roots," in Breitman, *Malcolm X Speaks*, 3–4.

33. Malcolm X, "The Ballot or the Bullet," in Breitman, *Malcolm X Speaks*, esp. 24–25.

34. See Fanon, *Black Skin, White Masks*, 111–12. Fanon talked about having his "corporal schema" reduced to a "racial epidermal schema," which was fixed as object in the white gaze. See also the introduction in this volume.

35. Cleage, *Black Christian Nationalism*, 79.

36. See Bourdieu, *Outline of a Theory of Practice*; Douglas, *Natural Symbols*.

37. X and Haley, *The Autobiography of Malcolm X*, 17.

38. X and Haley, *The Autobiography of Malcolm X*, 27.

39. Muhammad, *Message to the Blackman in America*, 103.

40. See Glaude, *Exodus!*, esp. 9, 163.

41. X and Haley, *The Autobiography of Malcolm X*, 356–57.

42. X, *By Any Means Necessary*, 59.

43. X, "Message to the Grass Roots," 20.

44. X, "Message to the Grass Roots," 4.

45. Breitman, *Malcolm X Speaks*, 4.

46. Breitman, *Malcolm X Speaks*, 3. These are Breitman's words.

47. Breitman, *Malcolm X Speaks*, 4–44.

48. Muhammad, *The True History of Master Fard Muhammad*, 157.

49. Breitman, *Malcolm X Speaks*, 41.

50. X, *By Any Means Necessary*, 159–61.

51. Robinson, *Black Nationalism in American Politics and Thought*, 34–50. See also X, *By Any Means Necessary*, 33–67; X, February 1965, 269–81.

52. X and Haley, *The Autobiography of Malcolm X*, 206.

53. X and Haley, *The Autobiography of Malcolm X*, 60.

54. Muhammad, *Message to the Blackman in America*, 165; Muhammad, *History of the Nation of Islam*, 26; Clegg, *An Original Man*, 5.

55. Shabazz, "Malcolm X as a Husband and Father," 136.

56. Shabazz, "Malcolm X as a Husband and Father," 136.

57. X, February 1965, 43.

58. X and Haley, *The Autobiography of Malcolm X*, 248.

59. X and Haley, *The Autobiography of Malcolm X*, 248.

60. Howard-Pitney, *Martin Luther King, Jr., Malcolm X and the Civil Rights Struggle of the 1950s and 1960s*, 127; X and Haley, *The Autobiography of Malcolm X*, 248.

61. X and Haley, *The Autobiography of Malcolm X*, 248.

62. Howard-Pitney, *Martin Luther King, Jr., Malcolm X and the Civil Rights Struggle of the 1950s and 1960s*, 122.

63. See Lincoln, *The Black Muslims in America*. This text was originally published in 1961. Lincoln later revised his position and insisted that the NOI was religious.

64. Essien-Udom, *Black Nationalism*.

65. X and Haley, *The Autobiography of Malcolm X*, 41, 53–54, 56–57.

66. X and Haley, *The Autobiography of Malcolm X*, 45.

67. X and Haley, *The Autobiography of Malcolm X*, 55.

68. West, *Prophesy Deliverance!*, 53–54.

69. X and Haley, *The Autobiography of Malcolm X*, 56–57, cf. 264.

70. X and Haley, *The Autobiography of Malcolm X*, 57.

71. X and Haley, *The Autobiography of Malcolm X*, 224.

72. X and Haley, *The Autobiography of Malcolm X*, 224–25.

73. X and Haley, *The Autobiography of Malcolm X*, 57.

74. X, *The End of White World Supremacy*, 48.

75. X, *The End of White World Supremacy*, 48. Notice the contrast: "black BUT" soft, delicate, and fine, as if black were in conflict with these characteristics.

76. X, *The End of White World Supremacy*, 48.

77. X, *February 1965*, 177–79. Malcolm mentions that he was under some control of Muhammad in something akin to a deep daze until after he left the NOI and woke up.

78. Howard-Pitney, *Martin Luther King, Jr., Malcolm X and the Civil Rights Struggle of the 1950s and 1960s*, 12.

79. X, *By Any Means Necessary*, 138.

80. X, *By Any Means Necessary*, 138.

81. X, *By Any Means Necessary*, 84, 93, 185.

82. Cone, *Martin and Malcolm and America*, 186.

83. Cone, *Martin and Malcolm and America*, 186.

84. Gomez, *Black Crescent*, 358.

85. Marable, *Living Black History*, 173; Evanzz, *The Messenger*, 175–77.

86. Cone, *Martin and Malcolm and America*, 186–87.

87. Muhammad, *The Supreme Wisdom*, vol. 1.

88. See, e.g., DeCaro, *Malcolm and the Cross*, 186, 189; DeCaro, *On the Side of My People*, 100; Gomez, *Black Crescent*, 356.

89. Leigh, *Circuitous Journey*, 138. These numbers vary. Some suggest that the NOI had as many as 20,000 members and others suggest as many as 250,000 members. Cf. Gomez, *Black Crescent*, 356.

90. DeCaro, *Malcolm and the Cross*, 185–86.

91. DeCaro, *On the Side of My People*, 110.

92. Robinson, *Black Nationalism in American Politics and Thought*, 35.

93. See Marable, *Living Black History*, 157.

94. X, "Message to the Grass Roots," 4.

95. Butler, *Bodies That Matter*, 31–32; Yancy, "Geneva Smitherman."

96. See, e.g., Smitherman, *Black Talk*.

97. Butler, *Bodies That Matter*, 10, 13; Yancy, "Geneva Smitherman" 277–78.

98. Malcolm X, "God's Judgment of White America (The Chickens Are Coming Home to Roost)," in X, *The End of White World Supremacy*, 133.

99. X, *The End of White World Supremacy*, 133.

100. Cone, *Martin and Malcolm and America*, 187.

101. Leigh, *Circuitous Journey*, 148.

102. DeCaro, *On the Side of My People*, 264.

103. Evanzz, *The Messenger*, 287. Evanzz reports that Malcolm announced his break with the NOI on NBC's *Today Show* on August 8, 1964.

104. X, *February 1965*, 22.

105. X, *February 1965*, 179.

106. See Muhammad, *Message to the Blackman in America*, 103. Muhammad describes the story of Yakub and how whites nearly degenerated into "wild beasts."

107. X and Haley, *The Autobiography of Malcolm X*, 374.

108. X, *By Any Means Necessary*, 190.

109. X, *February 1965*, 43.

110. X, *By Any Means Necessary*, 69–74, 163–66; X, *February 1965*, 75–107; Breitman, *Malcolm X Speaks*, 23–44.

111. Breitman, *Malcolm X Speaks*, 7–10, 23–24; X, *By Any Means Necessary*, 75–107; X, *The End of White World Supremacy*, 128; X, *February 1965*, 75–107.

Chapter Four: Warith Deen Mohammed and the Nation of Islam

1. Wallace D. Muhammad announced that he had changed his name to Warith Deen Mohammed in 1980. For the purposes of this chapter, I use his later name: Warith. See Lee, *The Nation of Islam*, 97; cf. *Bilalian News*, March 14, 1980. He used what he called the legal spelling "Mohammed," although he also said, "And Waarith Ud-Deen—we say Wallace, but Waarith Ud-Deen means inheritor of the religion or faith of Muhammad." See Dawan, *New Unabridged Historical Glossary*, 1:92, cf. 91.

2. Lee, *The Nation of Islam*, 92. See also *Chicago Tribune*, March 7, 1976, 38.

3. McCloud, *African American Islam*, 37–38.

4. Curtis, *Black Muslim Religion in the Nation of Islam*, 176; Lee, *The Nation of Islam*, 75; Marsh, *The Lost-Found Nation of Islam in America*, 69. However, Karl Evanzz lists Muhammad's death as February 24, 1975: Evanzz, *The Messenger*, 422.

5. Lee, *The Nation of Islam*, 78, 93.

6. Mohammed, *As the Light Shineth from the East*, 110.

7. Lee, *The Nation of Islam*, 94; Gibson, *A History of the Nation of Islam*, 71–84.

8. Lee, *The Nation of Islam*, 96.

9. Lee, *The Nation of Islam*, 81.

10. Curtis acknowledges the problem of the absence of scholarship and literature on Warith Deen Mohammed: see Curtis, *Islam in Black America*, 107.

11. See Mohammed, *An African American Genesis*; Mohammed, *As the Light Shineth from the East*; Mohammed, *Imam W. Deen Muhammad Speaks from Harlem, NY*, vols. 1–2; Mohammed, *Religion on the Line*. Cf. Clifton E. Marsh, "Interview with Imam Wallace D. Muhammad," in Marsh, *The Lost-Found Nation of Islam in America*, 160.

12. See, e.g., Dawan, *New Unabridged Historical Glossary*, vol. 1, which reproduces and defines the words and important concepts of Mohammed from *Muhammad Speaks* and *Bilalian News* during this time period. In addition, it includes an interview with Mohammed titled "The Meaning of Ramadan": Dawan. *New Unabridged Historical Glossary*, 1:74–92.

13. Mamiya, "From Black Muslim to Bilalian," 141.

14. Marsh, "Interview with Imam Wallace D. Muhammad," 160.

15. Gardell, *In the Name of Elijah Muhammad*, 101.

16. Marsh. "Interview with Imam Wallace D. Muhammad," 161.

17. Marsh, "Interview with Imam Wallace D. Muhammad," 162.

18. Curtis, *Islam in Black America*, 112.

19. Gardell, *In the Name of Elijah Muhammad*; Curtis, *Islam in Black America*, 112–13.

20. Mohammed, *As the Light Shineth from the East*, 113.

21. Mohammed, *As the Light Shineth from the East*, 113.

22. Mohammed, *As the Light Shineth from the East*, 13–23, 208.

23. Mohammed, *As the Light Shineth from the East*, 210; Lee, *The Nation of Islam*, 101.

24. Mohammed, *As the Light Shineth from the East*, 25–26.

25. Mohammed, *As the Light Shineth from the East*, 31–32.

26. See Muhammad, *The Supreme Wisdom*, 1:3–5; Muhammad, *The Supreme Wisdom*, 2:3.

27. It is important to note that as late as November 1976 (*Bilalian News*, November 14, 1976, 1, 20–21), the names "The Lost-Found Nation of Islam in the West" and "Universal Nation of Islam" were still being used for the organization: see Dawan, *New Unabridged Historical Glossary*, 4:183. Mohammed, *Religion on the Line*, 4.

28. It had gone from the Nation of Islam to the World Community of Al-Islam in the West to the American Muslim Mission (which eventually dropped the "American").

29. Marsh, "Interview with Imam Wallace D. Muhammad," 157.

30. Mohammed frequently expounds on the idea of the body directly and indirectly: see, e.g., Mohammed, *As the Light Shineth from the East*, 37–39, 45–49, 53–59, 70–71, 94–106, 140–49.

31. Mohammed, *As the Light Shineth from the East*, 38–39.

32. Mohammed, *As the Light Shineth from the East*, 39. Cf. Durkheim, *The Elementary Forms of Religious Life*, 9. What "eminently social" means as I use it to describe Mohammed is that religion first and foremost emphasizes the collective.

33. Mohammed, *As the Light Shineth from the East*, 56.

34. See, e.g., Mohammed, *As the Light Shineth from the East*, 38–39.

35. Mohammed, *As the Light Shineth from the East*, 56.

36. Mohammed, *As the Light Shineth from the East*, 73.

37. Mohammed, *As the Light Shineth from the East*, 73.

38. Mohammed, *As the Light Shineth from the East*, 81.

39. See Mohammed, *An African American Genesis*, Mohammed, *As the Light Shineth from the East*; Mohammed, *Religion on the Line*; Mohammed, *Imam W. Deen Muhammad Speaks from Harlem, NY*, vols. 1–2.

40. Jackson, *Islam and the Blackamerican*.

41. Mohammed, *Imam W. Deen Muhammad Speaks from Harlem, NY*, 1:1.

42. Mohammed, *Imam W. Deen Muhammad Speaks from Harlem, NY*, 1:28.

43. For examples of discussions of Islam's role in the enslavement of Africans, see Segal, *Islam's Black Slaves*.

44. Mohammed, *As the Light Shineth from the East*, 170; cf. Segal, *Islam's Black Slaves*, ix, 199–223.

45. Diouf, *Servants of Allah*, 1.

46. Hunwick and Powell, *The African Diaspora in the Mediterranean Lands of Islam*, ix, 51–64.

47. Mohammed, *An African American Genesis*, 4.

48. Muhammad, *The Supreme Wisdom*, 1:29.

49. Mohammed, *As the Light Shineth from the East*, 136.

50. Mohammed, *As the Light Shineth from the East*, 137–38.

51. See, e.g., Mohammed, *Imam W. Deen Muhammad Speaks from Harlem, NY*, 2:13–15, 104–5.

52. Mohammed, *As the Light Shineth from the East*, 138.

53. Mohammed, *Imam W. Deen Muhammad Speaks from Harlem, NY*, 2:95.

54. Mohammed, *Imam W. Deen Muhammad Speaks from Harlem, NY*, 2:96–99.

55. Mohammed, *An African American Genesis*, ix.

56. Mohammed, *An African American Genesis*, 68.

57. Mohammed, *An African American Genesis*, 44.

58. Mohammed, *An African American Genesis*, 42, 44.

59. Mohammed, *An African American Genesis*, 16.

60. Mohammed, *An African American Genesis*, 17.

61. Mohammed, *An African American Genesis*, 41.

62. See, e.g., Mohammed, *Religion on the Line*, 7–11.

63. Mohammed, *An African American Genesis*, 35.

64. Carson, *The Autobiography of Martin Luther King, Jr.*, 325; Mohammed, *An African American Genesis*, 34–35; Mohammed, *As the Light Shineth from the East*, 141–42.

65. Mohammed, *An African American Genesis*, 35.

66. Mohammed, *An African American Genesis*, 34–35.

67. Mohammed, *An African American Genesis*, 31–33.

68. Mohammed, *An African American Genesis*, 33.

69. Mohammed, *An African American Genesis*, 33.

70. Mohammed, *An African American Genesis*, 32.

71. E.g., Mohammed, *Imam W. Deen Muhammad Speaks in Harlem, NY*, 1:79.

72. Mohammed, *As the Light Shineth from the East*, 79.

73. Mohammed, *As the Light Shineth from the East*, 79.

74. Mohammed, *Imam W. Deen Muhammad Speaks in Harlem, NY*, 1:79. It is unclear whether he is suggesting the existence of a "Blackland" or something similar. It is uncertain what the corresponding geography is.

75. The name "Bilalians" appears in *Muhammad Speaks*, October 24, 1975, 2. See also Lee, *The Nation of Islam*, 89; cf. Dawan, *New Unabridged Historical Glossary*, 1:7, which locates the usage in *Bilalian News*, November 7, 1975. On Bilal ibn Rabah, see Abdul-Rauf, *Bilāl Ibn Rabāh*; Craig, *Bilal*. See also Marsh, *The Lost-Found Nation of Islam in America*, 270–71; McCloud, *African American Islam*, 75–76; Turner, *Islam in the African American Experience*, 225. See the discussion of Bilali Mohammed and Salih Bilali, slaves on the Georgia islands in the early nineteenth century, in Austin, *African Muslims in Antebellum America*, 85–113.

76. Curtis, *Black Muslim Religion in the Nation of Islam*, 66.

77. Mohammed, *As the Light Shineth from the East*, 91.

78. Mohammed, *As the Light Shineth from the East*, 7, 9–36. The American Academy of Religion address was entitled "The Evolution of the Nation of Islam."

79. Mohammed, *As the Light Shineth from the East*, 223–42, esp. 232.

80. Mohammed, *As the Light Shineth from the East*, 18; Mamiya, "From Black Muslim to Bilalian," 139.

81. Mohammed, *As the Light Shineth from the East*, 97.

82. Mamiya, "From Black Muslim to Bilalian," 139.

83. Abdul-Rauf, *Bilāl Ibn Rabāh*, 63–68.

84. Abdul-Rauf, *Bilāl Ibn Rabāh*, 25, emphasis added.

85. Abdul-Rauf, *Bilāl Ibn Rabāh*, iii.

86. Mohammed, *As the Light Shineth from the East*, 101, emphasis added.

87. Abdul-Rauf, *Bilāl Ibn Rabāh*, 58–61.

88. Abdul-Rauf, *Bilāl Ibn Rabāh*, 58.

89. Abdul-Rauf, *Bilāl Ibn Rabāh*, 57–61.

90. Abdul-Rauf, *Bilāl Ibn Rabāh*, 58–59.

91. Abdul-Rauf, *Bilāl Ibn Rabāh*, 59.

92. Abdul-Rauf, *Bilāl Ibn Rabāh*, 67.

93. Mohammed, *As the Light Shineth from the East*, 100.

94. Abdul-Rauf, *Bilāl Ibn Rabāh*, 68–70.

95. By 1985, however, the term *Bilalian* is rarely seen in Mohammed's writing, and by 1986 it is absent: see Mohammed, *African American Genesis*; Mohammed, *Imam W. Deen Muhammad Speaks from Harlem, NY*, vol. 2.

96. Mohammed, *As the Light Shineth from the East*, 110.

97. Mohammed, *As the Light Shineth from the East*, 102.

98. Mohammed, *As the Light Shineth from the East*, 102.

99. Mohammed, *As the Light Shineth from the East*, 128.

100. Mohammed, *As the Light Shineth from the East*, 121–22.

101. Mohammed, *As the Light Shineth from the East*, 123.

102. Mohammed, *As the Light Shineth from the East*, 109.

103. Mohammed, *As the Light Shineth from the East*, 206–27.

104. Mohammed, *As the Light Shineth from the East*, 27.

105. Mohammed, *Religion on the Line*, 128.

106. Mohammed, *W. Deen Muhammad Speaks from Harlem, NY*, 1:87.

107. Mohammed, *W. Deen Muhammad Speaks from Harlem, NY*, 1:86–87.

108. Mohammed, *W. Deen Muhammad Speaks from Harlem, NY*, 2:122.

109. Mohammed, *W. Deen Muhammad Speaks from Harlem, NY*, 2:122.

110. Mohammed, *W. Deen Muhammad Speaks from Harlem, NY*, 2:122.

111. Mohammed, *As the Light Shineth from the East*, 65.

112. Mohammed, *An African American Genesis*, 42.

113. Mohammed, *Religion on the Line*, 75.

114. Mohammed, *W. Deen Muhammad Speaks from Harlem, NY*, 1:130. In March 1977, he founded CRAID, which stands for Committee for the Removal of All Images That Attempt to Portray the Divine.

115. Mohammed, *Religion on the Line*, 75–76, 81–82.

116. Mohammed, *Religion on the Line*, 75.

117. Mohammed, *W. Deen Muhammad Speaks from Harlem, NY*, 1:74.

118. Mohammed, *W. Deen Muhammad Speaks from Harlem, NY*, 1:74.

119. Mohammed, *W. Deen Muhammad Speaks from Harlem, NY*, 2:29; Mohammed, *W. Deen Muhammad Speaks from Harlem, NY*, 1:48; cf. Mohammed, *Religion on the Line*, 65–66.

120. Mohammed, *W. Deen Muhammad Speaks from Harlem, NY*, 1:48.

121. Mohammed, *W. Deen Muhammad Speaks from Harlem, NY*, 2:132.

122. Mohammed, *W. Deen Muhammad Speaks from Harlem, NY*, 1:51.

123. Mohammed, *W. Deen Muhammad Speaks from Harlem, NY*, 1:89.

124. Mohammed, *W. Deen Muhammad Speaks from Harlem, NY*, 2:29–30.

125. Mohammed, *W. Deen Muhammad Speaks from Harlem, NY*, 2:29.

126. Mohammed, *Religion on the Line*, 68–89.

127. Mohammed, *Religion on the Line*, 69.

128. Mohammed, *W. Deen Muhammad Speaks from Harlem*, 2:30.

Chapter Five: Mothership Connections

1. Finley, "The Supernatural in the African American Experience," 242–44; Parliament, *Mothership Connection*, Casablanca, 1976. I also recognize Walker, *Mothership Connections*, but Parliament's record album, rather than Walker's book, was the inspiration for the title of this chapter.

2. See Farrakhan, *The Announcement*, 6.

3. See, e.g., Alexander, *The Farrakhan Factor*; Gardell, *In the Name of Elijah Muhammad*; Haskins, *Louis Farrakhan and the Nation of Islam*; Kelleter, *Con/tradition*; Marsh, *The Lost-Found Nation of Islam in America*; Marshall, *Louis Farrakhan*; Walker, *Islam and the Search for African-American Nationhood*.

4. See Finley, "The Meaning of 'Mother' in Louis Farrakhan's 'Mother Wheel,'" 434–65.

5. Gardell, *In the Name of Elijah Muhammad*, 119; J. Muhammad, *Closing the Gap*, x–xi, esp. xi.

6. Gardell, *In the Name of Elijah Muhammad*, 120; J. Muhammad, *Closing the Gap*, 110.

7. J. Muhammad, *Closing the Gap*, 114, 234–35.

8. J. Muhammad, *Closing the Gap*, 334–35.

9. J. Muhammad, *Closing the Gap*, 333.

10. Evanzz, *The Messenger*, 169; J. Muhammad, *Closing the Gap*, 333.

11. J. Muhammad, *Closing the Gap*, 334. The clarification in brackets is Muhammad's, not mine.

12. J. Muhammad, *Closing the Gap*, 334.

13. J. Muhammad, *Closing the Gap*, 334–35.

14. J. Muhammad, *Closing the Gap*, 335–37.

15. J. Muhammad, *Closing the Gap*, 336.

16. J. Muhammad, *Closing the Gap*, 336–37. See also J. Muhammad, *Closing the Gap*, 111–13; cf. Gardell, *In the Name of Elijah Muhammad*, 120–21.

17. X and Haley, *The Autobiography of Malcolm X*, 190, cf. 192; James, *The Varieties of Religious Experience*, 460–65.

18. Curtis, *Black Muslim Religion in the Nation of Islam*, 167–73.

19. Stuart Hall, "The Work of Representation," in Hall, *Representation*, 16.

20. See Farrakhan, *The Wheel and the Last Days*; Farrakhan, *The Announcement*, 6; Farrakhan, *The Reality of the Mother Plane*; Koppel, *An Interview with Louis Farrakhan*.

21. J. Muhammad, *Closing the Gap*, 338.

22. J. Muhammad, *Closing the Gap*, 338.

23. J. Muhammad, *Closing the Gap*, 338–39.

24. Farrakhan, *The Announcement*. A version of this press conference is printed with additional commentary from Tynnetta Muhammad and Jabril Muhammad in J. Muhammad, *Closing the Gap*, 377–88. The full text is also available online. See the Honorable Louis Farrakhan, "International Press Conference, J. W. Marriott Hotel, October 24, 1989," accessed January 5, 2020, http://www.noi.org/statements /transcript_891024.htm. T. Muhammad, *The Comer by Night*, 29–36. Mother Tynnetta is a spiritual interpreter of events in the Nation of Islam. Here she ties Farrakhan's international travels, numerology, and mystical practices to his UFO experience.

25. Farrakhan, *The Time and What Must Be Done*.

26. Bakker, *On Knowledge of God, Self and Enemy*, 61.

27. Farrakhan, *The Announcement*, 5–6.

28. Lieb, *Children of Ezekiel*, 206.

29. Koppel, *An Interview with Louis Farrakhan.*

30. See Denzler, *The Lure of the Edge*, 1–67, esp. 35–55.

31. See Hughes and Geduld, *A Critical Edition of "The War of the Worlds."*

32. Hughes and Geduld, *A Critical Edition of "The War of the Worlds"* 84; cf. *The War of the Worlds*, VHS, 50 mins., Learning Channel Great Books, Discovery Communications, Bethesda, MD, 1996.

33. Farrakhan, *The Announcement*, 6.

34. Farrakhan, *The Announcement*, 6.

35. Farrakhan, *The Announcement*, 6.

36. Farrakhan, *The Announcement*, 6.

37. Lieb, *Children of Ezekiel*, 180. Lieb suggests that at least a dozen such groups emerged after the death of Muhammad.

38. J. Muhammad, *Is It Possible That the Honorable Elijah Muhammad Is Still Physically Alive???*, 5–8.

39. Farrakhan, *The Announcement*, 7.

40. I explore Mother Tynnetta's discursive authority and her esoteric system of thought in Finley, "From Mistress to Mother."

41. Bakker, *On Knowledge of God, Self and Enemy*, 106–7.

42. T. Muhammad, *The Comer by Night*, 84.

43. See chapter 2 in this volume. See also E. Muhammad, *The Mother Plane.*

44. Cf. Farrakhan, *The Reality of the Mother Plane*; Farrakhan, *The Wheel and the Last Days.*

45. Ronald Reagan, "Remarks to Students and Faculty at Fallston High School," December 4, 1985, accessed January 5, 2020, https://commons.wikimedia.org/wiki/File:President_Reagan%27s_Remarks_to_Students_and_Faculty_at_Fallston_High_School_on_December_4,_1985.webm. See also Dolan, *UFOs and the National Security State*, an academic study of the US government's research on UFOs. It indicates consistent and concentrated attention to the subject by the by the United States.

46. Ronald Reagan, "Address to the 42d Session of the United Nations General Assembly in New York, New York," September 21, 1987, accessed January 5, 2020, http://www.reagan.utexas.edu/archives/speeches/1987/092187b.htm.

47. Farrakhan, *The Announcement*, 9–10.

48. Farrakhan, *The Announcement*, 9–10.

49. Farrakhan, *The Announcement*, 10–11. According to Farrakhan, the Federal Bureau of Investigation has been working to destroy the NOI since 1940 via the Counterintelligence Program (COINTELPRO).

50. Farrakhan, *The Announcement*, 13.

51. Farrakhan, *The Announcement*, 13.

52. Farrakhan, *The Announcement*, 13.

53. Farrakhan, *The Announcement*, 13.

54. See Alexander, *The New Jim Crow*.

55. Farrakhan, *The Announcement*, 14–15. The italics are in the original source.

56. See Jones, *Is God a White Racist?*; cf., e.g., Cone, *A Black Theology of Liberation*; Pinn, *Making the Gospel Plain*, esp. 54, 67, 170–80; Walker and Garnet, *Walker's Appeal and Garnet's Address to the Slaves of the United States of America*.

57. Farrakhan, *The Announcement*, 16.

58. Farrakhan, *The Announcement*, 16.

59. See, e.g., Finley, "The Meaning of 'Mother' in Louis Farrakhan's 'Mother Wheel'"; James, *The Varieties of Religious Experience*; Freud, *Introductory Lectures on Psychoanalysis*; Freud, *Three Essays on the Theory of Sexuality*; Jung, *Flying Saucers*; Kohut, "Forms and Transformations of Narcissism."

60. J. Muhammad, *Closing the Gap*, xix.

61. Lee, *The Nation of Islam*, 121. Lee cites Louis Farrakhan tying the teaching of the Mother Plane to Elijah Muhammad in *Final Call*, January 31, 1987, 2.

62. Farrakhan, *The Wheel and the Last Days*.

63. Farrakhan, *The Wheel and the Last Days*.

64. Farrakhan, *The Wheel and the Last Days*.

65. Farrakhan, *The Wheel and the Last Days*.

66. Farrakhan, *The Wheel and the Last Days*.

67. Farrakhan, *The Wheel and the Last Days*.

68. Farrakhan, *The Reality of the Mother Plane*.

69. Farrakhan, *The Reality of the Mother Plane*.

70. Farrakhan, *The Reality of the Mother Plane*.

71. Farrakhan, *The Time and What Must Be Done*.

72. Farrakhan, *The Wheel and the Last Days*. See also Koppel, *An Interview with Louis Farrakhan*; Farrakhan, *The Reality of the Mother Plane*.

73. Farrakhan, *The Wheel and the Last Days*.

74. Farrakhan, *The Reality of the Mother Plane*.

75. Farrakhan, *The Wheel and the Last Days*.

76. Lieb, *Children of Ezekiel*, 219.

77. Farrakhan, *The Wheel and the Last Days*.

78. Farrakhan, *The Wheel and the Last Days*; cf. Farrakhan, *A Torchlight for America*, 1–4.

79. Lieb, *Children of Ezekiel*, 219.

80. Farrakhan, *A Torchlight for America*, 25–26.

81. Farrakhan, *The Wheel and the Last Days*.

82. Farrakhan, *The Announcement*.

83. Walker, *Islam and the Search for African-American Nationhood*, 494–526.

84. Koppel, *An Interview with Louis Farrakhan*; cf. Farrakhan, *The Wheel and the Last Days*. Farrakhan claims that the Mother Plane followed him throughout his international excursion.

85. Koppel, *An Interview with Louis Farrakhan*.

86. Koppel, *An Interview with Louis Farrakhan*.

87. Farrakhan, *A Torchlight for America*, 51. Farrakhan says that the US government is angry with him because Libya loaned the NOI the smaller amount of $3 million without any collateral or interest.

88. Farrakhan, *The Wheel and the Last Days*.

89. Farrakhan, *The Wheel and the Last Days*.

90. Farrakhan, *The Wheel and the Last Day*. Note that this lecture was given a week later, on July 13, 1986.

91. At least one Navajo member, YoNasDa Lonewolf-McCall Muhammad, was also member of the NOI: see Louis Farrakhan, "The Common Destiny of Original People: Making a Productive Nation," FinalCall.com, August 1, 2006, accessed October 11, 2008, http://www.finalcall.com/artman/publish/article_2808.shtml. This article states that it reflects excerpts from Farrakhan's June 19, 1986, speech, but it is unclear when the article actually appeared.

92. Farrakhan, *The Wheel and the Last Days*.

93. Farrakhan, *The Wheel and the Last Days*.

94. Farrakhan, *The Wheel and the Last Days*.

95. Farrakhan, *The Wheel and the Last Days*; cf. Farrakhan, "The Common Destiny of Original People."

96. See chapter 2 in this volume, in which I argue that the Mother Plane is a vehicle that discloses ultimate reality, a gnosis that heretofore had been hidden from the world.

97. See Lieb, *Children of Ezekiel*, 201.

98. Lieb, *Children of Ezekiel*, 199–201.

99. Farrakhan, *Let Us Make Man*, 127–50. See also Makhubuti and Karenga, *Million Man March/Day of Absence*, 9–29. Lieb, *Children of Ezekiel*, 201. Lieb also suggests that this speech was one of the acts of "bearing witness" to the Mother Wheel.

100. See Farrakhan, *The Meaning of the F.O.I.*

101. See Koppel, *An Interview with Louis Farrakhan.*

102. Douglas, *How Institutions Think*, 3–4.

103. See Judith Bradford and Crispin Sartwell, "Voiced Bodies/Embodied Voices," in Bradford and Sartwell, *Race/Sex*, 192.

104. Lee, *The Nation of Islam*, 115; cf. *New York Times*, October 7, 1985, pt. 2, 4.

105. Koppel, *An Interview with Louis Farrakhan.*

Conclusion

1. Allen, "Religious Heterodoxy and Nationalist Tradition," 26.

2. Felber, *Those Who Know Don't Say*, 1.

3. Hucks, *Yoruba Traditions and African American Religious Nationalism*, 41–42.

4. Long, *Significations*, 211.

5. Long, *Significations*, 9.

6. Bourdieu, *Outline of a Theory of Practice*, 190–97.

7. Douglas, *How Institutions Think*, 3–4, 48–53, 112, 119; Douglas, *Natural Symbols*, 57–71; Gellner, "Sanctity, Puritanism, Secularism and Nationalism in North Africa."

8. See Bourdieu, *Distinction*, 1–2, 257–94.

9. Bourdieu, *Outline of a Theory of Practice*, 17, 72, 81–82, 111–12, 157, 165.

10. Bourdieu, *Outline of a Theory of Practice*, 72–82.

11. Bradford and Sartwell, "Voiced Bodies/Embodied Voices," 191–92.

12. Bourdieu, *Outline of a Theory of Practice*, 85.

13. Bourdieu, *Outline of a Theory of Practice*, 87.

14. Bourdieu, *Outline of a Theory of Practice*, 87.

15. Bourdieu, *Outline of a Theory of Practice*, 164–65.

16. Bourdieu, *Outline of a Theory of Practice*, 190–97.

17. E.g., Muhammad, *The Supreme Wisdom*, 1:33–24; Muhammad, *The Supreme Wisdom*, 2:16.

18. Ray, *Bourdieu on Religion*, 35, 50.

19. Douglas, *How Institutions Think*, 48–49.

20. Bourdieu, *Outline of a Theory of Practice*, 171–82, 190–97.

21. Douglas, *How Institutions Think*, 48–49.

22. Finley and Guillory, "'That Girl Is Poison'"; cf. Hill Collins, *Black Feminist Thought*, 69–96.

23. Butler, *Bodies That Matter*.

24. Bourdieu, *Distinction*, 257–60.

25. Curtis, "Islamizing the Black Body," 169, 177–78; Essien-Udom, *Black Nationalism*, 86, 104, 110; Lincoln, *The Black Muslims in America*, 24, 44, 79, 217; Mamiya, "From Black Muslim to Bilalian, 138, 145–48.

26. Bourdieu, *Distinction*, 114.

27. Cleage, *Black Christian Nationalism*, 102–3.

28. Cleage, *Black Christian Nationalism*, 102–3.

29. Cf. Cregan, *The Sociology of the Body*, 74–75.

30. On "naturalizing," see Bourdieu, *Outline of a Theory of Practice*, 164.

31. Bourdieu, *Outline of a Theory of Practice*, 17, 72, 81–82, 87.

32. Pierce and Williams, "And Their Prayers Shall Be Answered through the Womb of a Woman," 199.

33. Higginbotham, *Righteous Discontent*, 185–230.

34. See McClintock, *Imperial Leather*, 167–68.

35. See, e.g., Muhammad, *How to Eat to Live, Book 1*, 15, 33, 70.

Epilogue

I thank LSU's College of Humanities and Social Sciences for a generous Manship Summer Research Award in 2017 that provided the freedom to conduct the research for this epilogue; and thanks to Drs. Tamura A. Lomax, Fahima I. Ife, Biko M. Gray, and Lori L. Martin for their insightful feedback.

1. Abdul Khabeer, *Muslim Cool*.

2. Karim, *American Muslim Women*, 21.

3. I. Muhammad, *UFOs and the Nation of Islam*.

4. Tate, *Little X*; Taylor, "As-Salaam Alaikum, My Sister"; Taylor, "Elijah Muhammad's Nation of Islam"; Taylor, *The Promise of Patriarchy*; Rouse, *Engaged Surrender*.

5. See, e.g., Taylor, "As-Salaam Alaikum, My Sister," 192; Rouse, *Engaged Surrender*, 8.

6. Jeffries, "Raising Her Voice"; cf. Gibson, "Nation Women's Engagement and Resistance in the *Muhammad Speaks* Newspaper."

7. See Gibson, "Nation Women's Engagement and Resistance in the *Muhammad Speaks* Newspaper"; Sims, "An Analysis of Womanhood." See also Gibson, "Ebony Muhammad's *Hurt2Healing* Magazine and Contemporary Nation Women."

8. West, "Nation Builders," 219, cf. 12.

9. Bennett Muhammad, "Humble Warrioress," 26.

10. West, "Nation Builders."

11. West, "Revisiting Female Activism in the 1960s"; West, "Take Two."

12. Gibson and Karim, *Women of the Nation*, 2.

13. Sims, "An Analysis of Womanhood."

14. Sims, "An Analysis of Womanhood," 6–7, 109–10

15. Bennett Muhammad, "Humble Warrioress," ii.

16. Bennett Muhammad, "Humble Warrioress," 7, 103.

17. Jeffries, *A Nation Can Rise No Higher Than Its Women*, ix.

18. Jeffries, *A Nation Can Rise No Higher Than Its Women*, 3–9. She ignores most of the scholarship on women in the NOI that has been published since 2000, including all of my work.

19. Jeffries, *A Nation Can Rise No Higher Than Its Women*, 17.

20. See, e.g., Akom, "Reexamining Resistance as Oppositional Behavior."

21. Pierce and Williams, "And Their Prayers Shall Be Answered through the Womb of a Woman," 197.

22. Pierce and Williams, "And Their Prayers Shall Be Answered through the Womb of a Woman," 199.

23. Finley, "The Meaning of 'Mother' in Louis Farrakhan's 'Mother Wheel.'"

24. David Halperin, "UFOs, Louis Farrakhan, and the 'Mother Wheel'—The Scholarship of Stephen C. Finley," *Diary of a UFO Investigator* (blog), October 9, 2015, accessed August 25, 2017, https://www.davidhalperin.net/ufos-louis-farrakhan-and -the-mother-wheel-the-scholarship-of-stephen-finley; David Halperin, "UFOs, Louis Farrakhan, the 'Mother Wheel' . . . and 'Independence Day,'" *Diary of a UFO Investigator* (blog), October 22, 2015, accessed, January 5, 2020, https://www.davidhalperin.net /blog/page/10.

25. Curtis, "Science and Technology in Elijah Muhammad's Nation of Islam."

26. Finley, "The Meaning of 'Mother' in Farrakhan's 'Mother Wheel,'" 460.

27. Finley, "From Mistress to Mother"; Finley, "Hidden Away"; Finley, "Mathematical Theology."

28. See, e.g., Louis Farrakhan, "How to Give Birth to a God," *Final Call*, May 16, 2005 (updated), accessed August 17, 2017, http://www.finalcall.com/artman/publish /Minister_Louis_Farrakhan_9/How_To_Give_Birth_Toa_God_2001.shtml; Louis Farrakhan, "The Origin of Blackness," *Final Call*, April 8, 2001, accessed August 17, 2017, http://www.finalcall.com/columns/mlf/mlf_org-blackness06-19-2001 .htm; Louis Farrakhan, "Minister Louis Farrakhan's Speech at the Million Family March," *Washington Post*, October 16, 2000, accessed August 17, 2017, http://www .washingtonpost.com/wp-srv/metro/daily/oct00/1017speech.htm. Cf. Farrakhan, *Let*

Us Make Man. See also Pierce and Williams, "And Their Prayers Shall Be Answered through the Womb of a Woman."

29. Farrakhan, *Let Us Make Man,* 98–99.

30. Farrakhan, *Let Us Make Man,* 107–24.

31. Farrakhan, *Let Us Make Man,* 109.

32. Pierce and Williams, "And Their Prayers Shall Be Answered through the Womb of a Woman," 204.

33. Pierce and Williams, "And Their Prayers Shall Be Answered through the Womb of a Woman," 203–5.

34. Miyakawa, "Receiving, Embodying, and Sharing 'Divine Wisdom.'" While not specifically on the NOI, this essay is an exception.

35. Pierce and Williams, "And Their Prayers Shall Be Answered through the Womb of a Woman," 201–2.

36. See, e.g., Farrakhan, *Let Us Make Man,* in which Farrakhan mentions "wombs" multiple times in every speech on men and women.

37. Finley, "The Meaning of 'Mother' in Farrakhan's 'Mother Wheel,'" 458.

38. Gibson, "Nation Women's Engagement and Resistance in the *Muhammad Speaks* Newspaper," 1.

39. See, e.g., Taylor, "Elijah Muhammad's Nation of Islam," esp. 149. See also the chapter "Pork or Women: Purity and Danger in the Nation of Islam," in Witt, *Black Hunger,* 102–25. She also omits additional essays by Cynthia S'thembile West. Finley and Guillory, "'That Girl Is Poison.'"

40. Finley and Guillory, "'That Girl Is Poison,'" 8.

41. Farrakhan, *Let Us Make Man,* 90, cf. 27–28, 66.

42. Davis, *Women, Race and Class,* 224, cf. 222–44.

43. Davis, *Women, Race and Class,* 226.

44. Sims, "An Analysis of Womanhood," 4.

45. Farrakhan, *Let Us Make Man,* 41, cf. 118.

46. Finley, "The Meaning of 'Mother' in Farrakhan's 'Mother Wheel,'" 455; cf. Gardell, *In the Name of Elijah Muhammad,* 335.

47. Gardell, *In the Name of Elijah Muhammad,* 335; cf. Finley, "The Meaning of 'Mother' in Farrakhan's 'Mother Wheel,'" 455.

48. Finley, "The Meaning of 'Mother' in Farrakhan's 'Mother Wheel,'" 454–45; Hartman, *Lose Your Mother,* 98.

49. Lieb, *Children of Ezekiel,* 219.

50. Finley, "The Meaning of 'Mother' in Farrakhan's 'Mother Wheel,'" 455.

51. Farrakhan, *The Wheel and the Last Days*.

52. On Sister Clara Muhammad, see Amatullah-Rahman, "She Stood by His Side and at Times in His Stead"; Martin, *Black Women as Leaders*, 38–40; Finley and Guillory, "'That Girl Is Poison,'" 20.

53. Taylor, "As-Salaam Alaikum, My Sister," 177, cf. 183.

54. Louis Farrakhan, "Millions Justice March," video, *C-Span*, October 10, 2015, accessed January 5, 2020, https://www.c-span.org/video/?328654-1/millions-justice-march.

55. Ross, "Understanding Reproductive Justice"; Lindsey and Johnson, "Searching for Climax."

56. Farrakhan, "Millions Justice March."

Afterword

1. Louis Farrakhan, "The Criterion," video, July 4, 2020, https://www.noi.org/the -criterion.

2. See, e.g., Stephen C. Finley, "Esotericism, the Nation of Islam, and the African American Religious Experience w[ith] Dr. Stephen C. Finley," interview by J. G. Michael, audio, *Parallax Views*, May 21, 2021, https://parallaxviews.podbean.com/e /sfinley. See also Finley, "'The Secret . . . of Who the Devil Is,'" 156, 170 n. 8.

3. See Finley et al., *The Religion of White Rage*; cf. Stephen C. Finley, "The Religion of Whiteness and the Myth of Eternal Return: The Capitol Insurrection of January 6, 2021," unpublished typescript delivered via Zoom to Montclair State University, Montclair, NJ, March 31, 2021.

4. Finley, "The Meaning of 'Mother' in Louis Farrakhan's 'Mother Wheel,'" 454–55.

5. Lieb, *Children of Ezekiel*, 195–96.

6. Lieb, *Children of Ezekiel*, 196–97.

7. Betsy Klein, Kate Sullivan, and Maegan Vazquez, "Biden Says U.S. to Buy and Donate Half-Billion Doses of Pfizer's COVID Vaccine: 'We Know the Tragedy. We Also Know the Path to Recovery,'" CNN.org, June 10, 2021, https://www.cnn.com/2021/06 /10/politics/joe-biden-vaccine-us-leadership/index.html.

8. Finley and Gray, "God *Is* a White Racist."

9. Louis Farrakhan, "International Press Conference J. W. Marriott Hotel, Washington, D.C.: The Honorable Minister Louis Farrakhan," *Nation of Islam*, October 24, 1989, https://www.noi.org/oct-24-1989-press-conference.

10. Bialy and Loeb, "Could Solar Radiation Pressure Explain 'Oumuamua's Peculiar Acceleration?"

11. Alan Yuhas, "The Pentagon Released UFO Videos: Don't Hold Your Breath for a Breakthrough," *New York Times*, April 28, 2020, updated June 3, 2021, https://www .nytimes.com/2020/04/28/us/pentagon-ufo-videos.html.

12. John Greenewald Jr., "UFOs: The Central Intelligence Agency (CIA) Collection," *The Black Vault*, January 7, 2021, updated March 26, 2021, https://www.theblackvault.com/documentarchive/ufos-the-central-intelligence-agency-cia-collection.

13. John Kirby, "Statement by Pentagon Press Secretary John Kirby on Unidentified Aerial Phenomena Assessment," *U.S. Department of Defense*, June 25, 2021, https://www.defense.gov/Newsroom/Releases/Release.Article/2672732/statement-by-pentagon-press-secretary-john-kirby-on-unidentified-aerial-phenome.

14. Kirby, "Statement by the Pentagon Press Secretary John Kirby on Unidentified Aerial Phenomena Assessment."

15. Office of the Director of National Defense Intelligence, "Preliminary Assessment: Unidentified Aerial Phenomena (Intelligence Assessment)," June 25, 2021, https://www.dni.gov/index.php/newsroom/reports-publications/reports-publications-2021/item/2223-preliminary-assessment-unidentified-aerial-phenomena.

16. Office of the Director of National Defense Intelligence, "Preliminary Assessment," 5.

17. Lieb, *Children of Ezekiel*, 197.

Abdul Khabeer, Su'ad. *Muslim Cool: Race, Religion, and Hip Hop in the United States.* New York: New York University Press, 2016.

Abdul-Rauf, Muhammad. *Bilāl Ibn Rabāh: A Leading Companion of the Prophet Muhammad.* N.p.: American Trust Publications, 1977.

Akom, A. A. "Reexamining Resistance as Oppositional Behavior: The Nation of Islam and the Creation of a Black Achievement Ideology." *Sociology of Education* 76 (2003): 305–25.

Alexander, Amy, ed. *The Farrakhan Factor: African American Writers on Leadership, Nationhood, and Minister Louis Farrakhan.* New York: Grove, 1998.

Alexander, Michelle. *The New Jim Crow: Mass Incarceration in the Age of Colorblindness.* New York: New Press, 2010.

Allen, Ernest, Jr. "Identity and Destiny: Formative Views of the Moorish Science Temple and the Nation of Islam." In *Muslims on the Americanization Path?*, edited by Yvonne Yasbeck Haddad and John Esposito, 201–66. New York: Oxford University Press, 2000.

Allen, Ernest, Jr. "Religious Heterodoxy and Nationalist Tradition." *Black Scholar* 26, nos. 3–4 (1996): 2–34.

Allen, Ernest, Jr. "When Japan Was the 'Champion of the Darker Races': Satokata Takahashi and the Flowering of Black Messianic Nationalism." *Black Scholar* 24, no. 1 (2001): 23–46.

Amatullah-Rahman, Ajile Aisha. "She Stood by His Side and at Times in His Stead: The Life and Legacy of Sister Clara Muhammad, First Lady of the Nation of Islam." DHA diss., Clark Atlanta University, 1999.

Anderson, Victor. *Beyond Ontological Blackness: An Essay on African American Religious and Cultural Criticism.* New York: Continuum, 1999.

Austin, Allan D. *African Muslims in Antebellum America.* New York: Routledge, 1997.

Baker-Fletcher, Karen. *Dancing with God: The Trinity from a Womanist Perspective.* Atlanta: Chalice, 2006.

Bakker, Justine M. "On Knowledge of God, Self and Enemy: Secrecy, Concealment and Revelation in the Nation of Islam." Master's thesis, University of Amsterdam, 2013.

Baraka, Amiri. *Eulogies.* New York: Marsilio, 1996.

Bennett Muhammad, Kathy Makeda. "Humble Warrioress: Women in the Nation of Islam: A Comparative Study 1930–1975 and 1978–2000." PhD diss., Union Institute and University, Cincinnati, 2008.

Berg, Herbert. *Elijah Muhammad and Islam.* New York: New York University Press, 2009.

Beynon, Erdmann Doane. "The Voodoo Cult among Negro Migrants in Detroit." *American Journal of Sociology* 43, no. 6 (May 1938): 894–907.

Bialy, Shmuel, and Abraham Loeb. "Could Solar Radiation Pressure Explain 'Oumuamua's Peculiar Acceleration?" *Astrophysical Journal Letters* 868, no. 1 (November 20, 2018): 4–5.

Bourdieu, Pierre. *Distinction: A Social Critique of the Judgement of Taste.* Cambridge, MA: Harvard University Press, 1984.

Bourdieu, Pierre. *Outline of a Theory of Practice*, trans. R. Nice. Cambridge: Cambridge University Press, 1977.

Bradford, Judith, and Crispin Sartwell. *Race/Sex: Their Sameness, Difference, and Interplay*, edited by Naomi Zack. New York: Routledge, 1997.

Breitman, George, ed. *Malcolm X Speaks: Selected Speeches and Statements.* New York: Grove Weidenfeld, 1990.

Brown, Frank Burch. *Religious Aesthetics.* Princeton, NJ: Princeton University Press, 1993.

Butler, Judith. *Bodies That Matter: On the Discursive Limits of Sex.* New York: Routledge 1993.

Carew, Jan. *Ghosts in Our Blood: With Malcolm X in Africa, England, and the Caribbean.* Chicago: Lawrence Hill, 1994.

Cleage, Albert B., Jr. *Black Christian Nationalism: New Directions for the Black Church.* Detroit: Luxor, 1972.

Cleage, Albert B. "Myths about Malcolm X." In *Malcolm X: The Man and His Times*, edited by John Henrik Clarke, 13–26. Trenton, NJ: Africa World Press, 1991.

Clegg, Claude Andrew, III. *An Original Man: The Life and Times of Elijah Muhammad.* New York: St. Martin's Griffin, 1997.

Cone, James H. *A Black Theology of Liberation: Twentieth Anniversary Edition.* Maryknoll, NY: Orbis, 1990.

Cone, James H. *Martin and Malcolm and America: A Dream or a Nightmare?* Maryknoll, NY: Orbis, 1991.

Cooey, Paula M. *Religious Imagination and the Body: A Feminist Analysis.* New York: Oxford University Press, 1994.

Craig, H. A. R. *Bilal.* London: Quartet, 1977.

Cregan, Kate. *The Sociology of the Body: Mapping the Abstraction of Embodiment.* London: Sage, 2006.

Curtis, Edward E., IV. *Black Muslim Religion in the Nation of Islam, 1960–1975.* Chapel Hill: University of North Carolina Press, 2006.

Curtis, Edward E., IV. *Islam in Black America: Identity, Liberation, and Difference in African American Islamic Thought.* Albany: State University of New York Press, 2002.

Curtis, Edward E., IV. "Islamizing the Black Body: Ritual and Power in Elijah Muhammad's Nation of Islam." *Religion and American Culture* 12, no. 2 (2002): 167–96.

Curtis, Edward E., IV. "Science and Technology in Elijah Muhammad's Nation of Islam: Astrophysical Desire, Genetic Engineering, UFOs, White Apocalypse, and Black Resurrection." *Nova Religio* 20, no. 1 (2015): 5–31.

Davis, Angela Y. *Women, Race and Class.* New York: Random House, 1981.

Dawan, Adilah, comp. and ed. *The New Unabridged Historical Glossary and Source Index of English and Arabic Words Defined by W. Deen Mohammed*, vol. 1, *1975–78*. Chicago: QHB, 2005.

Dawan, Adilah, ed. *The New Unabridged Historical Glossary and Source Index of English and Arabic Words Defined by W. Deen Mohammed*, vol. 4, *2000–05*. Chicago: QHB, 2006.

DeCaro, Louis A., Jr. *Malcolm and the Cross: The Nation of Islam, Malcolm X, and Christianity*. New York: New York University Press, 1998.

DeCaro, Louis A., Jr. *On the Side of My People: A Religious Life of Malcolm X*. New York: New York University Press, 1996.

Denzler, Brenda. *The Lure of the Edge: Scientific Passions, Religious Beliefs, and the Pursuit of UFOs*. Berkeley: University of California Press, 2001.

Diop, Cheikh Anta. *The African Origin of Civilization: Myth or Reality*. Chicago: Lawrence Hill, 1989.

Diouf, Sylviane A. *Servants of Allah: African Muslims Enslaved in the Americas*. New York: New York University Press, 1998.

Dolan, Richard M. *UFOs and the National Security State: Chronology of a Cover-Up 1941–1973*, rev. ed. Charlottesville, VA: Hampton Roads, 2002.

Douglas, Mary. *How Institutions Think*, rev. ed. Charlottesville, VA: Hampton Roads, [1986] 2002.

Douglas, Mary. *Natural Symbols: Explorations in Cosmology*. London: Routledge Classics, 2003.

Douglas, Mary. *Purity and Danger: An Analysis of Concept of Pollution and Taboo*. London: Routledge, 2002.

Du Bois, W. E. B. *The Souls of Black Folk*. New York: Bantam, 1989.

Durkheim, Émile. *The Elementary Forms of Religious Life*, trans. Karen E. Fields. New York: Free Press, 1995.

Dyson, Michael Eric. *Making Malcolm: The Myth and Meaning of Malcolm X*. New York: Oxford University Press, 1995.

Eilberg-Schwartz, Howard. *God's Phallus and Other Problems for Men and Monotheism*. Boston: Pantheon, 1999.

Essien-Udom, E. U. *Black Nationalism: A Search for an Identity in America*. Chicago: University of Chicago Press, 1962.

Evanzz, Karl. *The Messenger: The Rise and Fall of Elijah Muhammad*. New York: Pantheon, 1999.

Fanon, Franz. *Black Skin, White Masks*, trans. C. L. Markmann. New York: Grove, 1967.

Farrakhan, Louis. *The Announcement: A Final Warning to the U.S. Government*. Chicago: FCN, 1989.

Farrakhan, Louis. *Let Us Make Man: Select Men Only and Women Only Speeches*, edited by Brother Yusuf and Sister Shah'Keyah. Atlanta: Uprising Communications, 1996.

Farrakhan, Louis. *The Meaning of the F.O.I.* Chicago: Honorable Elijah Muhammad Education Foundation, 1983.

Farrakhan, Louis. *The Reality of the Mother Plane*. 2 DVDs. Final Call, Chicago, 1987.

Farrakhan, Louis. *The Time and What Must Be Done, Part III.* 2 DVDs. Final Call, Chicago, 2010.

Farrakhan, Louis. *A Torchlight for America.* Chicago: FCN, 1993.

Farrakhan, Louis. *The Wheel and the Last Days.* DVD. FCN, Chicago, 1984.

Felber, Garrett. *Those Who Know Don't Say: The Nation of Islam, the Black Freedom Movement, and the Carceral State.* Chapel Hill: University of North Carolina Press, 2020.

Finley, Stephen C. "From Mistress to Mother: The Religious Transformation of Mother Tynnetta Muhammad in the Nation of Islam." In *Ain't I a Womanist Too?: Third Wave Womanist Religious Thought,* edited by Monica A. Coleman, 49–61. Minneapolis: Fortress, 2013.

Finley, Stephen C. "Hidden Away: Esotericism and Gnosticism in Elijah Muhammad's Nation of Islam." In *Histories of the Hidden God: Concealment and Revelation in Gnosticism, Esotericism, and Mysticism,* edited by April D. DeConick and Grant Adamson, 259–80. London: Acumen, 2013.

Finley, Stephen C. "Homoeroticism and the African American Heterosexual Male Quest for Meaning in the Black Church." *Black Theology* 5, no. 3 (2007): 305–26.

Finley, Stephen C. "Mathematical Theology: Numerology in the Religious Thought of Tynnetta Muhammad and Louis Farrakhan." In *Esotericism in African American Religious Experience: "There Is a Mystery"* . . . , edited by Stephen C. Finley, Margarita Simon Guillory, and Hugh R. Page Jr., 123–37. Leiden: Brill, 2015.

Finley, Stephen C. "The Meaning of 'Mother' in Louis Farrakhan's 'Mother Wheel': Race, Gender, and Sexuality in the Cosmology on the Nation of Islam's UFO." *Journal of the American Academy of Religion* 80, no. 2 (2012): 434–65.

Finley, Stephen C. "'The Secret . . . of Who the Devil Is': Elijah Muhammad, the Nation of Islam, and Theological Phenomenology." In *New Perspectives on the Nation of Islam,* edited by Dawn-Marie Gibson and Herbert Berg, 154–73. London: Routledge, 2017.

Finley, Stephen C. "The Supernatural in the African American Experience." In *Super Religion,* edited by Jeffrey J. Kripal, 231–46. Farmington Hills, MI: Macmillan Reference, 2017.

Finley, Stephen C., and Biko Mandela Gray. "God *Is* a White Racist: Immanent Atheism as a Religious Response to Black Lives Matter and State-Sanctioned Anti-black Violence." *Journal of Africana Religions* 3, no. 4 (October 2015): 443–53.

Finley, Stephen C., Biko Mandela Gray, and Lori Latrice Martin, eds. *The Religion of White Rage: White Workers, Religious Fervor, and the Myth of Black Racial Progress.* Edinburgh: University of Edinburgh Press, 2020.

Finley, Stephen C., Biko Mandela Gray, and Hugh R. Page Jr. "Africana Esoteric Studies and Western Intellectual Hegemony: A Continuing Conversation with Western Esotericism." *History of Religions* 60, no. 3 (2021): 163–87.

Finley, Stephen C., and Margarita Simon Guillory. "'That Girl Is Poison': White Supremacy, Anxiety, and the Conflation of Women and Food in the Nation of Islam." In *Women and Religion in the World,* vol. 7, edited by Darnise T. Martin, 3–27. Westport, CT: Greenwood, 2012.

Finley, Stephen C., Margarita Simon Guillory, and Hugh R. Page Jr., eds. *Esotericism in African American Religious Experience: "There Is a Mystery"* . . . Leiden: Brill, 2015.

Foucault, Michel. *Discipline and Punish: The Birth of the Prison*. New York: Vintage, 1979.

Frazier, E. Franklin. *The Negro Family in the United States*. Chicago: University of Chicago Press, 1939.

Freud, Sigmund. *Introductory Lectures on Psychoanalysis*, trans. James Strachey. New York: W. W. Norton, 1966.

Freud, Sigmund. *Three Essays on the Theory of Sexuality*, trans. James Strachey. New York: Basic, 1975.

Gardell, Mattias. *In the Name of Elijah Muhammad: Louis Farrakhan and the Nation of Islam*. Durham, NC: Duke University Press, 1996.

Gellner, Ernst. "Sanctity, Puritanism, Secularism and Nationalism in North Africa: A Case Study." In *Contributions to Mediterranean Sociology: Mediterranean Rural Communities and Social Change*, edited by J. G. Peristiany, 31–48. Paris: Mouton, 1963.

Gibson, Dawn-Marie. "Ebony Muhammad's *Hurt2Healing* Magazine and Contemporary Nation Women." In *New Perspectives on the Nation of Islam*, edited by Dawn-Marie Gibson and Herbert Berg, 31–45. New York: Routledge, 2017.

Gibson, Dawn-Marie. *A History of the Nation of Islam: Race, Islam, and the Quest for Freedom*. Santa Barbara, CA: Praeger, 2012.

Gibson, Dawn-Marie. "Nation Women's Engagement and Resistance in the *Muhammad Speaks* Newspaper." *Journal of American Studies* 49, no. 1 (2015): 1–18.

Gibson, Dawn-Marie, and Jamillah Karim. *Women of the Nation: Between Black Protest and Sunni Islam*. New York: New York University Press, 2014.

Glaude, Eddie S., Jr. *Exodus!: Race, Religion, and Nation in Early Nineteenth-Century Black America*. Chicago: University of Chicago Press, 2000.

Gomez, Michael A. *Black Crescent: The Experience and Legacy of African Muslims in the Americas*. New York: Cambridge University Press, 2005.

Gossett, Thomas F. *Race: The History of an Idea in America*. Dallas: Southern Methodist University Press, 1963.

Hall, Stuart, ed. *Representation: Cultural Representations and Signifying Practices*. London: Sage, 1977.

Hanegraaff, Wouter J. *New Age Religion and Western Culture: Esotericism in the Mirror of Secular Thought*. Albany: State University of New York Press, 1998.

Hartman, Saidiya. *Lose Your Mother: A Journey along the Atlantic Slave Route*. New York: Farrar, Straus and Giroux, 2007.

Hartman, Saidiya. *Scenes of Subjection: Terror, Slavery, and Self-Making in Nineteenth-Century America*. New York: Oxford University Press, 1997.

Haskins, Jim. *Louis Farrakhan and the Nation of Islam*. New York: Walker, 1996.

Higginbotham, Evelyn Brooks. *Righteous Discontent: The Women's Movement in the Black Baptist Church, 1880–1920*. Cambridge, MA: Harvard University Press, 2006.

Hill Collins, Patricia. *Black Feminist Thought: Knowledge, Consciousness, and the Politics of Empowerment*. New York: Routledge, 2000.

hooks, bell. *Black Looks: Race and Representation*. Boston: South End, 1992.

Hopfe, Lewis M., and Mark R. Woodward. *Religions of the World*, 10th ed. Upper Saddle River, NJ: Pearson Prentice Hall, 2007.

Howard-Pitney, David. *Martin Luther King, Jr., Malcolm X and the Civil Rights Struggle of the 1950s and 1960s: A Brief History with Documents*. New York: Bedford/St. Martin's, 2004.

Hoyle, Fred. *The Nature of the Universe*. New York: HarperCollins, 1960.

Hucks, Tracey E. *Yoruba Traditions and African American Religious Nationalism*. Albuquerque: University of New Mexico Press, 2012.

Hughes, David Y., and Harry M. Geduld. *A Critical Edition of "The War of the Worlds": H. G. Wells's Scientific Romance*. Bloomington: Indiana University Press, 1993.

Hunwick, John, and Eve Trout Powell. *The African Diaspora in the Mediterranean Lands of Islam*. Princeton, NJ: Markus Wiener, 2002.

Jackson, Sherman A. *Islam and the Blackamerican: Looking Forward to the Third Resurrection*. New York: Oxford University Press, 2011.

Jackson, Sherman A. *Islam and the Problem of Black Suffering*. New York: Oxford University Press, 2009.

James, William. *The Varieties of Religious Experience*. New York: Touchstone, 1997.

Jeffries, Bayyinah S. *A Nation Can Rise No Higher Than Its Women: African American Muslim Women in the Movement for Black Self-Determination, 1950–1975*. Lanham, MD: Lexington, 2014.

Jeffries, Bayyinah S. "Raising Her Voice: Writings by, for, and about Women in *Muhammad Speaks* Newspaper, 1961–1975." In *African American Consciousness: Past and Present*, edited by James Conyers Jr., 145–73. New Brunswick, NJ: Transaction, 2012.

Jones, William R. *Is God a White Racist?: A Preamble to Black Theology*. Garden City, NY: Anchor Press/Doubleday, 1973.

Jung, Carl G. *Flying Saucers: A Modern Myth of Things Seen in the Skies*, trans. R. C. F. Hull. Princeton, NJ: Princeton University Press, 1978.

Karim, Jamillah. *American Muslim Women: Negotiating Race, Class, and Gender within the Ummah*. New York: University of New York Press, 2008.

Kelleter, Frank. *Con/tradition: Louis Farrakhan's Nation of Islam, the Million Man March, and American Civil Religion*. Heidelberg, Germany: Universitätsverlag C. Winter, 2000.

Kickelmans, Joseph J. *Heidegger on Art and Art Works*. Dordrecht, Netherlands: Martinus Nijhoff, 1985.

Kohut, Heinz. "Forms and Transformations of Narcissism." In *The Search for the Self: Selected Writings of Heinz Kohut: 1950–1978*, vol. 1, edited by Paul H. Ornstein, 427–460. New York: International Universities Press, 1978.

Koppel, Ted. *An Interview with Louis Farrakhan*. DVD, 22 mins. Films for the Humanities and Sciences, Hamilton, NJ, 1998.

Kristeva, Julia. *Powers of Horror: Essays on Abjection*, trans. Leon S. Rudiez. New York: Columbia University Press, 1982.

Leder, Drew. *The Absent Body*. Chicago: University of Chicago Press, 1990.

Lee, Martha F. *The Nation of Islam, an American Millenarian Movement*. Lewiston, NY: Edwin Mellen, 1988.

Leigh, David. *Circuitous Journey: Modern Spiritual Autobiography*. New York: Fordham University Press, 1999.

Lévi-Strauss, Claude. *The Savage Mind.* Chicago: University of Chicago Press, 1966.

Lieb, Michael. *Children of Ezekiel: Aliens, UFOs, the Crisis of Race, and the Advent of the End Time.* Durham, NC: Duke University Press, 1998.

Lincoln, C. Eric. *The Black Muslims in America,* 3d ed. Grand Rapids, MI: William B. Eerdmans, 1994.

Lindsey, Treva B., and Jessica Marie Johnson. "Searching for Climax: Black Erotic Lives in Slavery and Freedom." *Meridians: Feminisms, Race, Transnationalism* 12, no. 2 (2014): 169–95.

Long, Charles H. *Significations: Signs, Symbols, and Images in the Interpretation of Religion.* Philadelphia: Fortress, 1986.

Makhubuti, Haki R., and Maulana Karenga, eds. *Million Man March/Day of Absence: A Commemorative Anthology.* Chicago: Third World, 1996.

Mamiya, Lawrence H. "From Black Muslim to Bilalian: The Evolution of a Movement." *Journal for the Scientific Study of Religion* 21, no. 2 (1982): 141–52.

Marable, Manning. *Living Black History: How Reimagining the African American Past Can Remake America's Racial Future.* New York: Basic Civitas, 2006.

Marable, Manning. *Malcolm X: A Life of Reinvention.* New York: Viking, 2011.

Marsh, Clifton E. *The Lost-Found Nation of Islam in America.* Lanham, MD: Scarecrow, 2000.

Marshall, A. *Louis Farrakhan: Made in America.* N.p.: BSB, 1997.

Martin, Lori Latrice. *Black Women as Leaders: Challenging and Transforming Society.* Santa Barbara, CA: Praeger, 2019.

McClintock, Anne. *Imperial Leather: Race, Gender, and Sexuality in the Colonial Context.* New York: Routledge, 1995.

McCloud, Amina Beverly. *African American Islam.* New York: Routledge, 1995.

Miyakawa, Felicia M. "Receiving, Embodying, and Sharing 'Divine Wisdom': Women in the Nation of Gods and Earths." In *Women in New and Africana Religions,* edited by Lillian Ashcraft-Eason, Darnise C. Martin, and Oyeroke Olademo, 29–52. Santa Barbara, CA: Praeger, 2010.

Mohammed, Warith Deen. *An African American Genesis.* Calumet City, IL: MACA Publication Fund, 1986.

Mohammed, Warith Deen. *As the Light Shineth from the East.* Chicago: W. D. Mohammed Publications, 1980.

Mohammed, Warith Deen. *Imam W. Deen Muhammad Speaks from Harlem, NY,* vol. 1. Chicago: W. D. Mohammed Publications, 1984.

Mohammed, Warith Deen. *Imam W. Deen Muhammad Speaks from Harlem, NY: Challenges That Face Man Today,* vol. 2. Chicago: W. D. Mohammed Publications, 1985.

Mohammed, Warith Deen. *Religion on the Line: Al-Islam, Judaism, Catholicism, Protestantism.* Chicago: W. D. Mohammed Publications, 1983.

Muhammad, Elijah. *Birth of a Savior.* Chicago: Coalition for the Remembrance of Elijah, 1993.

Muhammad, Elijah. *The Fall of America.* Phoenix: Secretarius MEMPS, 1973.

Muhammad, Elijah. *The Flag of Islam.* Chicago: Muhammad's Temple No. 2, 1983.

Muhammad, Elijah. *The History of Jesus' Birth, Death and What It Means*. Atlanta: Secretarius MEMPS, 1993.

Muhammad, Elijah. *History of the Nation of Islam*. Atlanta: Secretarius MEMPS, 1993.

Muhammad, Elijah. *How to Eat to Live, Book 1*. Chicago: Muhammad's Temple of Islam No. 2, 1967.

Muhammad, Elijah. *How to Eat to Live, Book 2*. Atlanta: Secretarius MEMPS, 1972.

Muhammad, Elijah. *I Am the Last Messenger of Allah*. Atlanta: Secretarius MEMPS, 1997.

Muhammad, Elijah. *Message to the Blackman in America*. Atlanta: Secretarius MEMPS, 1965.

Muhammad, Elijah. *The Mother Plane*. Maryland Heights, MO: Secretarius MEMPS, 1992.

Muhammad, Elijah. *Our Savior Has Arrived*. Atlanta: Secretarius MEMPS, n.d.

Muhammad, Elijah. *The Science of Time: The Time and Judgment When Self Tells the Truth on Self*. Atlanta: Secretarius MEMPS, 1993.

Muhammad, Elijah. *The Secrets of Freemasonry*. Atlanta: Secretarius MEMPS, 1994.

Muhammad, Elijah. *The Supreme Wisdom: Solution to the So-Called Negroes's Problem*, vol. 1. Atlanta: Secretarius MEMPS, n.d.

Muhammad, Elijah. *The Supreme Wisdom*, vol. 2. Atlanta: Messenger Elijah Muhammad Propagation Society, 2006.

Muhammad, Elijah. *The Tricknology of the Enemy*. Atlanta: Secretarius MEMPS, 1997.

Muhammad, Elijah. *The True History of Master Fard Muhammad*. Atlanta: Secretarius MEMPS, 2002.

Muhammad, Elijah. *Yakub: The Father of Man-Kind*. Atlanta: Secretarius MEMPS, 2002.

Muhammad, Elijah. *The Theology of Time: The Secret of Time*. Phoenix, AZ: Secretarius MEMPS, 2008.

Muhammad, Ilia Rashad. *UFOs and the Nation of Islam: The Source, Proof, and Reality of the Wheels*. Memphis: Ilia Rashad Muhammad and Nation Brothers, 2013.

Muhammad, Jabril, ed. *Closing the Gap: Inner Views of the Heart, Mind and Soul of the Honorable Minister Louis Farrakhan*. Chicago: FCN, 2006.

Muhammad, Jabril. *Is It Possible That the Honorable Elijah Muhammad Is Still Physically Alive???* Phoenix: Nuevo, 2007.

Muhammad, Tynnetta. *The Comer by Night, 1986*. Chicago: Honorable Elijah Muhammad Educational Foundation, 1986.

Outlaw, Lucius T. *On Race and Philosophy*. New York: Routledge, 1996.

Pierce, Paulette, and Brackette F. Williams. "And Their Prayers Shall Be Answered through the Womb of a Woman: Insurgent Masculine Redemption and the Nation of Islam." In *The Gender of Agency and the Place of Nationality*, edited by Brackette F. Williams. 186–215. London: Routledge, 1996.

Pinn, Anthony B., ed. *Making the Gospel Plain: The Writings of Bishop Reverdy C. Ransom*. Harrisburg, PA: Trinity Press International, 1999.

Pinn, Anthony B. *Terror and Triumph: The Nature of Black Religion*. Minneapolis: Fortress, 2003.

Ray, Terry. *Bourdieu on Religion: Imposing Faith and Legitimacy*. London: Equinox, 2007.

Robinson, Dean E. *Black Nationalism in American Politics and Thought*. Cambridge: Cambridge University Press, 2001.

Rojcewicz, Richard. *The Gods and Technology: A Reading of Heidegger*. Albany: State University of New York Press, 2006.

Ross, Loretta. "Understanding Reproductive Justice: Transforming the Pro-choice Movement." *Off Our Backs* 36, no. 4 (2006): 14–19.

Rouse, Carolyn Moxley. *Engaged Surrender: African American Women and Islam*. Berkeley: University of California Press, 2004.

Segal, Ronald. *Islam's Black Slaves: The Other Black Diaspora*. New York: Farrar, Straus and Giroux, 2001.

Shabazz, Betty. "Malcolm X as a Husband and Father." In *Malcolm X: The Man and His Times*, edited by John Henrik Clarke, 132–43. Trenton, NJ: Africa World Press, 1990.

Sims, Toni Y. "An Analysis of Womanhood: The Portrayal of Women in the Nation of Islam Newspaper: *The Final Call* 1982–1995." DA diss., Clark Atlanta University, 2001.

Smitherman, Geneva. *Black Talk: Words and Phrases from the Hood to the Amen Corner*, rev. ed. Boston: Houghton Mifflin, 2000.

Spillers, Hortense. "Mama's Baby, Papa's Maybe: An American Grammar Book." *Diacritics* 17, no. 2 (1987): 64–81.

Tate, Sonsyrea. *Little X: Growing Up in the Nation of Islam*. Knoxville: University Press of Tennessee, 2005.

Taylor, Ula Yvette. "As-Salaam Alaikum, My Sister: The Honorable Elijah Muhammad and the Women Who Followed Him." *Race and Society* 1, no. 2 (1998): 177–96.

Taylor, Ula Yvette, "Elijah Muhammad's Nation of Islam: Separatism, Regendering, and a Secular Approach to Black Power after Malcolm X." In *African American Consciousness: Past and Present*, edited by James Conyers Jr., 29–41. New Brunswick, NJ: Transaction, 2012.

Taylor, Ula Yvette. *The Promise of Patriarchy: Women and the Nation of Islam*. Chapel Hill: University of North Carolina Press, 2017.

Taylor, Wayne. "Premillennium Tension: Malcolm X and the Eschatology of the Nation of Islam." *Souls* 7, no. 1 (2005): 52–65.

Tsoukalas, Steven. *The Nation of Islam: Understanding the "Black Muslims."* Phillipsburg, NJ: P&R, 2001.

Turner, Richard Brent. "Edward Wilmot Blyden and Pan-Africanism: The Ideological Roots of Islam and Black Nationalism in the United States." *Muslim World* 87, no. 2 (1997): 169–82.

Turner, Richard Brent. *Islam in the African American Experience*, 2d ed. Bloomington: Indiana University Press, 2003.

Walker, Dennis. *Islam and the Search for African-American Nationhood: Elijah Muhammad, Louis Farrakhan and the Nation of Islam*. Atlanta: Clarity, 2005.

Walker, David, and Henry Highland Garnet. *Walker's Appeal and Garnet's Address to the Slaves of the United States of America*. North Stratford, NH: Ayer, 2008.

Walker, Theodore, Jr. *Mothership Connections: A Black Atlantic Synthesis of Neoclassical Metaphysics and Black Theology*. Albany: State University of New York Press, 2004.

Washington, Booker T. *Up from Slavery*. Oxford: Oxford University Press, 1995.

West, Cornel. *Prophesy Deliverance!: An Afro-American Revolutionary Christianity*. Louisville: Westminster John Knox, 2002.

West, Cynthia S'thembile. "Nation Builders: Female Activism in the Nation of Islam, 1960–1970." PhD diss., Temple University, Philadelphia, 1994.

West, Cynthia S'thembile. "Revisiting Female Activism in the 1960s: The Newark Branch of the Nation of Islam." *Black Scholar* 26, nos. 3–4 (1996): 41–48.

West, Cynthia S'thembile. "Take Two: Nation of Islam Women Fifty Years after Civil Rights." In *African American Consciousness: Past and Present*, edited by James Conyers Jr., 29–41. New Brunswick, NJ: Transaction, 2012.

Wilson, Amos. *Black-on-Black Violence: The Psychodynamics of Black Self-Annihilation in Service of White Domination*. New York: Afrikan World Infosystems, 1990.

Witt, Doris. *Black Hunger: Food and the Politics of U.S. Identity*. New York: Oxford University Press, 1999.

X, Malcolm. *By Any Means Necessary*. New York: Pathfinder, 1992.

X, Malcolm. *The End of White World Supremacy: Four Speeches*, edited by Benjamin Karim. New York: Arcade, 1971.

X, Malcolm. *February 1965: The Final Speeches*. New York: Pathfinder, 1992.

X, Malcolm, and Alex Haley. *The Autobiography of Malcolm X*. New York: Ballantine, 1987.

Yancy, George. "Geneva Smitherman: The Social Ontology of African American Language, the Power of *Nommo*, and the Resistance and Identity through Language." *Journal of Speculative Philosophy* 18, no. 4 (2004): 273–99.

Yancy, George. "Whiteness and the Return of the Black Body." PhD diss., Duquesne University, Pittsburgh, PA, 2005.

Young, Iris. "Five Faces of Oppression." In *Oppression, Privilege, and Resistance: Theoretical Perspectives on Racism, Sexism, and Heterosexism*, edited by Lisa Heldke and Peg O'Connor, 55–71. New York: McGraw-Hill, 2004.

Muhammad, Elijah (Continued)
black bodies, 5–6, 16–17, 18, 35, 37–39,
40; the prayer service, 57–58; on race
and the aesthetics of taste, 82–83; relationship with Fard Muhammad, 18, 22,
28–29, 63; the religious body, 9, 46, 49,
58, 135; renaming practices, 44, 53–54;
Saviour's Day address, 36, 78, 132–33;
as still alive on the Mother Plane, 34,
141–42, 148, 151, 199; succession of,
102–3; symbolic out-of-place bodies,
46–47, 79, 100; valorization of Bilal,
117; views on homosexuality, 56, 60; the
Yakub mythology, 16, 21–28, 44–45
Muhammad, Fard: Farrakhan's vision of
Muhammad and Fard on the Mothership, 198; as still alive on the Mother
Plane, 199
Muhammad, Fard (Master Fard): on
black bodily phenotypes, 26, 27; divine
status of, 18, 21–22, 41, 61, 63, 66–67;
Farrakhan's longing to see, 147, 148;
Farrakhan's vision of Muhammad and
Fard on the Mother Wheel, 135, 139–43,
147, 148, 151, 154–55, 191; foundation of
the Nation of Islam, 15, 17–18; image of,
140; Mohammed's reinterpretation of
the teachings of, 102, 104, 105–6, 107–8,
122–23; name, 54; prophetic acts and the
birth of Warith Mohammed, 103; race
and cosmology of the Yakub mythology,
22, 24, 28–29; racial mythology, 17–18,
65–67, 123–24, 127, 172; relationship with
Elijah Muhammad, 18, 22, 28–29, 63; as
the source of dietary knowledge, 50; as
still alive on the Mother Plane, 34, 142,
148, 151; theosophy, 62–63
Muhammad, Ilia Rashad, 175
Muhammad, Jabril, 138, 141–42, 147, 153
Muhammad, Tynnetta, 138, 142, 153, 180
Muhammad, Wallace D. *See* Mohammed,
Warith Deen
Muhammad Ibn Abdullah, 33, 102, 120–21
Muslim Girls Training and General Course
in Civilization (MGT-GCC), 47, 57

Naeem, Abdul Basit, 106
Nation of Islam (NOI): activism, 152–53; as
a black nationalist movement, 2, 74, 159,
210n57; control over women's bodies,
58–60, 186–8; devil imagery, 9, 16–17,
23, 31–32, 59; dietary rules, 44, 50–52,
64, 166; distinct NOI black bodies, 9, 46,
48–49, 72, 135; education and discipline,
55–57; engagement with the black body,
2–3, 4–5, 6–8, 27, 31; Farrakhan's leadership of, 101, 102–3, 139–41; foundation
of, 15, 17–18, 21–22, 48, 190; gender
markers of the body, 2–3; global image
of, 1–2, 6; immigrant Muslims in, 107–8,
126–28; intraracial discrimination, 2–3;
as the Lost-Found Nation of Islam, 132;
Malcom X's divergence from, 90–98;
Martin Luther King's criticism of, 87;
Masonic influences on, 63, 78, 154;
Mohammed's leadership of, 101, 103–5,
106, 126–27; Muslim Girls Training
and General Course in Civilization, 57;
perception of the in-place black body,
5–6, 15, 16; perichoretic politics of racial
uplift, 48, 161; politics of respectability,
47; the prayer service, 57–58; racial
uplift ideologies, 46–48; reconstruction of black bodies, 161–62; relations
within the global community, 153, 155,
192; as a religious nationalist group,
2, 7, 158–61; renaming practices, 44,
53–54, 133–34; reproduction of white
supremacist hierarchies, 161–63, 167,
170–71, 172–73; scholarship on, 2, 159;
scholarship on women in the Nation
of Islam, 174–79; temple planting
by Malcom X, 92–93; transition to a
Sunni Muslim organization, 101, 104,
105, 107, 128; as World Community of
al-Islam in the West (WCIW), 101, 106,
107–8, 128, 132
National Association for the Advancement
of Colored People (NAACP), 84
National Security Study Memorandum
200, 198

white supremacy: and the African American experience in Mohammed's thought, 114–16; African American foods, 82; black bodies as other, 4, 7; Christianity and, 35–36, 38–39, 40–41, 44; counter-significations of Malcom X and, 76–77; devilish white people discourses, 9, 16–17, 23, 31–32, 59, 74, 78–79, 80–82, 96–97, 124; the discursive white normative gaze, 2, 32, 88, 115, 123–24; Mohammed's figure of the foreigner, 123–28, 129; NOI's reproduction of white supremacy's hierarchies, 161–63, 167, 170–71, 172–73; the in-place black body and, 4–5, 6–8; stereotypes of black inferiority, 27, 85–86, 122; subordination of black bodies, 7, 8, 16, 160–61

whiteness: concept of, 4; Muhammad's critique of whitenized black bodies, 16, 18, 35–36, 38–39, 41–42, 44, 86; perichoretic politics of racial uplift, 48, 161

Williams, Brackette F., 47–8, 171, 178, 181

women: control over women's bodies, 58–60; dress codes, 54–55, 58; embodiment of in the Nation of Islam, 175–77, 179–88; experiences of systemic violence, 18; in the *Final Call* newspaper, 176, 177–78; Frazerian reform narratives, 47–48, 178–79; metaphysical masculinity, 161, 180; in Mohammed's thought, 116; Muhammad's agrarian metaphors for the bodies of, 168, 181–82; politics of respectability, 47, 161, 171; the prayer service, 58; scholarship on women in

the Nation of Islam, 174–79; social mobility and black women's bodies, 48; wheels/women/womb intersections, 179, 180–85; white devil's enslavement of, 59–60. *See also* gender

Women's Convention of the National Baptist Convention, 47, 161

Woodson, Carter G., 114

World Community of al-Islam in the West (WCIW), 101, 106, 107–8, 128, 132

Wright, Daunte, 194

Yakub mythology: (re)incorporation of the other, 32; black bodies in, 15, 26–27, 61, 64–66; Christianity as an instrument of oppression, 22, 30, 31, 32–33, 34–35, 44–45; destruction of the original people, 25; devilish white people, 23, 31–32, 80, 97, 124; esotericism in, 62; God's own body, 170; in Malcom X's thought, 79–80, 92; in Mohammed's thought, 105; the Mother Plane within, 34, 67–68, 72, 141–42, 143, 147–48; Muhammad's critique of whitenized black bodies, 18–19; in Muhammad's thought, 16, 21–25, 26, 27–28, 44–45; narrative, 21, 22–25, 33–34; the Original People in East Asia, 25–27; race and cosmology of the Yakub mythology, 22, 24, 28–29; scholarship on, 16; self-creation of God and the cosmos, 22–25; as theological phenomenology, 16, 21–22; written script in, 24–25; Yakub and the creation of the white race, 6, 27–33, 65, 82–83

Young, Iris, 18–19

Printed in the USA
CPSIA information can be obtained
at www.ICGtesting.com
LVHW021116080124
768370LV00003B/58

9 781478 018773